THE DESOLATE CITY

THE DESOLATE CITY

❧

REVOLUTION
IN THE
CATHOLIC CHURCH

❧

ANNE ROCHE MUGGERIDGE

1817

HARPER & ROW, PUBLISHERS, SAN FRANCISCO

CAMBRIDGE, HAGERSTOWN, NEW YORK, PHILADELPHIA, WASHINGTON
LONDON, MEXICO CITY, SÃO PAULO, SINGAPORE, SYDNEY

For John Muggeridge

Library of Congress Catalog Card Number: 86-45170

FIRST U.S. EDITION

Excerpt from "Growth, (Hopefully) in Wisdom, Age and Grace"
by Charles E. Curran, from *Journeys*, Gregory Baum, ed. © 1975 by
The Missionary Society of St. Paul the apostle in the State of New York.
Reprinted by permission of Paulist Press.

86 87 88 89 90   10 9 8 7 6 5 4 3 2 1

Contents

❧

INTRODUCTION

❧

How doth the city sit desolate that was full of people: how is she become as a widow that was mistress among nations. Among her lovers there is none to comfort her: all her friends have despised her, they are become her enemies. All her gates are broken down: her priests sigh, her virgins grieve, and she is oppressed with bitterness. And from the daughter of Sion all her beauty is departed.

When I was young, I very much loved Tenebrae, the noble tragic night Office of Holy Week, intoned, some of it in complete darkness, by unaccompanied male voices in the austere, penitential Lenten plainchant. The verses quoted above come from the *Lamentations of Jeremiah* upon the fall of Jerusalem, Matins, First Nocturn, of the Office of Holy Thursday, sung in the night of Wednesday in Holy Week. They used to make my soul shiver with sorrow. Now they describe to me what has happened to another holy city, the Catholic Church. For Catholicism is today like a city ravaged by war. The spires have fallen, the wells are poisoned, the government is in exile. Those citizens who cannot bear to flee wander sadly through the ruins, trying to salvage objects not too damaged to be useful. Families are divided, neighbours turned cold.

Catholicism is not just a religion: it is a country of the heart and of the mind. No matter how resolutely they turn their backs on it, people born within it never quite shed their accents. And there are a great many who cannot emigrate, no matter how uninviting living conditions become. We may freeze within it; we would die outside it.

"I belong to the race of people," wrote the great Catholic novelist François Mauriac, "who, born in Catholicism, realize in earliest manhood that they will never escape from it, never leave it. They were within it, they are within it, and they will be within it for ever and ever." To this race I also belong. The present work attempts to understand recent catastrophic convulsions in my native land.

ONE

REVOLUTION: THE BACKGROUND

This book is an attempt to explain the complete and extraordinarily rapid collapse of the Catholic world in which I grew up, a society still in 1960 at the peak of confidence and unity. Since the Catholic Church is a human society, the oldest continuous government in the world, it is both possible and illuminating to compare events within it with similar events in secular society. I argue that a revolution is taking place within the Roman Catholic Church, a classic revolution in the pattern of those that from time to time convulse and transform secular human societies.

In the first two chapters of this study I try to trace the pedigree of the controlling idea behind the present revolution, which, I contend, is that view of authority that has variously been called the Protestant principle, the anti-dogmatic or anti-hierarchical principle, or liberalism. I see this idea as the opposite of the Catholic idea of authority and of the direction in which it flows. This Catholic idea might be called the hierarchical principle, the belief that moral authority derives from God and is exercised in the Church by direct commission from Christ and through the apostolic succession. The Catholic Church has always resisted the Protestant principle of authority, basing its opposition on both universal natural law and on the scriptural account of the Fall of Man. The appeal from private judgement alone has been rejected by the Church whenever it has appeared, from the Acts of the Apostles to the modernist movement of the late nineteenth and early twentieth centuries, which attempted to adapt Catholic beliefs to developments in science.

This section also examines two earlier attempts during the modern (post-Renaissance) period to force the Catholic Church to accept the Protestant principle of authority as its governing idea. The first of these attempts was the Protestant Reformation, or, as I prefer to call it, the Protestant revolution, since I do not accept its own description of its intentions and activities. Protestantism, in large part a defensive reaction to the unsettling challenges of the explosive New Learning of the Renaissance, fell back upon the individual authority of a private faith, the direct, unmediated approach to God. The Catholic Church, although it once again expelled the Protestant principle, was unable to contain the damage; the Protestant principle became institutionalized within Christendom.

The second revolutionary attempt that I will examine is the modernist crisis of the late nineteenth century: its Protestant ancestry, its principles, assumptions, and methods. It is modernism, I will argue, that has reduced religion to mere sentiment, has alienated tens of millions of Catholics from their faith, and is well on its way to destroying the Catholic Church.

DEFINITIONS AND LABELS

Catholics, of course, believe that the Church is not just a human society; it is also a divine one, instituted by Christ while He was on earth to teach in His name. They believe, therefore, that it is infallible and indefectible; that is, it cannot err in matters of faith and morals, and it cannot ultimately fall away from the truth. Thus, the Church leads a life both natural and supernatural, independent on the one hand of secular society, while on the other inextricably bound to whatever human society it finds itself sojourning with.

One traditional Catholic way of approaching this mystery has been to think of the Church as both She and It: She, the spotless mystical Bride of Christ; It, the all too human and fallible visible temporal organization. The Church as It makes its way through history burdened by the effects of original sin; the Church as She keeps It free from error in matters of faith and morality. She and It are not two churches, nor even two aspects of one church, but an inseparable unity of body and soul, the same unity that exists in every human being. The Church of faith and the Church of history are one.

This traditional image, now largely discarded, made it possible for Catholics to love and obey the Church while disagreeing with certain prudential decisions of its governors, or even while personally abominating those governors. The sinful behaviour of priests and prelates often makes pious Catholics anti-clerical, yet those same Catholics will with unshaken faith receive absolution and the Body of Christ from the hands of a loose-living priest, as they once did dogma from a Borgia pope.

Nowadays, when one wants to say that "Catholics believe" some particular thing it is always necessary to qualify one's remarks. During the Second Vatican Council and for a short period after it, *liberal* and *conservative* were reasonably useful terms with which to describe

Catholic positions, but their time is long past. Before the Council, "liberal" and "conservative" Catholics *believed* the same things in matters of faith and morals. (Later in this book I will cite evidence to show that even in the matter of birth control, which in 1968 was to provide the flashpoint for the revolution, "liberal" Catholics, as late as 1963, still accepted and practised with conspicuous fidelity the traditional teaching of the Church.) But if the "liberal" of the 1950s and early 1960s was "conservative" in doctrine and morality, he or she was "progressive" and reform-minded in other areas of Catholic discipline. Ironically, at the beginning, "liberal" Catholics were for *more* Catholicism rather than, as now, for less. They wanted more and better preaching, more decorum and splendour in the liturgy, expansion of every apostolate. They criticized the clerical laziness, which, they said, had reduced the parish churches to the level of "ecclesiastical filling stations." They wanted to elevate the religious style of Catholic popular culture, to replace the "Viennese Masses" with Gregorian chant, to strip what they considered superstitious excesses from popular devotion. Though totally loyal to the Pope, they deplored the stranglehold that the Roman curial bureaucracy had in the past century acquired over every aspect of life in the universal Church, and they wanted to emphasize the local Church. Above all, they longed for a Catholic Church that would be, as James Hitchcock, the American historian, puts it in summarizing their hopes, "more open, more honest, less authoritarian and more humane than at present."[1]

Hitchcock himself is a perfect case in point of the pre-Conciliar "liberal" now redefined against his inclinations as a "conservative." In a rueful preface to his 1971 book *The Decline and Fall of Radical Catholicism*, Hitchcock repudiated the now pejorative label "conservative." Still laying claim to the title of "progressive," he listed credentials that might have described any young liberal Catholic of his generation: dismissed in 1959 from the editorship of a Catholic college newspaper "in a classic censorship dispute"; participant in the St. John's University strike of 1966, the first to challenge the power of the hierarchy to fire dissenting faculty; author of an exposé of chancery machinations; active in the effort to evict ROTC from college campuses; worker in Eugene McCarthy's campaign for the Democratic nomination. Yet today James Hitchcock is the leading "conservative" Catholic intellectual in America, co-founder of practically every post-Conciliar counter-revolutionary society or publication of importance, tireless opponent of the anti-orthodox radicalism that has become the establishment position in the Church.

During the Conciliar period, the liberal reform was captured by the revolution in a manner I shall discuss later. Arbitrary redefinition by this revolution has overtaken other great reform-minded "liberals" of the Conciliar years, including Popes Paul VI and John Paul II. The enthusiastic Conciliar reformer Karol Wojtyla remained, after his elevation to the papacy, probably far more "liberal" and "progressive" in politics and economics than most of his flock, yet this position has not saved him from being portrayed, within and without his Church, as *the* archconservative authority figure, rigidly traditionalist, completely lacking in compassion for the human predicament, the leading enemy of the modern quest for personal freedom. As the revolution progressed, many "liberals" abandoned the orthodox beliefs they had once shared with Paul VI and John Paul II. The "liberal" position became instead one of public dissent from Catholic doctrine, while those who held to the older definition of "liberal Catholicism" were dismissed as "conservatives," "reactionaries," "fundamentalists."

There is today, and it is a pity, no position within the Catholic Church that is at once both "liberal" and orthodox. It is now safe to say, for instance, that *all* those described as "liberals" reject the Church's teaching on contraception.[2] But "liberal" dissent is now much broader than this one issue. Indeed, if one judges from their published writings and private conversations, one would assume that very many "liberal Catholics" are now actually agnostics, or at most deists.

As liberalism rapidly progressed towards unbelief, those Catholics who had unwillingly endured the sobriquet "conservative" began to describe themselves as what they always knew they were: *orthodox*. In 1965, to use the term *orthodox* of oneself seemed self-righteous; it smacked of old sectarian wars and heresy-hunting. Today, *orthodox* is merely a factual definition of an historic, though now minority, religious position. One no longer says, for example, that "Catholics believe" that the Church was instituted by Christ the Son of God while He was on earth and is continued through the apostolic succession; one says that "orthodox Catholics believe" this. That definition certainly includes the present incumbent of the Chair of Peter, and presumably the several thousand bishops who put their names to the latest official Catholic reaffirmation of the above proposition, the *Dogmatic Constitution on the Church*, *Lumen Gentium* of the Second Vatican Council. Conversely, *non-orthodox* Catholics believe that Christ was no more than a man, though in some undefined way specially made use of by God to show us what it means to be fully human. He neither founded a church nor established a succession of authority. For these post-Conciliar "liberal" Catholics the Church is a human society only, its institutions – the priesthood, the episcopacy, the papacy, the sacraments – having developed gradually during the centuries after Christ's death to meet the needs of the Christian community.

Extraordinary as it may seem, in these few years since Vatican II reconfirmed the Church's traditional system of belief, *non-orthodox*

Catholicism has become the dominant, virtually unchallenged persuasion of every level of the Catholic academy and civil service, while the bishops who enthusiastically endorsed the Council documents now not only tolerate but openly support dissenters. Many of the people who teach with the Church's mandate think of the Catholic Church as a human society only, one moreover in very bad condition because earlier misconceptions of its nature long kept its citizens from adapting it to changing times. They believe that its system no longer meets the needs of modern men and women, that its world view perpetuates inequalities among them. The institutional Church is, for them, no more than a government that has lost its legitimacy and is therefore justly subject to revolution.

Orthodox Catholics have been slow to recognize and admit the profoundly revolutionary nature of the disorder within the post-Conciliar Church for the very reason that for them the transcendental reality of the Church seems to preclude the concept of true revolution within it. When I try to argue that revolution is precisely what is taking place, they quote the Petrine Promise – that Christ will remain with the Church He founded upon Peter until the end of time, so that "the Gates of Hell will not prevail against it" – and remind me of other moments in the long, chequered history of the Church when "things were even worse than they are now." I, too, of course, share the long-term optimism of such Catholics, but I also think that, ironically, the very solidity of their faith has kept from many such Catholics the realization that what is called "dissent" or "pluralism" within the Church is in reality an increasingly confident revolution, which, if successful, will radically transform the world view, morality, dogma, and discipline of the Roman Catholic Church.

Therefore, I say, let us prescind for a moment, for the sake of argument, from our idea of the Church as a divinely constituted, infallible body, and think of it as a human political organization under pressure from hostile outside systems. Then the lines of the classic revolution going on within Catholic society will clearly emerge. Let us look at the lineaments of revolution first of all in the abstract, and then let us supply names and faces.

ANATOMY OF A REVOLUTION

A revolution, according to the *Oxford English Dictionary*, is a sudden and fundamental change in a society, a radical disruption of organic development and continuity, ending in the complete overthrow of the established government by those who were previously subject to it and the forcible substitution of a new form of government.

A revolution begins with a major change in the relationships among the groups within a society. One group feels strongly that it is being kept from exercising the power or having the status it thinks it deserves. The aggrieved class is not necessarily inspired to revolt by oppression and degradation; often, perhaps generally, revolution is instigated by the group immediately below the rulers. The members of this group may be equal if not superior to the rulers in intellect and competence and therefore are most irritated by exclusion from what they consider their just prerogatives. This subordinate class realizes that as long as it goes on proclaiming and implementing the policies of the government, it will remain subordinate. Therefore, the first step is to stop obeying while remaining in office as long as possible in order to make revolutionary use of the symbols of power.

At the beginning of a revolution, the radical intent is hidden or disguised, since a ruling power will resist an open attempt at overturning it. If the revolutionaries show their hand too soon, they risk liquidation by the still powerful government. Since no political system is likely to allow itself to be fundamentally changed by legal means, revolutionaries have to resort to subversion and illegal means. Every occasion is exploited in order to use the authority of the government to discredit the government. The revolutionaries' resolute withdrawal of legitimacy from the existing order becomes known to the society at large.

As the revolutionaries succeed in isolating the government from the mass of the governed, the government's prestige declines rapidly. It may not dare to use force against the rebels, lest successful defiance further discredit it. Therefore, it tries conciliatory gestures, which the revolution correctly interprets as weakness. As the government becomes increasingly unable or unwilling to govern, the revolutionaries throw off all pretence that their movement is merely a logical development of the old system or a legal reform. They make clear their separation from the old world view, constantly contrasting the bad old ways with the progressive new ones. Intense propaganda is directed at making the old ideas and disciplines seem outmoded and ridiculous and the new ones inevitable and irresistible. The interests and grievances of other groups in the society are sympathetically addressed and the advantages of the proposed new order touted. In this way, key groups in the society are revolutionized, while those who refuse to be co-opted are demoralized by being made to feel that they have been rendered irrelevant by the irresistible force of progress.

Often a revolution simmers for a long time before it boils over. When it does, the incident that triggers its official bid for power is often such as would have passed without reaction in an earlier, prerevolutionary period. Now, when the revolutionaries feel sufficiently strong, the event is represented as being an insult too gross to be borne, the symbol of all the injustice the failing system has ever perpetrated upon a helpless society.

When a revolution meets and wins this first great trial of strength, opposition to it virtually collapses. There is a rush from the hitherto unrevolutionized parts of the society to identify with the goals, the panache, the success of the revolution. Private axes are ground for free at the revolutionary whetstone. Incredible conversions to the revolutionary ideology on the part of those who lately enforced the opposite ideology occur overnight. Members of the ruling class co-operate with the revolution, not necessarily out of conviction but often in an attempt to direct or at least to mitigate revolutionary fervour. These elements in the threatened government are as hostile to the conservatives (that is, the loyalists to the old order and therefore putative counter-revolutionaries) as are the dominant rebels.

Moderates are co-opted or neutralized, conservatives frozen out or destroyed, extremists given their head. Any nascent opposition is hopelessly split, quarrelling among itself. A feature of a rising group is its ability to put aside its differences until victory is assured; therefore, in contrast to the loyalist opposition, the revolution seems invincibly single-minded. The pace of reform is speeded up so that when the situation finally settles down, the break with the past will be irrevocable. The revolutionaries move to ensure permanent control over the sources and channels of power.[3]

The worldwide society that is the Catholic Church is at the point at which the revolution controls most of the channels of power. The government has been discredited and isolated; radical reform is accelerating, and a united counter-revolution is not yet under way. Let us look back and trace the steps by which this situation has come to pass.

The revolution has been a long time brewing. It is impossible, when tracing the history of an intellectual movement, to say with confidence, "This is where it began." It might be said by a really scrupulous religious anthropologist that the principle of insubordination originated with Lucifer's *non serviam*, I will not obey. ("The Devil," said Dr. Johnson, "was the first Whig.") The Book of Genesis, that glorious account of what man is like, which seems more true every time one meditates on it, tells us that the principle of insubordination, the spirit of lawlessness, the anti-hierarchical principle, is as old as creation. The mutinous spirit personified as Lucifer, expelled from heaven by the archangel Michael's successful counter-revolution, subverted man in Eden. Why God created intelligences who would reject Him is part of the mystery of free will. The Fall was the consequence of our being allowed to choose to disobey, the consequence of His having made us in His own image and likeness: men, not clocks.

It is a commonplace of psychoanalytic theory that revolution is the struggle of the sons against the father, an explanation particularly seduc-

15

tive when applied to a revolution within the Catholic Church, where the highest authority is actually called Papa, pope. Psychohistorians attempt to understand revolution as the complex psychological response of certain types of personality when critical moments of personal history coincide with certain external events.[4] This method can be taken to exotic lengths, as in John Osborne's play *Luther*, which attributes the Protestant Reformation to Luther's balky digestive system. However, psychohistory, by exposing the revolutionary's hidden impulses, has at least rehabilitated the motives of loyalists who refuse to join with a revolution. In our times, the loyalist is usually abused as a man afraid of freedom, psychologically infantile, the fascist-leaning possessor of an "authoritarian personality," in Theodor Adorno's famous phrase. But psychohistory indicates that, in practitioner Peter Shaw's words, it does not follow that revolutionaries "necessarily represent[ed] psychological types more highly evolved in personal traits of independence than their contemporaries."[5] Yet even if psychohistory's secular version of Genesis was sound and one could use it to explain why a man like St. Bernard of Clairvaux, tireless scourge of ecclesiastical corruption and great reformer though he was, nevertheless accepted the Church's claim to divine authority while Martin Luther, under rather better conditions, would not, there would be little one could do to make the course of history run nearer to one's heart's desire.

What makes a true revolution different in kind from other rearrangements of political power resulting from wars, dynastic struggles, and elections is that the group that is determined to seize power is answering something more profound than the simple natural desires of greed or ambition, or the sensible desire to replace bad governors with good ones. A revolution intends to overthrow not only the regnant authority but the *idea of authority* by which the regnant authority claims the right to govern. Thus, for example, the murder and replacement of the English King Richard II by his cousin Bolingbroke was not a revolution; as Henry IV, Bolingbroke continued to exercise the idea of kingship by which his predecessors had ruled. Whereas the execution of Charles I by Oliver Cromwell was a true revolution, since it shattered forever in England the idea that the supreme political authority lay in an anointed king invested in his power from above by God rather than from below by some combination of "the people."

THE PROTESTANT REVOLUTION

Perhaps it is rather too baroque to hark back to the Garden of Eden for the genesis of the present revolution within Catholicism. Yet it is necessary to look back about five hundred years to the Protestant revolution of the sixteenth century for the modern source of the present revolution. The Protestant Reformation, as it called itself, was a genuine revolution, a totally radical challenge to the regnant idea of religious authority, with radical political, economic, and cultural consequences. The Protestant Reformation, in its insistence on the supremacy of private judgement over external authority, raised opposition to authority to the level of a theological principle. It institutionalized in Christendom a new consciousness that was to have enormous political and religious consequences: the idea of the rejection, on principle, of hierarchy.

God remained for Protestantism the supreme arbiter, and Protestants, like Catholics, accepted the Bible as His inerrant revelation. The great difference occurred over the question of who should interpret this authoritative word of God to the individual Christian. Catholics maintained from the Catholic understanding of Scripture that it should be the Church, founded by Christ upon Peter to teach authoritatively: "Upon this Rock I shall build my Church" (Matthew 16:18); "Going therefore, teach ye all nations" (Matthew 28:19). Protestants rejected the Catholic account of authority. No one, they said, should dare to stand between man and God. The individual soul, enlightened by the Holy Ghost, should be free to interpret the Bible for its own salvation. The seat of authority is within.

The principle of private judgement is the anti-hierarchical principle. Its logical consequence is anarchy, the acknowledgement of no external authority at all. Antinomianism, the conviction that the law no longer has the power to bind, is a state quickly reached in revolutions.[6] The logic of the Protestant principle did not escape the most enthusiastic of the early Reformers nor those who resisted them. Their revolutionary religious principle led extremist Protestants, such as the Anabaptists, to reject all constituted authority. Thomas Munzer, a Lutheran pastor, turned the peasant uprisings in southern Germany in 1525 into a war to establish a communist society. In 1534 the fanatical John of Leyden seized the town of Münster and established for a year an anarchical "new Zion," in which were enacted scenes of religiously inspired debauchery and frenzy paralleled in history only in the maniacal socialist society of Jonestown. (No commentator on Jonestown seems to have noticed the extraordinary likeness to the Anabaptist Münster.)

Not all Reformers became antinomian, tore off their clothes, took four wives, or beheaded unsatisfactory spouses with their own hands in the market place. Luther co-operated with the Protestant princes, preaching a bloodthirsty policy of extermination against the rebellious peasants. Yet the Anabaptists, the Hutterites, the Adamites, and the multitude of other revolutionary sects were justified in claiming that

17

their doctrines were the logical corollaries of Luther's own doctrines of private judgement and the priesthood of all believers; they bitterly reproached him with having betrayed the Reformation, a charge echoed in the nineteenth century by the infinitely more sophisticated but equally logical Adolf von Harnack, the German theologian who initiated the modern rejection of the Reformation as well as of Catholic dogmatic formulations.

The principle of *sola scriptura*, Protestantism's watchword, cannot be strictly applied if any semblance of community is to be preserved. Luther and Calvin hastened to re-establish a religious government that made the same claim to interpret the Scriptures authoritatively as had the Catholic Church. Thus they were able, to some extent, to restrain the antinomian tendencies they had released.

The Catholic Church itself had suffered many earlier antinomian outbursts, but had hitherto managed to suppress them. In the sixteenth century, a combination of geopolitical circumstances, one of them being the increasing pressure of the Turks upon Europe's borders, occupied the powers of the Holy Roman Empire and the papacy, leaving them unable to contain the revolution. After the Turks were finally defeated at the battle of Lepanto in 1571 (even though the Anabaptists had been praying for their success, willing to put aside pacifism if the Turks failed to destroy the Christian political and social order), a strong Counter-Reformation flowing from the great Council of Trent (1545-1563) expelled the revolution and its governing principle from the Catholic Church, but with great loss. The unity of Christendom was destroyed. The anti-dogmatic principle was established within Christendom, out of reach of the Church's curb. Catholicism virtually disappeared from large areas of Europe, to many of which, the Scandinavian countries, for example, it has never managed to return. The Counter-Reformation failed to re-establish a public Catholic presence in Britain, where by the end of Elizabeth I's reign there remained only about sixty thousand Catholics. Not until 1895 were English Catholics restored to most civil liberties. (They are still excluded from succession to the throne.)

Ideas have consequences. Protestantism having, in Peter Berger's words, "cut the umbilical cord between heaven and earth . . . threw man back upon himself in a historically unprecedented manner."[7] From the Reformation's central idea about the direction in which authority flows, there developed the distinctive movements and institutions of the modern world – the Enlightenment, the French Revolution, Romanticism (and its glorification of the lonely rebel), popular sovereignty, liberalism, capitalism, egalitarianism, feminism, Marxism. Thus, "Protestantism served as a historically decisive prelude to secularization."[8] Armed with the Protestant political idea, Cromwell broke the idea of kingship. The levelling ideas of Cromwell's Puritans, expelled from England's more "Catholic" brand of Protestantism, migrated to the New World, establishing there the Protestant principle, securing it by a late War of Religion, the American Revolution, with fateful consequences for the future of what we now term the West.[9]

The Catholic political idea is hierarchy, which Catholicism claims to derive from nature as well as from revelation. The Protestant political idea is egalitarianism, which it derives from its religious principle of personal autonomy. Since egalitarianism cannot exist in practice for any length of time, Protestant reformers set up hierarchical orthodoxies of their own as soon as they were free of the parent body, structures protected by distinctive cultural symbols and possessing large coercive and punitive powers. However, Protestant orthodoxy cannot long remain unfractured because of the logic of its own dynamics. Private judgement prevailing, the Reformation immediately divided and divided again into sects, each time setting up a narrower orthodoxy or a wilder antinomianism.

"The spirit of lawlessness came in with the Reformation," said John Henry Newman. There could be no givens, no supreme authority, where this spirit prevailed. It prevails in the modern world, but until very lately the Catholic Church successfully resisted it.

THE CHURCH AND LIBERALISM

The Church is often accused of not coming to terms with modernity, of having maintained since the Reformation "a fortress mentality." This description is accurate in the sense that the Church knows that coming to terms with the Protestant principle would mean not only the abdication of what it believes to be its divinely appointed authority but also ultimately the loss of its faith in God. The Church watched the steady erosion of Christian faith within the Protestant communions and acted to check the tendency to make religion a private matter wherever it appeared within Catholicism. When one considers the length of time since the Reformation successfully institutionalized its religious revolution, and the extraordinary pressures upon the Church because of this institutional grounding, one has to admit that the Catholic Church has given the Protestant principle an admirable run for its money. Perhaps it is sheer weariness in the face of increasing odds that is causing elements within the Catholic hierarchy to consider throwing in the towel now.

In the nineteenth century, John Henry Newman described the progress of liberalism, which he termed "the anti-dogmatic principle," within the Church of England and predicted with tragic accuracy what would happen to the deposit of faith "if Liberalism once got a footing" within Anglicanism.[10] He would today be saddened but not surprised to learn that an Anglican bishop has written a prayer to be used by doctors about to perform abortions, and that the Episcopalian bishop of New York has ordained a self-described lesbian to that church's priesthood. Newman saw the Catholic Church as the only defence against "the spirit of lawlessness." Throughout the nineteenth century, the Catholic Church resisted the importation into its sytem of the anti-dogmatic principle. In the 1830s it crushed the political liberalism of Felicité de Lammenais, Henri Dominique Lacordaire, and Charles Montalembert, French Catholics who urged the Church to "baptize the French Revolution" by accepting the doctrines of popular sovereignty, separation of Church and state, and liberty of conscience. When the liberal program was condemned by Rome in the encyclical *Mirari vos* (1832), Lammenais broke with the Church, revealing himself as a radical republican and socialist. Most of his colleagues submitted to Rome.

The Church's opinion of popular sovereignty was strengthened by the widespread insurrections of 1848. Religious liberalism, the adaptation of Catholic doctrine to modern demands, was even more suspect than political liberalism. Both were exhaustively condemned by Pius IX in the encyclical *Quanta Cura* and in the *Syllabus of Errors*, both issued in December 1864. Pius IX has been charged with locking the Church into a "citadel mentality" through a confusion of true with false liberalism by his misreading of the signs of the times and his failure to adjust the Church to new political realities.[11] Pius IX's condemnations, in particular the *Syllabus of Errors*, were to some degree a disillusioned reaction; Pius IX had been something of a liberal himself until the revolution of 1848, when he was forced to flee from Rome. The *Syllabus* is an extreme though logical restatement of the Church's traditional attitude towards the Protestant principle and its political developments; it ends by denying the proposition "that the Roman Pontiff can and ought to reconcile himself and reach agreement with progress, liberalism and modern civilization." That denial seemed, in the early idealistic days of Catholic Liberalism and throughout the 1950s, to be a suicidally intransigent position. Now, ironically, in the post-industrial, post-Christian, post-liberal age, Catholics on the left, utterly disenchanted with the society that is the outcome of the political developments Pius IX condemned, often speak and act as if they had written his words themselves.

In practice, of course, the Church coexisted in spite of its principled reservations with the new kinds of secularizing governments that took power in the nineteenth century, as it has always coexisted with governments good and bad. Yet it has never accepted democracy, the modern account of authority, as a religious or moral revelation, or even as a better, juster social arrangement, since it springs from a false principle of the source of authority. Even in the United States, where the Church has enjoyed wide freedom, its historical stance has been as an adversary to government, except for the brief honeymoon in the 1950s, when it seemed about to accept the American Jesuit John Courtney Murray's very influential political theology that there is no necessary dichotomy between "the American proposition" and "the Catholic proposition."

The Church's opposition on principle to the Protestant account of authority long survived Pius IX and Pius X. The following words were read over the radio on the morning of a provincial election in Quebec in 1956:

> Sovereign authority, by whatever government it is exercised, is derived solely from God, the supreme and eternal principle of all power. . . . It is therefore an absolute error to believe that authority comes from the multitudes, from the masses, from the people, to pretend that authority does not properly belong to those who exercise it, but that they have only a simple mandate revocable at any time by the people. This error, which dates from the Reformation, rests on the false principle that man has no other master than his own reason.[12]

Even today, after all the hopeful talk at the Vatican Council of man's coming of age in the modern world, even though John Courtney Murray's liberal concept of religious pluralism was enshrined in one of the Council's documents (*On Religious Liberty*), the papacy remains cool towards the dominant political and economic system of the West, what is now called "democratic capitalism." A hostile note was present in the political statements of John XXIII and of Paul VI, and even more powerfully in those of John Paul II. Nor is it generally perceived how large a part the traditional opposition to the Protestant principle and its secular developments plays in the opposition of the present-day Catholic left to the distinctive political system of the West, especially in its American, that is, most Protestant, manifestation.

The papacy, however, although it refuses to look upon democracy and capitalism as being either necessary or moral, has historically opposed even more fiercely the levelling ideas of socialism and communism. Liberalism, though undoubtedly, in Newman's words, the halfway house to atheism, is nevertheless preferable to its terminus, the atheist, materialist systems of socialism and communism. Therefore, in practice, except for a short, controversial period of détente during Paul VI's *Ostpolitik* (his attempt to soften up the governments of the Soviet east bloc towards the Church by the appointment to eastern European sees of only those bishops acceptable to the Communist governments), the modern papacy has chosen the political system of the

21

West over the only available alternative. This position is, however, no longer that of the Catholic leftists who dominate the powerful post-Vatican II agencies that direct the Catholic Church's enormous social-justice efforts. Catholic leftists have long abandoned what now seems the mild liberalism of the nineteenth century and pre-Vatican II period; now they espouse the cause of undemocratic socialism. In the manner of John of Leyden's Anabaptists in the sixteenth century, the Catholic Left now looks to other barbarians from the East, the Communist commissars, to bring in the Kingdom of God on earth. Ironically, it is the modern papacy, in the person of John Paul II, that has become in effect the principal defender of the liberal values of the West.

༺∿༻

TWO

THE FIRST MODERNIST CRISIS

༺∿༻

It is accepted wisdom, even to some extent among orthodox Catholics, that if the early benign liberalism of Felicité de Lammenais and his colleagues had not been so violently suppressed it would have evolved into a Catholic synthesis of the best in the old world view and the best in the new. Instead, this theory goes, exasperation and frustration drove liberals into excesses and out of the Church, as in the case of Lammenais, or underground to plot in bitterness a new challenge, this time one more dangerous to authority. The same charge is made concerning the suppression and condemnation of modernism, the movement of religious liberalism in the Catholic Church, which developed in the nineteenth century under the influence of the liberal Protestant school of biblical criticism.

In the middle of the nineteenth century, the papacy, lacking secular powers, had been unable to do very much to resist the progressive liberalization, that is, secularization, of the various nation states. After a vigorous restatement of its principles, it resumed wary coexistence with pagan governments, something of which it has had much experience in its history. But in the sphere of doctrine, of maintaining the purity of the deposit of faith, it had lost none of its moral authority or nerve, and had no intention of allowing the anti-dogmatic principle to be invited into its own domain. Pope Leo XIII, during whose mildly liberal papacy modernism had first gone public, taking alarm at the direction in which modernist scholars like the French priest Alfred Loisy were taking biblical criticism, issued in 1893 the encyclical letter *Providentissimus Deus*, which reasserted the inerrancy of Scripture. Pius X followed in July 1907 with a sweeping condemnation, *Lamentabili Sane*, of sixty-five modernist positions, and in September of the same year with the encyclical *Pascendi, On the Doctrines of the Modernists*, which described modernism as "a synthesis of all heresies," since "it is not possible to admit one part without admitting all." Loisy and George Tyrrell, an Irish Jesuit, were excommunicated when they refused to reconsider their positions. An oath against modernism was required of all priests, seminary professors, and religious superiors. The thoroughgoing condemnation of modernism and the vigorous carrying out of measures against it scattered the movement at its beginning and postponed revolution in the Catholic Church for sixty years. That this involved excesses in the exercise of spiritual authority can be admitted without accepting the charge that Pius x turned the Church into a police state. Acting on delations from sources whose identities were not revealed, Rome sometimes investigated and harassed orthodox scholars. (The recent bestowing by John Paul II of a cardinal's hat on Father Henri de Lubac was recognition of and apology for unwarranted suspicion, just as a similar gesture by Leo XIII had removed a cloud from the great Newman.) But what of the typical defence of the modernists, such as the following by Dr. A.R. Vidler, the noted Anglican historian:

> It is no doubt the case that some of the modernists were too much under the spell of current (evolutionary, immanentist, or pragmatic) fashions of thought, and, when driven to extremes by oppressive measures, advocated ideas it would be difficult, if not impossible, to reconcile with historic Christianity, but this was after they had been made more or less desperate by the Church's refusal to look in the face the questions that they had raised. It is an unwarranted assumption that they would have gone to such lengths if they had been treated by the authorities with respect and understanding. On behalf of the Roman authorities it may be said that they were responsible for the government of a Church the vast majority of whose members were peasants so that pastoral solicitude inclined them to protect the faith of simple believers, however much they might scandalize the educated in the process. Nonetheless, it may seem in retrospect that a Church which made such august claims for itself as did the Church of Rome, ought to have been able to handle the modernist crisis without resorting to panic measures, and to have been able to discriminate between what was important and what was not, and also to have availed itself of the services of honest, intelligent and devoted men who were doing their best to face genuine problems that would certainly have to be faced sooner or later.[1]

This kind of criticism assumes that modernists were intent on a reform of degree, not of kind, that they wished only to tidy up anomalies and embarrassing anachronisms, and that they would be content with being just a little liberal. This was not the case.

What the modernists intended was a revolution in religious thinking that would have altered Christian belief far more radically than had the Protestant Reformation. The working principle of modernism was that the discoveries of modern science had rendered obsolete and ridiculous much of the traditional language of Christian belief. To make

Christianity intellectually "credible" again and thus "more habitable for men of contemporary culture,"[2] the miraculous and mythical had to be stripped away, leaving only that kernel capable of scientific verification. Christian propositions left unsupportable by science but which nevertheless contained useful truths about human existence were to be reinterpreted to meet the new physical conditions and psychological demands of modern life and constantly thereafter modified by the lived experience of the Christian community.

The logic of their leading principle necessitated that the nineteenth-century modernists quickly found themselves propounding ideas "impossible to reconcile with historic Christianity," though perhaps at the beginning, like Luther before them, they did not fully understand the logic of their enterprise until the opposition of the Church forced them to think their premises through. Yet the speed and startling frankness of their reaction after it became clear that the gradual undermining of the traditional mode of belief was not going to be tolerated any longer just as plausibly suggests that the most influential and committed modernists, Alfred Loisy and George Tyrrell, for instance, abandoned their cover only when there was no more to be hoped for from a policy of dissimulation. Loisy revealed in his angry memoirs that he had lost his faith long before publication of his ideas brought him into conflict with the authorities of the Roman Catholic Church: "What I was beginning to believe regarding the Bible, Jesus, the Christian principles and their origins, was the absolute negation of any supernatural character for religion whatever." He also boasted that he had designed his early teaching to have about it "an air of innocent candor which, it was hoped, might prevent too much attention being paid to the daring character of its innovations."[3] As for Tyrrell, "the father of modernism," the publication shortly after his death in 1909 of his spiritual autobiography, *Christianity at the Crossroads*, made it clear that his doctrinal radicalism must have been fully developed by the time of Pius x's condemnation of his ideas, although he was still attempting to conceal the extent of his rejection of the Catholic faith. Such dissimulation on the part of modernism's stars should be called what it is: intellectual dishonesty.

There were indeed genuine problems facing the Church in the nineteenth century, but it quickly became clear that the modernist attempt to resolve them by the application of the scientific method was not going to shore up the traditional faith of Christianity. Major elements of Christian belief are simply not susceptible of that kind of physical verification. What imaginable scientific tests would, for example, "prove" to the non-believer the reality of the virginal conception of Jesus? Therefore, a revolutionary shift in the interpretation of the Christian Scriptures was necessary. The whole body of creedal propositions had to be removed and translated from the historical level of things that actually, physically happened in time to the psychological level, from the objective to the subjective, from the actual to the ideal. In this way, educated modern men could continue to adhere to a "Christian revelation" separated from the outmoded cultural concepts through which it had been transmitted.

Let us take an example of modernist translation of the key doctrine of Christianity: the Resurrection of Jesus. How is a modern Christian to assent to the creedal formula, "On the third day He rose again from the dead"? Not as an historical fact, says Rudolf Bultmann, the chief of modernist demythologizers, since "an historical fact which involves a resurrection from the dead is utterly inconceivable."[4] Nor as a bare-faced lie, as in the high-priestly effort at demythologizing reported at the end of St. Matthew's Gospel: the disciples, having stolen Christ's body while the guards were sleeping, put about the story that He was risen from the dead. That avenue, with its naturalist bypaths (such as that Jesus, though mortally wounded, recovered for a time during which He was seen by various people, but later died of His wounds), is closed to anyone who retains a shred of Christian faith. So we readily admit that "*something* happened" to account for the indisputable fact that the disciples came to believe that Jesus had come back from death. But we now explain that happening as a psychological, not a physical, event, and therefore speak not of "the Resurrection" but of "the resurrection experience." The psychological explanation takes two forms. The earlier modernist, George Tyrrell, explained it this way: the phenomena were "real" but in what way?

> Were they determined from without or within; did they belong to that series of regular sequences which exists for all, or to that which exists for one alone? Did they reveal what we call the external world, or the spirit and faith of the beholder? . . . What they saw was a vision, the spontaneous self-embodiment, in familiar apocalyptic imagery, of their faith in His spiritual triumph and resurrection, in the transcendental and eternal order – a vision that was external-ized by the very intensity of their faith, that seemed something given from outside; a vision that was purposive and symbolic of a reality which, though inwardly apprehended, was in no sense subjective; a vision that was divine, just because the faith that produced it was divine.[5]

It is easier to believe in a physical resurrection than in this extraordinary manufacture. Consequently, today's modernists have dropped the vision hypothesis. The disciples, they say, saw no phenomena of whatever origin; the revelation was of a different order of reality. As the disciples pondered upon Christ's life among them, its true significance gradually unfolded as the revelation of a new mode of living, of relating to each other. They realized that He had led them to a breakthrough in their apprehension of what it meant to be fully human, and this revelatory experience released in them a new spirit of love and forgiveness. In this spirit, Jesus may be truly described as having transcended His death, to have remained "alive" among His followers. He was present in the prophetic spirit released in the early Christian community. Today, the authentic voice of Christ can be discerned in the voices of those crying for liberation from various forms of oppression.[6] All intellectual content has been removed from the Resurrection proposition of the Creed. The "resurrection experience" is entirely subjective.

The major awkwardness faced by proponents of a psychological understanding of the propositions of the faith is how to deal with the indisputable fact that the Gospels present them as factual statements about physical events that took place in history. How does one deal with the moving and detailed accounts, some claiming to be eyewitness, of encounters with a physically convincing risen Christ, encounters during which the disciples examined His wounds and picnicked with Him by the Sea of Tiberias? The Church has from the outset offered them to us as actual episodes in history. Today, after all the reportorial discrepancies have been carefully noted, the Gospel accounts still convey the conviction and immediacy of contemporary versions of spectacular events.

Modernists deal with this awkwardness by having recourse to the historical-critical method of interpretation. By means of this method, the evangelists can be shown to have told not lies but stories. As Jews whose religious imaginations were shaped by the Messianic prophecies, the disciples of Christ could understand His suffering and death only in terms of their great national myth. They expressed what His life had come to mean to them in Messianic language, and also in concepts borrowed from the more ancient nature myths of the dying and resurrected god, current among neighbouring pagan cultures. By the use of form criticism and of generic criticism, modern scholars identified the class of literature in which the evangelists embodied their concepts – allegory, maxim, poetry, folk tale, myth, parable, midrash, history, morality play. Such identification determines what response is required of us. By the use of another historical-critical tool, redaction criticism, any scriptural account can be moved back to its earlier form, stripped of the additions, decorations, interpolations, interpretations, borrowings, by which generations of editors overlaid its basic statement. Thus, the Christ of faith can be scientifically separated from the Christ of history.

Modernists are thus able to retain the creedal formulas while at the same time emptying them of their traditional meaning, indeed of any historical or objective content whatever. There is no logical place for the demythologizer to stop. Early modernists taught that Christ only belatedly became conscious that He was the Messiah. Soon, having reassigned His supposed claims about His divinity and mission to much later Christian apologists, modernist scholars came to see Christ as no more than an extraordinary man who so perfectly carried out the will of God that He might in a sense be called one with God. Contemporary feminist theologians dispense even with a human Christ, claiming that He can no longer "represent redemptive personhood" to modern women.[7]

Demythologizers, having stripped down the Gospels, conclude that Jesus Himself was the proto-modernist: "Judging from the core sayings and parables, there is absolutely no basis for assuming that Jesus shared the cosmological, mythological, or religious ideas of his contemporaries."[8] What comfortable words for the thoroughly modern modernist – Jesus Himself was a demythologizer.

This is the outcome of the hopeful attempt "to make the Church more habitable for men of contemporary culture." It was a curious idea in any case, new in Christendom, that the Church should adapt the faith to suit the world rather than the other way around, or that the "contemporary" intellectual, of whatever age or culture, should expect to find being a Christian comfortable.

The effect of modernism on the individual soul is either the rapid loss of Christian faith altogether or a curious and rather touching brand of pious agnosticism, whereby one believes the little one respectably can, according to modernism's own very arbitrary canon, while at the same time practising far beyond one's rational acceptance, out of loyalty, or patriotism, or from a heart too won in childhood ever to be alienated.

There were pious modernists a century ago and there still are. I know many and respect them, though I think that a more contradictory and exasperating religious position is difficult to imagine. The contradiction between profession and practice is an admission of despair at the failure of modernism's attempt to heal the Protestant breach between faith and reason. The hopeful tools of the modern scientific method had failed to establish a rational belief for a modern faith, or rather, the system proposed had proven too cold and too cynical to satisfy the religious heart. Which means that, ironically, if the modernist needs to go on believing, he must do it by tacitly accepting that the split between faith and reason is irreparable, and he lives by what he no longer believes can be rationally justified.

Underlying what might be called modernist fideism is a curious irony that has become apparent at this late stage of the modernist effort: modernists are themselves engaged in the very enterprise they are committed to destroying – that is, the construction and maintenance of mythology. I am indebted to a young Catholic scholar, survivor of the first generation of official modernist Catholic catechesis,[9] for this insight: that modernists are in fact *mythologizers*, not *de*mythologizers. The Church experienced and afterwards always taught the events of Christ's life as *history*, not as myth, parable, allegory, or epic poetry. The Church thinks of the Gospels differently from the way it thinks of the Book of Jonah, or the Book of Job, or the Song of Solomon. The Church firmly holds that, as the great Anglican scholar, Bishop Stephen Neill, put it, "A Christ who is in any way at all less than historical is not the Christ of the Gospels, or of the Church, or of faith, or of glory."[10] Modernists, on the contrary, are engaged paradoxically in turning history into myth, by means of the mythological language and concepts of the secularized late twentieth century. In the process, they have turned the historical person, Christ, from man and God into an idea. Catholic modernists have ended up with the worst of both worlds, the loss of the historic faith they were born into, and the betrayal of their modernist principles that becomes necessary if they long to live as if that faith were still alive. The modernist program, far from revitalizing the Church, nearly destroyed it. The "educated" are still "scandalized," the "simple believers" are driven away.

This is a result of the attempt to construct a modern Catholic synthesis of human and divine knowledge through the assumptions and methods that the liberal Protestant school of biblical criticism worked out in the nineteenth century. For liberal Protestant scholars, dogma was a Greek accretion to Christ's simple message and had to be abandoned. Only the ethical content of the Gospels, "the essence of Christianity," as Adolf von Harnack, the greatest of the liberal school, put it, should be retained. Harnack taught that the Reformation would not be completed until faith cancelled dogma. For Harnack, as for the earliest Protestant reformers, subjective religious experience was the only valid authority for the Christian life: "The Kingdom of God comes by coming to the individual, by entering into his *soul* and laying hold of it."[11]

Nineteenth-century Catholic modernists began as apologists for Catholic dogma against Harnack and his school, but they quickly adopted the same liberal Protestant assumptions. They did so in part because there was no equally exciting Catholic working model of biblical exegesis among the fragmented systems of nineteenth-century Catholic thought. Yet there was a contemporary biblical movement loyal to the tradition (which made it less exciting for young bloods), which they might have joined. Newman was doing his great work on the development of doctrine and on the "illative" or inferential aspect of belief. Neo-Thomism was under way with the blessing of Leo XIII. The choice, for whatever reasons, of the liberal Protestant model, itself a phenomenon of the death of Protestant orthodoxy, meant that the content of the faith proposed for the modern Catholic Church would be defined by the authority of agnostic Protestants who rejected any concept of a teaching authority.

The original and continuing prestige of the historical-critical method depends on its claim to scientific objectivity. Catholics who dispute its findings are immediately charged with ignorance, superstition, fundamentalism, and obscurantism. Even bishops are told to stay out of a field in which they have no credentials. Yet the method does not deserve the blind obedience modernist scholars give it. It is not scientifically objective. Its hypotheses cannot be subjected to the kind of rigorous control and verification that the scientific method demands. Also, the historical-critical method is heavily dependent upon arbitrary assumptions that masquerade as evidence but originate in the researcher's own bias. Anyone who, for example, sets out with Rudolf Bultmann's agnostic, naturalist convictions – "the incredibility of a mythical event like the resuscitation of a dead person"[12] – is unlikely to find that the Resurrection actually happened, after all.

For example, a key "finding" upon which the authority of the historical-critical system rests is its dating of the Gospels. The lateness of the Gospel accounts is an assumption, not an historically established fact, made necessary by another assumption: that most of the claims the Gospels quote Christ as having made about Himself, His mission, and His Church are actually the theological reflections and political interpretations of Christians who lived several generations after Christ and who were reacting to conditions in which the developing Christian community found itself. The historical-critical "finding" here is that the Church created the tradition, not the other way around. Another crucial assumption – that Mark's Gospel was the first and was the source of Matthew and Luke – rests largely on the accident that Mark does not contain certain material awkward to liberal exegetes, such as the establishment of the Church upon Peter and the miracles accompanying the birth of Jesus.

Another unsupported assumption is the existence of the famous "Q" document (from the German *Quelle*, source). There is no compelling reason to believe that Q ever existed, except in the imagination of revisionist scholars, yet modernists continue to refer to it as if they had it open beside them in a recent annotated edition. Faithful Q: no modernist could leave home without it. With the help of Q, authentic-sounding "research" can be produced that is actually founded only on currently fashionable assumptions. James Breech, a Canadian biblical scholar, to take a recent glaring example, relies heavily on Q in his reduction of the Gospels to a guide to better personal relations: "The most informative saying of Jesus historically is the following, recorded by both Matthew and Luke from their source, Q"; ". . . the advice given by an early Christian teacher which was collected in Q"; "The Q version of these parables, then, together with their introductions, give evidence of early Christian thinking, but do not provide evidence of how Jesus might have connected the kingdom and his parables"; "We have seen that Q had already transformed that story into a question . . ."[13] (Breech's simple faith in this unsupported liberal dogma didn't stop him from calling me credulous for holding to the traditional Christian interpretation of the Gospels.) Adolf von Harnack actually went as far as to "reconstruct" Q.[14]

It is now widely recognized, though not yet in Catholic circles, how strongly liberal Protestant biblical scholarship was coloured by rationalist assumptions and presuppositions so that the historical-critical method it developed was anything but a tool for neutral scholarship.[15] "All that historical criticism can establish is the fact that the first disciples came to believe in the Resurrection," says its most eminent modern practitioner, Rudolf Bultmann. That is because it keeps itself poverty-stricken by dismissing out of hand the most important body of evidence, the Catholic tradition, the continuity of what the Church has believed and since apostolic times taught about Christ's life on earth. For the orthodox scholar, the tradition is the test of the truth of his findings; for the modernist, the tradition is inadmissible hearsay evidence. Yet the Scriptures themselves, the texts for all this higher criticism, come to us through the tradition, selected, canonized, and authoritatively interpreted by a teaching Church. It must always be remembered that it was the tradition that created the Church, not the Church the tradition. What the Church remembers in the tradition is the actual earthly life of Jesus Christ. For the tradition, the Christ of faith *is* the Christ of history. The exclusion of this most Catholic source is the chief deficiency of the historical-critical method, a deficiency built into it by the mind-set of its inventors. It is difficult at present to be fair to modern biblical criticism, considering the devastation it continues to produce. The Church recognizes its legitimate, if limited, uses. Names like Bishop Stephen Neill, the great Anglican scholar, or Stephen Clark and Hans Urs von Baltasar, modern Catholic scholars, remind us that reason and faith can still be compatible in biblical scholarship. You don't have to be agnostic.

It has not been difficult for its critics to divest the historical-critical method, at least as it is generally used, of its claims to scientific objectivity. It will be more difficult to extricate biblical scholarship from the modernist myth that has animated so much of its history, the myth that the discoveries of modern science have so qualitatively changed the human mind, so caused it to evolve, that it physically cannot believe what it could two thousand years ago. "It is impossible," says Rudolf

Bultmann, "to use electric light and the wireless and to avail ourselves of modern medical and surgical discoveries and at the same time to believe in the New Testament world of spirits and miracles."[16] "If the truth of the New Testament proclamation is to be preserved, the only way is to demythologize it."[17] This working myth of the reigning school of thought is actually a piece of chronological snobbishness, as C.S. Lewis put it, that cannot stand up to humble Christian reflection. When was it ever easy for "educated contemporary man" to believe that a corpse came back to life and rose from the grave? Easier for the brilliant pagan Augustine than for Edward Schillebeeckx? Easier for Saul of Tarsus than for Raymond Brown? For Thomas Aquinas than for Charles Curran? For Catharine of Siena than for Rosemary Ruether? Even Thomas the Apostle was unable to believe until he had the evidence of his hands and eyes. (Modernist scripture scholars say, of course, that this is a later story invented to strengthen belief in Christ's Resurrection.)

The problem of how best to reconcile the findings of history and science with the faith as handed down through the ages faces the Church in this as in every age. But if a new synthesis is needed, it cannot be that proposed by modernism. No common ground in which to anchor a new synthesis exists between scholars who deny the rational basis of Christian dogma and the Church, which put itself on record for modern times as continuing "firmly and with absolute constancy to hold that the four gospels . . . whose historical character the Church unhesitatingly asserts, faithfully hand on what Jesus Christ, while living among men, really did and taught for their eternal salvation until the day He was taken up into heaven" (*Dei Verbum*, 19).[18] Vatican II sanctioned scriptural scholarship but drew limits: "All of what has been said about the way of interpreting Scripture is subject finally to the judgment of the Church, which carries out the divine commission and ministry of guarding and interpreting the word of God" (*Dei Verbum*, 12).

So in the end it comes back to the old question of authority: Whose? For the modern Catholic, the authority of the Bible still cannot be separated from the authority of the Church. "Sacred theology rests on the written word of God, together with sacred tradition as its primary and perpetual foundation" (*Dei Verbum*, 24). Very many Catholics still believe on the authority of the Bible that Jesus Christ was the Son of God, and they accept the Bible on the authority of the Church. If any link in the chain of belief is broken, Catholics will stop trying to lead the difficult Christian life as described by the Gospels. Tens of millions have already made this rational decision. If not a reasonable faith, then none at all. Their religious imagination cannot be nourished by briefly fashionable academic theories. They have yearning hearts, not itching ears. Not for them the reduction of revelation to what one feels at any given moment, nor windy self-deceiving raptures about a Christ-less, Church-less Christianity:

> When the revelation is truly understood as God's revelation, it is no longer a communication of teachings, nor of ethical or historical and philosophical truths, but God speaking directly to me, assigning me each time to the place that is allotted to me before God, i.e. summoning me in my humanity which is null without God, and which is open to God only in the recognization of its nullity. Hence there can be only one "criterion" for the truth of revelation, namely this, that the word which claims to be the revelation must place each man before a decision – the decision as to how he wants to understand himself, as one who wins his life and authenticity by his own resources, reason and actions, or by the grace of God.[19]

These words, written by the greatest of the modernist fathers, Rudolf Bultmann, in his "inquiry into the possibility of religion without myth," are a classic statement of the Protestant principle in its late form. The revelation, whatever it is, now has no intellectual content whatever, uses no human channels, and accepts a radical antithesis between grace and nature. God speaks "wordlessly but directly" to "my humanity," refraining however from any suggestion as to what I should do. Revelation means each man's process of self-understanding, which, translated into action with no guidance from either God or nature, is yet in some mysterious way validated by grace. Belief in some power called "God" is retained, but only by a departure from modernist reason, for there is no more scientific proof for the existence of God than for the Resurrection. This is a God with reality only in the individual consciousness. One is God unto oneself.

Modernism as a theological system has been around long enough to allow it to be judged by its fruits, among which are the virtual disappearance of the Anglican Church, the Methodist Church, and other liberal Protestant bodies, and the recent staggering depopulation of the Catholic Church. Religious liberalism, Newman's "anti-dogmatic principle," has proven, as he predicted, "too cold a principle to prevail with the multitude."[20] Most Christians probably would still agree with Newman: "Dogma is the fundamental principle of my religion. I know of no other religion; I cannot enter into the idea of any other sort of religion; religion, as a mere sentiment, is to me a dream and a mockery."[21] But dogma means authority. Dogma means *Church*:

> The final conclusion, even if it disappoints some people, is that human beings are made in a certain way and not otherwise. When truth comes to them, they congregate around it, speculate along the lines it suggests, surround and protect it with a network of human and

objectual relationships. This is then what is called an institution. Religious truth is no exception, it too gives rise to institutions, the only way of protection and continuity known to man.[22]

The reduction of religion to experience, to sentiment however noble, must end in the disappearance of Christianity. Certain unaffiliated Christians are given to saying hopefully that the Church will die but Christianity will survive. It will not. The remythologized, privatized, sterilized, materialistic religion proposed by modernists in the nineteenth century and today cannot create or nurture a believing community now any more than some psychological "resurrection experience" could have created the electrifying and missionary belief of the apostles. Modernism is entirely a creature of the academy, where it continues to infect young minds, in the same way that the young Alfred Loisy was seduced by the rationalist ideas of his famous professor at the Collège de France, Ernest Renan. The individual modernist may cling to some shreds of faith by ingenious sleight-of-mind, but his is a one-generation construct, dying with its professor, not a living faith to inspire his culture and hand down to his children.

For what, in actual practice, should the critical, mature modernist Christian do when, for instance, he gathers his children around him to celebrate Christmas? Should he read Luke's Christmas Gospel and sing the Christmas carols as if they were true, even though he believes them to be crude and primitive theology? After all, the rest of his society has no scruples about doing this, the pagans and the department stores. Or if this seems too cynical, too dishonest, ought he rather, in the manner of early socialist Sunday schools, to devise a passionately rationalist catechesis, swap German for German, chant a passage from Bultmann instead of "Joy To The World!"; ought he to gather his little ones about the Crib, light the candles, and read Raymond Brown instead of St. Luke on the virginal conception of Jesus: "My judgment in conclusion is that the totality of the scientifically controllable evidence leaves an unresolved problem."[23] How their eyes will shine, how their little hearts will burn within them as they hear these holy words! How touched they will all be as the littlest child reverently places a shining question mark in the empty manger. And how they will rejoice when they find their stockings, which they have hung up to a Protestant parody of a Catholic bishop, stuffed with subscriptions to *Concilium*, *Catholic Update*, *National Catholic Reporter*, and *The Tablet*.

Pious modernists recognize this difficulty, with the result that what has already happened in liberal Protestant practice is now developing in the Catholic Church – that is, the establishment of a two-tier religion, one for the class, one for the mass. Recently, a priest was recounting to me the details of a modernist theory about the Eucharist of which he had just enthusiastically made the acquaintance. When I said that this theory would shake the faith of his parishioners who would realize at once that it was irreconcilable with what the Church teaches, he replied, "No, no, no! I would never say that from the pulpit. They can't understand these things. It would only upset them."

This now common attitude reveals an intolerable élitism utterly foreign to Catholicism but inherent in modernism. Modernists have historically felt that only a chosen few can reach their higher development of religious belief and that therefore the kindest thing to do is to free the non-intellectual masses from the most onerous restraints of religion, the sexual, and then leave them in peace. The Gnostic separation of the believing community into *perfecti* and *auditores* is the oldest Christian heresy. Whenever it raised its ugly head, the Church hammered it.

George Tyrrell wrote that Catholicism was "a personal religion lived by what must always be a small minority of professed Catholics," an élite that the hierarchy cynically smothers because "as a rule, it pays better to cater for the groundlings rather than for the elect few."[24] In Renan's revealing construct, Caliban, the ignorant believer, works and pays and keeps the whole enterprise going, thus freeing Prospero, the intellect, to think and rule, and Ariel, the spirit of religion, to fly at liberty. Raymond Brown, having blown up the concept of the virginal conception of Jesus, spares a thought for the feelings of Caliban and the groundlings: "But as we discuss Mary's virginity, we must assure all those ordinary people in our churches, the 'little' people who happen to be God's people, that in our quest we 'experts' have not forgotten that we too must obey the biblical injunction . . . that all generations, even this 'nosey' generation, shall call her blessed."[25] Jolly decent of him.

With mention of Raymond Brown, the subtlest and most influential of the post-Vatican II generation of neo-modernists, we reach the present stage of the revolution. But before we proceed to examine contemporary neo-modernism, we must look at the transitional stage of the revolution in the Catholic Church, the period between the crushing of the first modernist uprising and the Second Vatican Council.

THREE

ᗉᔗ

INTERIM: THE REVOLUTION UNDERGROUND

ᗉᔗ

Only about forty priests throughout the world refused to take the oath against modernism. One honours them for their integrity, since many other modernists on seminary and Catholic university faculties came to some accommodation with their consciences and went on teaching, though not publishing, their ideas. It is said by defenders of the early modernists that the Church reacted far more violently than the situation deserved, that there was in fact no organized modernist movement with a coherent program and disciples. While it is probably true that no single modernist held all the positions condemned by *Pascendi* and *Lamentabili*, all modernists shared that attitude towards belief and authority that Newman described as "deep, plausible scepticism." Or, as Ludwig Ott put it in his classic definition of modernism: "The cognitional theoretical basis of Modernism is agnosticism, according to which human rational cognition is limited to the world of experience."[1]

This attitude towards belief and authority survived the condemnation of modernism and was successfully communicated to generations of impressionable undergraduates without one incriminating word's being committed to print. The smile, the raised eyebrow, the incredulous little laugh, the mock serious reading – Alfred Loisy described Ernest Renan doing it and the glee of his class when "a tall ecclesiastic" slammed out of the classroom in disgust. Everyone of my generation who went past high school in Catholic education knew a Jesuit or a Dominican who was a past master of debunking body language. Or had, as I did, a French professor who, assigning *Candide*, said gleefully, "This is on the Index, of course. The only books worth reading are on the Index."

There is no point in wondering how many among those "liberal religionists" stranded after 1910, or of the priests they later instructed, harboured "a real antipathy or anger against revealed truth." Perhaps more often it was, as Newman wrote of the same kind of intellectual in his own time, a matter of "an animosity arising from almost a personal feeling; it being a matter of party, a point of honour, the excitement of a game, or a satisfaction to the soreness or annoyance occasioned by the acrimony or narrowness of apologists for religion, to prove that Christianity or that Scripture is untrustworthy."[2] There was, and is, only too often valid reason for that soreness and annoyance. What Catholic has not felt thus against even the most orthodox of priests and prelates? Churchmen exercising power in the cause of sacred truth too often act like secular governors, arrogantly and without compassion; these faults may be simply those connected with power but they are even less tolerable in men claiming to speak in the name of God.

This is a perennial and insoluble problem. Yet alert doctrinal vigilance is the only way the Church can preserve the faith. Corrections, definitions, and, as a final resort, condemnations and explusions did not start with Pius x. At the Council of Jerusalem (51 A.D.), St. Paul restrained the new Church from hiving itself off into a narrow Judaizing sect. At Nicaea (325 A.D.), the doctrine of the Trinity was defended and defined and Arius was condemned. Chalcedon (451 A.D.) defined the full humanity and full divinity of Christ and condemned Nestorius. Official protection of doctrine and repudiation of heretics are indispensable to the retention of the faith by the universal Church. The magisterium has periodically had to intervene whenever prolonged periods of doctrinal confusion distracted and alienated believers. A way of life cannot endure without agreed-upon principles.

The believer does not, of course, live the Christian life by propositions alone. He may not even be able to articulate them if pressed. But he could not live as a Christian at all if the propositions did not exist. Christianity as a way of life was founded upon the proposition that since Christ rose again from the dead, those who followed Him would also triumph over death. That, as St. Paul realized, is the argument for our belief. Unless the church energetically maintains this and related creedal propositions and confidently presents them to each generation as reality, the Christian vision will disappear, or rather trickle away into the warm slop of sentimentality and high-minded social meddling that is the end condition of many post-Christian Protestant bodies.

"Authority, not reasoned argument, extinguished the crisis," wrote Gabriel Daly, a recent Catholic historian of the modernist period.[3] The complaint about the Church's refusal to engage in argument is not true – years and decades of open argument preceded every major exercise of doctrinal authority in the Church's history. And the insinuation that Catholic authority is *per se* irrational is an insult. All that Daly's standard charge means is that once again the Church did not accept reasons and arguments that contradicted constant Christian teaching. Authority must have the final word; that is what entitles it to be called "authority." Modernism, like Arianism and Nestorianism before it, simply failed in its first bid to become authoritative. True, too, though Daly intends it disparagingly, is his remark that "Catholic theology and spirituality had been conditioned over a long period to accept this *modus operandi* as characterizing the specific difference between Catholicism and Protestantism."[4] Indeed it had, through two thousand years of resisting the Protestant principle of authority, whatever it called itself.

Underlying the notion that if the Church debated longer there would be an end to religious crises is the very modern proposition that truth is the end product of a dialectical process that results in the unification of opposites into a truth transcending both, a concept foreign to Scripture's self-understanding, or to that of the Catholic Church at any time in its past. The Church does not consider itself a debating society. The rare general councils called when doctrinal confusion becomes intolerable "are not conferences where theologians beat out an understanding, a *modus vivendi*. They are assemblies where authorized, or rather authoritative, witnesses testify to what the Church actually believes on the point at issue."[5] The intention is always, in the words of the Council of Trent, "to preserve the purity of the Gospel." When the Church (after many years of arguing with him) announced in 1979 than Hans Küng was no longer to be considered a *Catholic* theologian, it was acting in a manner entirely consistent with its conception of its mission in history.

In the late twentieth century, the Church has still not changed its mind about the nature of truth. Vatican II spoke of truth as something valid for all time, revealed by God through the Scriptures and in the unwritten tradition, both sources "to be accepted and venerated with the same sense of loyalty and reverence." To this "sacred deposit," the "heritage of faith," the whole Church must "remain always steadfast," "holding, practising and professing" it "in a single common effort" (*Dei Verbum*, 9, 10). The modern Church perseveres in believing that truth is objective and immutable, and in rejecting the idea that it is subjective, relative, historically conditioned, and evolving. Modernists, for their part, continue to maintain that all doctrinal construction is relative, that the locus of revelation is experience, and that doctrine develops, not as the flower from the seed, as in the older image, but as the human being from the fish, in evolutionary jumps.

A radical theory of theological evolution was essential to modernism if revolutionary doctrines were to be presented as legitimate developments of scriptural revelation such as those the Church had ratified in the modern dogmatic definitions of the Immaculate Conception and Assumption of Mary and the infallibility of the successor of Peter. During their period of eclipse, modernists sought an orthodox outlet for their evolutionary ideas. Their early attempt to co-opt Newman's theory of the development of doctrine was abandoned, since Newman's thought, though non-scholastic, was nonetheless implacably dogmatic and non-relativist, the whole of his personal and public life having been dedicated to resisting the anti-dogmatic principle in Anglicanism, and later its importation into the Roman Catholic Church. Modernists fared much better by attaching themselves to the charismatic figure of the Jesuit paleontologist Pierre Teilhard de Chardin, whose para-scientific theory of cosmic evolution became the vehicle for their ideas about radical development in the structures and dogmas of the Church.

At first glance, Teilhard seems an unlikely modernist hero, being by his own description "at the antipodes of modernism." He rejected modernism's attempt to diminish Christ, believing instead that "the 'success' of the Christ of Christianity is due to the association of his birth (which gives him the value of a *fact* or concrete *element* in the world) and his resurrection (which lets us grant him superhuman and, as it were, cosmic attributes)."[6] For Teilhard, the Incarnation was a synthesis between Christ and the universe, and the Resurrection a necessity of cosmic evolution. He quite literally adored the Mass, believing that in the Transubstantiation, when Christ transforms bread and wine into His body and blood, we see the beginning of the transfiguration of matter into God which must happen to the whole cosmos as the end of evolution. Unlike modernists, he had no thought of "deducing Christian dogmas from a mere inspection of those qualities which, according to the light of reason, characterize the structure of the world."[7]

Moreover, he had opinions deeply embarrassing to twentieth-century liberals, who took great pains to keep them hidden from his public. He was innocently and openly racist, approved of fascism – "a necessary phase" – and of the "civilizing" intervention of Italy in Ethiopia, believed in genetic engineering "not only to master scientifically the maladies and phenomena of counter-revolution . . . but to produce . . . a superior human type."[8] He celebrated war, technology, and the atom bomb, was anti-democratic and anti-egalitarian. The Piltdown forgery duped him but he went on defending it. The synthesis of science and faith that he proposed drew devastating criticism both from secular scientists like Peter Medawar and from his great Catholic humanist contemporaries, Etienne Gilson and Jacques Maritain, all of whom considered it mystical flim-flam; Gilson accurately described it as "theology fiction." Altogether, not an obvious bearer of the modernist standard.

Yet, from before the First World War through the Second Vatican Council, he was the single most important figure for modernist survival. If he had not existed, modernists would have had to invent him, which, in large measure, is what they did, glossing over embarrassing defects in his personality and scholarship while using his celebrity status and his theory of the cosmos evolving towards divinity to transport their own process theology. Henri de Lubac, a leading expositor of his ideas, warned that Teilhard and "teilhardism" should not be confused, claiming that apparent apostles of Teilhard's theories were actually propagandizing for their own quite different theories. The evolutionary transfiguration Teilhard prophesied was not at all identical with the revolution in religious consciousness envisioned by modernists, yet they used his vision to legitimate the latter, as successfully and as cynically as Charles Dawson had exploited the budding scientific reputation and innocence of the young Teilhard to validate the Piltdown forgery.

Teilhard's "synthesis" of faith and science was an extraordinary construct, wildly singular (he confessed he was "the only one to have *seen*!"), either mystically beautiful and true, or tawdry and spurious, as one's tastes dictate, a sunrise-hued broth of emotional French piety, Bergsonian metaphysics, provincial prejudices, and genuine religious imagination. It appealed to the type of perfectly orthodox Catholic who had earlier made a cult of the mystical French airman Antoine de Saint-Exupéry. But the interesting Catholic novelist Flannery O'Connor also admired Teilhard, doubting whether "any Christian of this century can be fully aware of his religion until he has reseen it in the cosmic light which Teilhard has cast upon it."[9] (O'Connor, a liberal but no modernist, qualified this judgement after the Church's *Monitum* [warning] of 1962: "His failure was the failure of a great and saintly man. . . . His life of faith and work can be emulated even though his books remain incomplete and dangerous."[10]) He has, and to some extent deserves, his orthodox defenders, among them the Jesuit Cardinals Jean Danielou and Henri de Lubac. He was treated relatively gently by the Vatican, the 1962 *Monitum* about ambiguities and "grave errors" in his work being milder than a relegation of them to the Index of prohibited books. The *Monitum* is still in force, although in 1981, the centenary of his birth, the Vatican praised him for "the witness of the unified life of a man imbued to the depths of his being by Christ." (The Vatican's praise, however, came from Secretary of State Cardinal Agostino Casaroli while the Pope lay near death from an assassination attempt. Later, Casaroli issued a reminder that the official warning about Teilhard's work was still in effect.)

Teilhard believed that evolution proceeds through a build-up of psychic energy until a boiling-point is reached, whereupon a jump occurs to a higher level of complexity. Such a jump took place, he believed, when our animal ancestors broke through into consciousness. We are now on the threshold of another jump as the organization of human psychic energy leads to the emergence of a common human soul. According to Teilhard, an envelope of conscious thought, which he dubbed the "noosphere," now surrounds the biosphere, the physical world.

Evidence of this emerging communitarian consciousness is to be found in the rapid political socialization of human societies, a sign of "the completion of hominization," which Teilhard welcomed.

It is easy to see how attractive Teilhard's idea of irresistible evolution towards a higher understanding was for men who wanted to challenge not only earlier formulations of truth but also the very idea that truth could ever be immutable, absolute. Man is "becoming," carried forward on an advancing wave of consciousness, a mystical flux in which nothing can be fixed. The only absolute is change. Radical change is thus not to be feared, but is holy, since it brings us always closer to identity with God. As human consciousness expands, the simpler, cruder understandings of reality that earlier satisfied it can no longer be accepted. The evolving mind is now physiologically unable to tolerate them. Understanding has shifted from the historical and physical to the cosmic and spiritual plane. This evolution of man's religious understanding cannot be resisted, though probably only a minority of men have yet experienced an evolutionary breakthrough. Perhaps, indeed, only a few members of a species ever do initiate increased "complexity consciousness," but these are the future; lower strains die off, as they are meant to. Here is Tyrrell's élite again, exotically redefined.

The change from an historical to a psychological understanding of Scripture is the core of the modernist attempt to rescue the Christian message. It is ironic that Teilhard was co-opted to this endeavour, for the one thing he could never be accused of is thinking metaphorically about Catholicism. For him, the evolution of mind and matter towards unity with God was as physical and historical a phenomenon as the rocks and bones he studied. However, though Teilhard, as he insisted, may not have been a modernist in the classical sense, his method was identical with that of modernism, in that it allowed the language of a dogma to be retained while it simultaneously emptied it of its traditional intellectual content.

A case in point is Teilhard's treatment of the presence of evil in the world. In Scripture, sin enters the world through the conscious decision of the first man and woman to disobey God, a moral choice. For Teilhard, evil was rather "a statistically inevitable by-product of a universe in the course of unification with God."[11] Sin is a natural feature in the structure of the world. Just as failures, bad starts, and wrong directions leading to extinction are accompanying features of natural evolution, so sin is inseparable from cosmogenesis. It is the condition of multiplicity struggling towards unity. In this account, sin may still be said to be "original," but obviously not in the way the Old and New Testaments understand the term.

Just as obviously, Teilhard's understanding destroys the traditional Christian understanding of the Atonement and the Redemption – that as sin and death entered the world by one man, Adam, so by one man,

Christ, the new Adam, sin and death were overcome. The implications of Teilhard's theories were noted by Church authority, which condemned them, though without naming him, in Pius XII's encyclical *Humani Generis* (August 12, 1950).

This one example of Teilhard's singular modernism indicates his multifaceted usefulness to theological revolutionaries. Its value for doctrinal reformulation is immediately apparent. Just as important was the use of his teaching on sin to justify political and social revolution. The modern development by Gregory Baum and other liberation theologians of Teilhard's concept of sin as structural rather than personal has informed the present attack by Catholic intellectuals on the governing political and economic systems of the West.

Though Teilhard himself maintained a patrician aloofness from politics, his theory that modern collectivizing movements (including Fascism and Marxism) announced a new level in the emergence of a unified consciousness helped to make radical socialism religiously respectable, even necessary, despite the fact that the Church had hitherto condemned it. Much of the present enthusiasm of Catholic intellectuals for left-wing revolutionary movements, in particular those with strong religious coloration, as in Nicaragua, claims support from Teilhard's thought. Gregory Baum, a Canadian liberation theologian and a leading Teilhardist in the years just before and during Vatican II, believes that the Council documents, especially that on the Church in the modern world, *Gaudium et Spes*, embodied Teilhard's thought, though without explicit reference to him. Certainly Teilhardian language is constantly resorted to by *Gaudium et Spes*: "an evolution towards unity, a process of wholesome socialization"; "a new age of human history"; "things in their mutable and evolutionary aspects"; "the human race is involved in a new stage of history."

It is also possible to trace to Teilhard the inspiration for much of "the global village" thinking of the powerful post-Vatican II bureaucracies, for collectivist activities like the Basic Christian Communes, and for the idea that a synthesis between Christianity and Marxism is inevitable. Initially cool to Marxism, Teilhard came to teach that "the Christian and the Marxist ways must eventually come together because in the nature of things everything that is faith must rise and everything that rises must converge."[12] In 1948, as the Communists marched to victory in China, Teilhard wrote to a friend: "Who can tell whether, in the very interests of the Kingdom of God, a good dose of Marxism is not the thing to save us?"[13] In 1966, a symposium on the "Christian-Marxist encounter" concluded that "Teilhard has brought home to both Christians and Marxists that their respective interpretations of history are as much in evolutionary movement as history itself."[14]

A further important insight for which neo-modernists are indebted to Teilhard de Chardin is that the revolutionary Catholic intellectual ought never to leave the Catholic Church. Earlier doctrinal controversies had ended with the expulsion of the revolutionaries and their ideas and with the magisterium of the Church still firmly holding the power of interpretation and definition. Teilhard's career suggested that this suicidal course was not inevitable. Like the modernists he believed that the Church had reached "a time of mutation, a necessary reformation, much more profound than that of the xvith century . . . a matter not of institutions and morality but of faith."[15] Teilhard thought that a new Christology was about to give birth to "the religion of the future." Aching from the Church's repudiation of his life's work, having "no illusions" about Rome, he still saw "no better way to promote what I hope for" than by "sincere attachment to the 'phylum' whose development I expect. . . . I see only in the Roman stem, taken in its entirety, the biological support vast enough and differentiated enough to bring about and to support the expected transformation."[16] He believed with all his heart "that if Christianity . . . is indeed destined to be the religion of tomorrow, it can only be through the living, organic, axis of its Roman Catholicism that it can hope to be a match for, and assimilate to itself, the great modern currents of humanitarianism."[17] What madness then, to amputate oneself from that "biological necessity," the Catholic phylum.

This is not to say that Teilhard's attachment to the Church was entirely from political design. He truly believed that "nothing spiritual or divine can come to a Christian, or to one who has taken religious vows, except through the Church or his Order."[18] He would be horrified by today's continuous parade of dissident religious who insult the Church in the media. That was not part of his legacy. His major contribution was the perception that the Catholic Church not only possessed but also *was* a unique communications system through which reforming ideas could be disseminated very successfully *"malgré toute Encyclique."*[19] Teilhard's own success was a heartening example. Though much is made by his supporters of his wonderful obedience to unreasonable prohibitions, it is a fact that all his "suppressed" work was in wide circulation during his lifetime in mimeographed copies, with his knowledge and without his hindrance. His ideas aroused more excitement while under a ban than when they were finally published with Rome's permission, a natural case, perhaps, of the spice of disobedience lending enchantment to the view. One could manage, obviously, without an *imprimatur*, and if one avoided open confrontation, one could count on a good long run.

Contrary to its popular image, Rome is cautious and Rome is slow to the point of lethargy. Even if one jumps up and down yelling heresies it generally takes at least a couple of decades to get excommunicated. Rome is almost pitifully eager to accept a plausible explanation; it is, in spite of what its critics say, extremely reluctant to separate even the most reprobate from communion with the Church. The Church never forgets its chief responsibility: to save sinners, not to cast them into outer darkness. It was only Hans Küng's repeated public refusal over many years to explain his views that forced a foot-dragging Vatican into its recent mild move against him; while Edward Schillebeeckx's more artful fencing should ensure his heresies at least another few years in which to flourish.

Teilhard himself had learned a salutary lesson from the fate of the earlier modernist, fellow-Jesuit George Tyrrell. That imprudent and irascible Irishman had virtually taunted the Church into making an example of him. Teilhard, on the other hand, submitted his works to an authority whose judgement he did not respect, and signed a Roman document setting out the traditional doctrine on original sin with this continuing inner reservation: "I am resolved to continue quite simply along my own way in a direction which seems to me to point exactly towards the dogmatic realism that Rome wants and is asking for."[20]

Today's revisionists likewise refuse to let the Vatican's doctrinal intransigence cramp their style. Rosemary Ruether recommended in 1973 that radicals should stay in the Church and propagandize along the academic grapevine, "create a discussion group, a new school or a publication or simply talk with friends."[21] Gregory Baum recently counselled patience to an exasperated reformer: "I recommend that you not be too annoyed by the Church's non-modern slowness to change. Don't make enemies of the hierarchy. Take the good things and run with them." He gave as an example his defence of the Canadian bishops' controversial anti-capitalist pastoral.[22]

In 1984, when it became clear that a counter-revolution centred on the papal magisterium was at last under way, Hans Küng invoked Teilhard's example: "We have to do what the theologians . . . did in the 1950s under the authoritarian regime of Pius XII. He . . . deposed a lot of professors. . . . Rahner, Congar, Teilhard de Chardin were all suppressed, but they quietly continued working to prepare the future. In a period like this, people must remain, rather than be driven out. The best thing is to stay, to fight and to work and prepare for the future. It is the wrong method to get out."[23]

Teilhard handled suspicious ecclesiastical authority in a masterful way throughout a long, controversial, and highly public life, proving that even the most extreme revolutionary could survive, even thrive, in the Church if he played his cards right. Despite his image of being above the fray, innocent and unworldly, he was as capable of cunning as any out-numbered guerrilla. Explaining his decision to go to South Africa in 1950 to investigate *Australopithecus*, he wrote: "I feel the moment has come for me to disappear for a time from Paris, where things are getting 'too hot' for me personally. In the last six months the press has been speaking too much about me and my indiscretions. From that point of view, it would be better to give Rome the impression that I am delving back into what people down there call 'pure science.' "[24]

Today's reformers, as they grow rapidly more numerous, can afford to be less cautious. Still, the most eminent North American biblical theorist, Father Raymond Brown, the undisputed leader in the English-speaking Church of the attempt to reinterpret and reformulate basic Catholic doctrines, has been able to keep the hierarchy guessing. Both his admirers and foes feel quite sure of what he is up to: the destruction of the traditional basis of certain key doctrines such as the virginal conception of Jesus, the subject of his most controversial book.[25] It is pretty safe to say that most of the multitudinous post-Vatican II attempts at adult and teacher re-education rely on Brown's works. (In my small, out-of-the-way town, it took only two weeks for sophistries from a series of lectures delivered here by a disciple of Brown's on Brown's version of the "Infancy Narratives," the Gospel stories about Christ's birth, to work their way into local elementary classrooms. A complaint from me drew an earnest, "Oh, but aren't you aware that the Church is rethinking these formulations?" – that is, the doctrines of the divinity of Christ, the virginal conception of Jesus, Mary's perpetual virginity).

Fellow demythologizer, the much franker John L. McKenzie, s.j., reproached Brown for equivocation: "As the author of some remarkably reserved, not to say evasive lines on just these questions, I must admire the deftness with which Brown skirts thin ice here. Brown manages to avoid saying there is no historical evidence for the Davidic descent of Jesus, for the birth of [sic] Bethlehem or for the virginal conception, at the same time affording ample evidence for the perceptive reader to draw this conclusion."[26]

Presumably bishops read just as perceptively as the rest of us. Yet by frequent and passionate avowals of orthodoxy and piety very reminiscent of Teilhard's, and by angry claims to ill-usage by "ultraconservatives," "fundamentalist Catholics," and "right-wing vigilantes," Brown has actually manoeuvred the bishops into an attempt to silence not Brown himself but those who take exception to his methods and findings. It is very unusual for bishops to defend theologians, yet Brown has been publicly defended, and his critics condemned in intemperate language, by important American bishops such as James Rausch, Thomas Whealon, Timothy Manning, and John Quinn.[27] He has managed this brilliant feat by couching his theories in language just ambiguous enough to enable today's unselfconfident authorities to avoid a confrontation they don't feel up to.

"Not uncommonly at a given moment in history," Monsignor George Kelly, an American sociologist, writes, "a single figure can epitomize an entire school of thought. . . . Among American Catholics, only Brown belongs in the small company of those who . . . have almost single-handedly refashioned the thinking of important segments of the Church body on vital matters of doctrine and practice."[28] Kelly's appreciation of Brown's significance is undoubtedly correct. Raymond Brown occupies in present-day revolutionary theology the place that Teilhard de Chardin filled for interim underground radicals: the cutting edge of modernism, the successful example of coexistence. I predict that Brown will be around long after his vain and intemperate colleague, Hans Küng, has blustered himself out of the Church.

It is to Teilhard de Chardin more than to any other twentieth-century source that Brown and his school owe their healthy existence. He was the one great publicly tolerated successful modernist (I use the term despite earlier qualifications) in the half-century since the suppression of the modernist movement. His attempt at a synthesis of faith and science gave hope to pious modernists who passionately longed to make the Christian message once again "respectable" to modern society. More importantly, he supplied language and concepts to the growing number of agnostic Catholics, that is, Catholics who despair of any knowledge of God except as some kind of "redemptive immanence" in the individual heart that makes a man more conscious of his human brotherhood. For these Christ-less Christians, faith is translated into a Teilhardian consciousness "that man is always more than man and that he is on the way to a destiny that transcends him."[29] In this way, it is possible for even atheists to believe.

"Every sentence about God can be translated into a declaration about human life. This enables us to speak of God in a language drawn from the ordinary conversation and concepts taken from the description of human life, its fears and its hopes, its pitfalls and its expansion. This sort of secular language about the divine demands no metaphysical commitment and hence will be understood by the people of the present culture."[30] The words are Gregory Baum's and the very title of the book from which they come – *Man Becoming: God in Secular Experience* – is itself a summary of what the large school of agnostic socialist Catholics to which Baum belongs derived from Teilhard's thought. In Baum's own thought, modernist immanentism reaches a conclusion which, though dignified and even moving, is not the same as Teilhard's. Teilhard's synthesis of "Faith in the Forward" and "Faith in the Upward" has been reduced to a radical secularism where the "horizontal" vision expands and the "vertical" fades away. God as "Thou" becomes "the transcendent mystery creatively present in man's coming to be"; prayer is "the turning in on the mystery of one's own history." Baum has written elsewhere that today God can be encountered *only* in the horizontal dimension, that is, in one's neighbour; the community collectivized along radical socialist lines is God redemptively present. This most committed Teilhardian therefore proposes that the Church "compose a creed which proclaims the Gospel of Christ and declares the divine redemption present in human life in ordinary secular language. . . . It is possible to proclaim the Gospel without mentioning God by name."[31]

But besides his system, his vocabulary, and his example, there is one more thing for which today's theological revolutionaries have to be grateful to Teilhard de Chardin: that is, the establishment of the rebel Catholic religious as modern media star. Of course, the press in anti-Catholic countries had always gladly featured any story likely to discredit the Roman Church, but in the main they had had to make do with lionizing unsavoury characters like the dreadful Giacinto Achilli, Newman's persecutor. Teilhard was a genuine lion, with what might be called a photogenic career from early on. There was Piltdown and then Peking man, the romantic *Croisière jaune* (Citroën's publicity-stunt crossing of the interior of China with Teilhard along as resident naturalist), and the very noisy "silencing" and "exile." Teilhard may not have indecently courted publicity but he certainly didn't shun it. Julian Huxley, the militantly anti-Christian evolutionist, took him up in England, and his post-war trips to America fed an excited interest in him there. Any stick will do to beat the Catholic Church with, as Ronald Knox observed; throughout the 1940s and 1950s Teilhard was the really big stick in media and academic anti-Catholic polemic. He served the simple, traditional purpose of the Church's enemies, to inflict as many-coloured a shiner as possible.

The Church's treatment of Teilhard became the latest link in the catena of grievances, a worthy addition to Galileo and the Inquisition. (I remember in particular a certain Catholic-baiting professor who had for years tormented me about Teilhard scrambling gleefully over a pile of firewood I was stacking in his eagerness to brandish before my eyes the first English edition of *The Phenomenon of Man*. I wish I had flattened him with the chunk of maple I was holding throughout his loud triumph.)

In the years before the Second Vatican Council, a period of lean pickings for anti-Catholics, with the Catholic Church at perhaps its best ever state of discipline, doctrine, and morale, Teilhard was revered as a persecuted prophet. One doesn't hear much about him now. An occasional radical-chic prelate will employ his jargon – at the 1974 Roman Synod French Archbishop (now Cardinal) Etchegaray urged his colleagues "to have the courage to accept the today of God in the dynamism of the provisional." Teachers in Catholic high schools will sometimes treat their students to an exotic taste of the evolutionary

Christ. New York's Governor Mario Cuomo quotes him incessantly when defending his own "pluralistic" stance on abortion, claiming that Teilhard taught him a less gloomy and negative view of faith than the one he grew up in. And he is still good for a warm line in the secular media: journalist Mary McGrory, in the course of defending Cuomo, noted that Teilhard "wrote more about the beauty of the world than about sin."[32] But the media are glutted with anti-Catholic Catholics who peddle much more interesting wares than Teilhard's, sexual and political rebellions undreamed of by earlier modernists. Upon the great, classically Catholic thinkers of his time, such as Etienne Gilson, Christopher Dawson, and Marshall McLuhan, Teilhard has made no impact at all.

Modernists no longer need him. His star seems to have set as far as theological modernism is concerned, but he brilliantly served its purpose. All the laity and most of the clergy encountered unprepared the cultural and religious revolution that accompanied Vatican II. Not so the handful of modernists who had kept the flame alive, who had survived in Teilhard's bright shadow, and who, as Council theological experts, or *periti*, succeeded in permeating the entire atmosphere of the Church with what had once been the dream of an avant-garde group of revolutionaries. These men came prepared ruthlessly to let loose the famous "spirit of Vatican II," born of the Teilhardian dogma that change is God.

FOUR

THE REVOLUTION SURFACES

There are, as noted earlier, certain features common to revolutions: an aggrieved class, a climate conducive to radical change, a weakened government, a triggering incident, a moderate phase stressing continuity with the old order, a radical phase proclaiming a new order, consolidation and institutionalization *or* counter-revolution. This chapter will look at the first three of these features.

Such a study cannot, of course, be carried out quite as neatly as this outline suggests. It is difficult enough to gain any real understanding of so complex a thing as a revolution when one has to observe it only in a single nation; how much more difficult in the universal society of the Catholic Church. For Catholicism is unique: so amazingly simple in its single clear line of religious authority, so incredibly complex in its relationship with the secular powers of the world. Catholicism inhabits two cities: the City of God and the City of the World. All we can see is what is happening to the institutional Church in the worldly city; this we can document with statistics and personal witness. But every Catholic knows that there is far more going on than we can see or understand. The battle being waged is for the soul of the Church, and a Power other than those in the Vatican or the national episcopal conferences or the Catholic academy will decide what the Catholic Church will eventually answer to the only question that matters: "What think you of Christ? Whose son is He?" (Matthew 22:42).

Always mindful of this mystery, I begin my study of the present revolution and of the upheavals in the society of the Catholic Church during the past twenty-five years or so, that is, in what is called the Conciliar period, from about 1960 to the present, or to date it more precisely, the period that began with Pope John XXIII's surprise announcement to the College of Cardinals on January 25, 1959, of the calling of an ecumenical Council, and which ended with the Extraordinary Synod called by Pope John Paul II for November 26 to December 8, 1985, to review the manner in which the Council decrees have been implemented.

Since I am considering the Catholic revolution thematically rather than chronologically, parts of this discussion may anticipate, backtrack upon, or overlap each other. The phases of a revolution do not, for example, follow each other in an orderly manner. The moderate and radical stages overlap, or even coincide with each other during the period of political ferment. Only later do the strongest personalities establish their own firm line of authority. Also, as is the case at present, the revolution is busily proceeding with the business of institutionalizing itself in the power structures at the same moment as a serious counter-revolution picks up steam. Therefore, subjects I mention in one place will turn up in others, and events will appear out of their chronological place. However, the governing structure of the argument throughout will be that which I have outlined.

AN AGGRIEVED CLASS

Within the Catholic Church, the aggrieved class ripe to join a hopeful-looking revolution was provided by that large group of Catholic theologians and university professors, for the most part priests and religious, to whom the Church delegated its task of instruction in the faith. Members of this group were highly educated in comparison with parish priests and Catholic laity, and very highly motivated, since their concentration of interest was undiluted by family or secular concerns. They were the Church's élite front-line troops and they knew it. Yet they were excluded from any real power in the Church's governing structure. Also, many of them chafed under the tight doctrinal and disciplinary control of the Vatican. The modernist suppression still rankled.

In the immediate post-Second World War years, at least in Europe and North America, greater numbers of Catholics began to move into the middle class. This shift, which was completed by the time of the Council, brought a rapidly increasing demand for Catholic higher education and increased pressure on the religious orders to provide it. Much of the cost of this expensive education was sacrificially borne by the various orders. But now that the Church was not the only career open to the clever, poor, working-class, or ethnic Catholic, some members of the teaching orders began to resent their position of underpaid and lowly employees. Morale was high, but one increasingly began to hear complaints like the following, from an exemplary young religious priest of my acquaintance in the early 1960s: "I'm paid four thousand dollars and I'm worth forty thousand."

Before the Council, theology was almost exclusively the preserve of ordained priests and male religious. Nuns and lay Catholics were trained in apologetics, arguments, and proofs for Catholic doctrine. This situation had begun to change by the end of the 1950s, a departure that favoured the revolution, since laymen, being less vulnerable to career pressure, are less easy for the Church to control. George Tyrrell's mentor, the modernist layman Baron Friedrich von Hügel, escaped unscathed while Tyrrell was destroyed. While it was still unwise for priests to attack publicly the Church's teaching on birth control, Michael Novak, a lay theologian (who claims "to have stimulated the first public dissent on this question in English"), published (early in 1964) the first dissenting article on the subject to appear in America.[1]

One should not exaggerate the extent of the disaffection and discontent. Much of it was, as Newman recognized, the natural "soreness and annoyance" that loyal and able subordinates feel under unappreciative authority. In the Church, as in the world, Dr. Johnson's epigram on Otway too often describes how the Catholic loyalist is treated: "He . . . had . . . the common reward of loyalty; he lived and died neglected." This habitual condition of people who give their lives to the work of the Church, if they are unable to sustain by prayer the effort of remembering that they are really working for Christ, provides fertile ground for recruits when genuine revolutionary discontent surfaces.

In the Catholic Church, the magisterium – the teaching authority of the Pope alone, and of the bishops united with the Pope – makes claim to be the guardian and interpreter of the revelation of God to man. The Church's authority derives from this claim to authoritative interpretation. To overthrow the government of the Church, it is therefore necessary to seize the power of interpreting the Scriptures and the tradition. No one better understands this imperative, or is better placed to effect it, than the professional class of theologians and teachers upon whom the Church depends so heavily for the propagation of the faith. This group has in the course of the past twenty-five years moved from a supportive to an adversary role. Its mass defection has produced the present revolutionary situation.

Much has been written on the role of the intellectual in modern secular society. The dynamics of the relationship operate in the same way in the Church. Indeed, secular descriptions of the role of the intellectual use terms suggested by religious society. Samuel Taylor Coleridge's coinage "the clerisy" is often used today of the New Class – the writers, academics, and bureaucrats who are carrying out the profound cultural and political revolution in the secular society of the West. Julien Benda used the old Catholic term "clerks" of the modernist intellectuals who, he thought, had betrayed their trust by embracing relativism. Paul Hollander, in his brilliant recent study, applies the religious term "pilgrims" to those western intellectuals who, since the Russian Revolution, have succumbed to the totalitarian temptation.[2]

As among secular intellectuals, the cause of the "*trahison des clercs*" among Catholic intellectuals has been their loss of faith in the controlling values of their society. In the Church, the class of dissenting clerks is now called by its critics "the parallel hierarchy"; its creators and defenders call it "the second magisterium" (the coinage of Richard McCormick, s.j.) and demand that "the first magisterium" be directed by its findings.[3]

One note is indicated here. The clerisy did not at the beginning of the revolution include the parish clergy. These were mostly secular (did not belong to religious orders), less theoretically inclined, more practically educated. Actual pastoral contact with the laity, rather than with ideas about them, quickly dispels romanticism about the priestly People of God, and educates parish priests into the cosmological, extrarational dimensions, vertical and mystical, which the human heart requires of religion. It is my own impression that many of the parish priests in place at the beginning of the revolution are still largely unconverted to its world view. Young priests educated after that period have all to some degree been infected, but even here one often finds upon acquaintance that their apparent modernism is more style than substance. The parish clergy might have been expected to be natural allies of the revolution, since they suffer most from the bishop's whims and the laity's unresponsiveness. But the historic jealousy of the secular clergy towards the regulars, nursed by the condescending attitude of the regulars, prevents an alliance. Parish priests, therefore, cannot as a body be considered co-opted by the revolution.

A CLIMATE CONDUCIVE TO CHANGE

The Catholic Church came out of the Second World War in good shape. Even in the defeated countries of Europe the Church had increased its moral stature by resistance and martyrdom. Many bishops and thousands of priests and nuns were imprisoned; many died with their people, giving the Church new names to rejoice in – Jozsef Mindszenty, Stefan Wyszynski, Titus Brandsma, Maximilian Kolbe, Edith Stein. The only shadow on the Church's record, the charge that it could have done more to help the Jews, was a canard started in quarters that had done nothing at all. In fact, the Church saved more than any other agency. Even in Germany, the Church's supposed "silence" about Nazi crimes is a calumny. Before Hitler came to power, the German bishops had condemned Nazi racism in a number of pastoral letters and public denunciations. Nazi party members were forbidden Christian burial. The Catholic Centre Party habitually allied itself with the Social Democrats in opposition to both Nazis and Communists in the pre-Hitler years.

In the election that brought Hitler to power, the traditionally Catholic areas of Germany voted against the Nazis.[4] In 1937 Pius XI condemned the Nazis' racist philosophy in an encyclical written in German and smuggled into Germany, *Mit Brennender Sorge, With Burning Sorrow.* In 1941 the "Lion of Münster," the great bishop Clemens von Galen, preached sermons so powerful against the Nazi euthanasia program that the Nazis halted the mass killings for a time. The bishop escaped arrest because he was protected by the aroused populace. Pius XII destroyed his planned follow-up of *Mit Brennender Sorge* after a strong anti-Nazi statement by the Dutch bishops caused a retaliatory round-up of Dutch Jews during which the Carmelite philosopher Edith Stein was arrested, to die in Auschwitz. When the Church couldn't help the Jews, at least it joined them in prison. Cardinal Stefan Wyszynski, in his prison memoirs, notes that he was the only member of his ordination class who escaped the concentration camp; seven died in Dachau; of the six who survived concentration camps, several soon died from the results of torture and medical experimentation. It is estimated that well over half the Polish Catholic clergy were imprisoned by the Nazis.[5]

After the war there was general goodwill between the Church and the governments of the West. The Church had considered the war against Hitler to have been a just war, and fought it with no qualms. Moreover, it came into the post-war period with a record of unswerving opposition to the other totalitarianism – communism. There were, until very lately, few Catholic entries in the shameful history of fellow-travelling by western intellectuals. Many bishops and priests went, like Cardinal Mindszenty, from Nazi to Communist jails. By 1950 the Church in China, succumbing to Teilhard's "good dose of Marxism," had been crushed, its priests murdered or in prison, where some still languish, unsung by the selectively indignant, leftist, Catholic social-justice organizations. In the political arena, the post-war Christian Democratic parties kept Europe from going Communist; in the post-war Italian election, Pius XII used his enormous moral prestige to save Italy from electing a Communist government.

The floods of post-war refugees and immigrants looked to the Church for comfort and assistance in their new countries. Catholic schools, novitiates, and seminaries overflowed. The horrors of war and the dis-illusionments of peace impelled many exceptional converts into the Church. There was an extraordinary flowering of the missionary effort in Africa, Asia, and Oceania. The Catholic presence among the suffering and poor was everywhere expanding and effective. Half a century of unrelaxing vigilance had brought the Church to a pitch of discipline and doctrinal unanimity that it had never reached before and perhaps never will again. It had taken four centuries, but the magnificent reform of the Council of Trent was at last fully realized. Catholics treated with condescending amusement the perennial Protestant stories about loose-living priests and nuns and venal bishops. They had not been true for a long time. Now, may God have mercy on His Church, they are true again, and those of us who grew up in the reformed Catholic Church find the shock almost unendurable.

Catholic society could not expect to remain immune to the disruption of manners and morals that accompanies major wars, or the general restlessness and impatience with authority in their aftermath. Yet the extent to which Catholics had been alienated by the pressures and disruptions of war and secularization has been exaggerated. Before and during the Council, one heard a great deal about how the Church was losing its attractiveness to the world and how the best of its own lay people were turning away in despair. However, the statistics do not support these contentions. For instance, a concrete measure of the Church's attractiveness to the world is the figure for conversions. The number of conversions increased sharply during the period from the end of the war to the Council. In the United States alone, in 1945 there were 84,908 converts; in 1960 there were 146,212. In England and Europe, the increase was comparable, while there took place in Africa an amazing missionary triumph on the scale of the early medieval conversions of the Anglo-Saxons, Germans, and Franks. Young Catholics, despite the temptation of newly opened secular horizons, dedicated themselves in unprecedented numbers to the arduous celibate life of total service of Christ and the world. In the United States in the period 1945-1960, the number of seminarians grew from 21,523 to 39,896; the number of sisters from 138,079 to 168,527; the number of priests, from 38,451 to 53,796.[6] This rate of growth continued, except for converts, throughout the Council years. In the United States, the number of seminarians peaked at 48,992 in 1965; by 1984 there were only 11,262. The number of sisters reached a high of 181,421 in 1966; by 1984, it had fallen to 118,027. The peak for priests was reached in 1968 with 59,803. The decline here is less precipitous; in 1984 there were 57,891 priests, secular and religious. Canadian statistics before 1968, when the Canadian Catholic Conference of Bishops started collecting them, are fragmentary and unreliable. In 1968 there were 50,565 sisters, 1,901 seminarians, and 14,971 priests; in 1983 there were 37,214 sisters, 12,375 priests, and the CCCB had stopped officially separating permanent deacons from seminarians in its statistics.[7]

Perhaps time will correct our judgement, but for orthodox Catholics who grew up before the Council and are dismayed by the collapse of Catholicism after it, Vatican II seems to have served the sole purpose of kicking over a flourishing and expanding religious community. Nor is the reformers' case for Catholic alienation supported by the experiences and memories of those of us who were mature Catholics before the Council, any more than by the statistics. Let us take one instance only, the issue upon which Catholic sociologists sympathetic to the revolution, Andrew Greeley and Joseph Fichter, for instance, argue that the Church foundered: given the example of secular society, post-war Catholics might have been expected to exert pressure for change at the point of the Church's teaching on birth control. Since 1930, the Catholic Church had been alone in its opposition to artificial contraception. Yet lay people, especially those described by Cardinal Paul-Emile Léger at the Council as "the best," in whose interest changes must be made in sexual ethics, had well into the 1960s accepted the teaching without rancour and practised it as best they could, often with heroism. Discussion of the doctrine before the Council centred on how best to obey it. During the Council years, theologians softened up the ground for dissent; in 1968 they led the rejection of *Humanae Vitae*. Even in this most intimate of lay concerns, the revolution was clerical in instigation and execution.

The Second Vatican Council, which both sides in the struggle now going on in the Church credit with creating a revolutionary climate, was not in itself a revolutionary event. The sixteen documents that proceeded from it reaffirmed traditional Catholic doctrine and morality, even in the vexed area of sexual ethics. It is more accurate to say of the Council that it was accompanied by a revolution not of its own making, a revolution imported into it by a disaffected group of clerical intellectuals. It is true that Catholic society at large remained well into the 1960s relatively unshaken by the secularizing pressures that were devastating mainline Protestant bodies. But many Catholic theologians were already in a frame of mind that made them passionately sympathetic to the aims of the cultural revolution that was beginning to sweep through secular society in the West in the early 1960s.

The general cultural climate was at that time vastly different from that during the first modernist attempt. In the 1960s, neo-modernists could draw enormous support from influential levels of secular society. The leading features of the cultural revolution within secular society were: the complete secularization of existence (that is, the removal of religion from any power to influence political or social behaviour), the privatization of morality, sexual libertinism, hatred of all hierarchies, a settled opposition to all constituted authority, which translated into an automatic adversary position towards one's society. It was this fully developed state of the revolution against the Catholic principle of authority that the clerical radicals introduced into the Council, when, as *periti*, they served as advisers to the national hierarchies. Like the earlier modernists, the radical Catholic intellectuals wanted to save the world by speaking to it in its own secular language, which would "be understood by the people of the present culture." When the Council called these radicals into the process of consultation on the Church's nature and future, it unwittingly acted for the revolution as did King Louis XVI when he called the Estates General into session at the beginning of the French Revolution.

Only two of the documents of Vatican II, the *Dogmatic Constitution on the Church, Lumen Gentium*, and *Divine Revelation, Dei Verbum*, were termed "dogmatic." The others were described as "pastoral," a distinction upon which both radicals and conservatives seized, the radicals "in order to obtain the passage of certain formulations with a modern tendency," as Edward Schillebeeckx, a leading radical theologian at the Council, admits; the conservatives to discredit these new departures as "merely pastoral," not having the force of doctrine. "This gap between 'doctrinal' and 'pastoral,' which was used as a pawn, will continue to have a bearing on the interpretation of the council and is, in my opinion, one of the most important shadows cast on the council debates, to which I have never been able to resign myself."[8] Schillebeeckx is correct. The double voice of the Council has been a major cause of the post-Conciliar confusion in the Church.

Initially, and, I think, in the long run, the distinction between "doctrinal" and "pastoral" worked to the advantage of the magisterium, in that the Council ended with the reaffirmation of traditional Catholic doctrine, an incredible achievement given the revolutionary pressures and the brave new world euphoria that overcame even the most sober bishops. Yet this reaffirmation was achieved at a price: the acceptance, sometimes in the same document, of *both* the traditional teaching and "certain formulations with a modern tendency." As a result both radicals and orthodox Catholics can point to the same document as supporting their doctrinal positions. For instance, section 50 of the "pastoral" *Constitution on the Church in the Modern World* can be read as both reaffirming *and* denying that procreation is the primary end of marriage. Or to take another very important example: section 8 of the "dogmatic" *Constitution on the Church, Lumen Gentium*, seems to undercut its own identification of the Church of Christ with the Catholic Church.[9]

However, the "dogmatic" content in the Vatican II documents far outweighs "the certain formulations of a modern tendency" inserted by the radicals. For instance, few if any of the startling and demoralizing liturgical and disciplinary changes that began before the Council ended were in fact ordered by it. And, though Pope Paul VI had reserved for himself the ultimate decision about birth control, the Council had in fact reiterated the historic teaching on contraception. Yet in the immediate aftermath of Vatican II, anyone unfamiliar with the actual documents – and that meant almost everyone, Catholic and secular – could be forgiven for believing that the Church had discarded or radically revised most of its basic teachings. For the revolutionary element in the Council ("a very small minority," according to Hans Küng, who should know) waged and won a brilliant propaganda war in comparison with which their failure to change the actual legislation of the Church faded into irrelevance. For what did it matter what the documents actually said, when it was by the revolutionary "spirit of Vatican II" that they were going to be interpreted? Küng was right when he said that this spirit, once the preserve of avant-garde dreamers, "has permeated the entire atmosphere of the Church, due to the Council."[10]

After the Council some conservatives, most notably Archbishop Marcel Lefebvre and his followers, decided that ambiguities in some of the Council's documents, "time bombs" as Lefebvre called them, cast serious doubt on the validity of the Second Vatican Council. Lefebvre set up his own seminaries and parishes to remain faithful to the pre-Conciliar tradition. Most orthodox Catholics did not take this route. Instead, once they had decided to accept the validity of the Council, they set out to use the Council's own distinction of dogmatic versus pastoral against the revolution as aggressively as the revolution was now using it in its implementation of Vatican II. Orthodox Catholics brandished the *Dogmatic Constitution on the Church* and ignored the *Pastoral Constitution on the Church in the Modern World*. Whereupon the revolution fell back on "the spirit of Vatican II" and complained to the bishops that their efforts at renewal were being hampered by legalistic "document flashers." At the present stage of the revolution, in the mid-1980s, the Council is dismissed by radicals as "a profoundly conservative event." "The Council was important in changing much of the style of Roman Catholicism as an institution," writes journalist Peter Nichols. "But at this distance in time, it looks like another piece of evidence for the innate conservatism of deep-rooted institutions."[11]

It is clear now that there were in effect two councils, the "conservative" Council, which is now realized to have been a brilliantly clever doctrinal holding-operation, and the radical Council, the enormous media event with its revolutionary stars and its box-office appeal. Media coverage was for the most part enthusiastically biased in favour of the emerging revolution. Internationally famous journalists like Henri Fesquet, the influential religion editor of *Le Monde*, and Robert Kaiser, Rome bureau chief for *Time*, built up during the Council years an extraordinary rapport which often looked like a collaboration on strategy with certain Council fathers and *periti*. These journalists reported the Council as a war of liberation against sinister forces of oppression, with the Pope and the curia cast as the vicious reactionary oligarchy and certain bishops and theologians as gallant freedom fighters. They even used military language – "another shot was fired today"; "the conservative forces were routed." Henri Fesquet, in his posturing, interminable (1,128 pages plus index) insider's report, *Le Journal du Concile*,[12] spoke of Cardinal Léger's intervention on birth control as "a bombshell" and of the destruction by the "Rhine Group" (the alliance of German-speaking bishops) of the curia's carefully drafted schema as "a demolition exercise." The use of military images by Council journalists was so pronounced that Michael Davies, paramount historian of the revolution, ironically added to it, terming the liberal German initiative in the Council "a blitzkrieg."

I urge anyone interested in the revolutionary psychology that created "the spirit of Vatican II" to read the classic example of sympathetic secular reporting, *Inside the Council*, by the influential leader of the English-speaking pack, Robert Kaiser.[13] Liberals who reread it today must feel as embarrassed by its uninhibited triumphalism as do present-day conservatives when reminded of the papalotrous excesses of some nineteenth-century Ultramontanists. This time the metaphor is naval, as indicated by these chapter headings: "Sailing Orders," "Dry Dock," "Down the Slips," "A New Crew," "Charting New Waters," "The Winds of Change," "The Barque of Peter," "Underway." Of the Rhine Group's first procedural triumph, Kaiser wrote: "To the intense satisfaction of many, Cardinal Liènart and Cardinal Frings blew the Holy Office list of commission candidates into figurative bits before the eyes of all. . . . I felt the whole thing significant enough to cable New York (beyond deadline time) . . . 'So-called liberal minority aren't going to have anything crammed down their throats by Italian Curia. Today demonstrated they have strength to avoid that possibility. This clearly going to be real parliament of Church.' "[14]

Kaiser personalized the opposing forces in the struggle for the Church in two elderly cardinals, Alfredo Ottaviani of the Holy Office and Augustin Bea, S.J., first head of the Vatican Secretariat for Christian Unity. Ottaviani was made to represent the old Church, Bea the new; they became symbols of what Kaiser hoped was happening at the Council. "Cardinal Alfredo Ottaviani, Secretary of the Sacred Congregation of the Holy Office, may have typified the [reactionary] spirit. The motto on his coat of arms reads *Semper Idem* – Always the same . . . the logical consequence of such a spirit could mean death for any organization into which it fused."[15] For Kaiser, "Ottaviani incarnated the old order, its obstinacy, its refusal to change, its admitted strength, an antique cast in ancient bronze, silently unmalleable, quietly unreceptive."[16] He described "Ottaviani's permanently furrowed forehead raftering the low compact skull curving back abruptly like the refusal to a direct question . . . sphinx-like immobility."[17] Bea was described in different language: "the tiered, tranquil architecture of his head, the powerful domelike skull-casing"; Bea "saw the need for an intellectual breakthrough"; Bea, scholar and intellectual, his eyes "observant, penetrating, flickering with sudden deep intelligence."[18]

In both cases, Kaiser's characterization was false; Bea was no more a radical or a modernist than Ottaviani was a Renaissance despot or closed-minded integrist. Both were brilliant orthodox scholars; Ottaviani was a noted historian and wit, a compassionate and charitable priest much loved in the poorest part of Rome, where he was born. In 1963, at Harvard, Bea had warned against unreasonable expectations for ecumenism: "Compromise on points of faith which have already been defined is impossible. . . . Nor is there a possibility that the Church – even in its zeal for eventual union – will ever be content with a recognition of 'essential dogmas' or that she will reverse or withdraw the dogmatic decrees drawn up at Trent."[19] Ottaviani wouldn't have changed a word of that. But Kaiser's myth-making was triumphantly successful. It set the pattern of discrediting what Ottaviani stood for because a man like him stood for it, and of reading into Bea, because of the exciting possibilities for modernism suggested by his new job, the promise of a Catholic retreat from historic creedal certainty. The typology persisted, in Xavier Rynne's books on the Council, in Malachi Martin's exaltation of Bea in *Three Popes and a Cardinal*, in Peter Nichols's *The Pope's Divisions*, in Bishop Remi de Roo's remarks on the CBC program *Catholics*.

The sympathetic interaction of radical elements inside and outside the Council can be traced clearly in the journalistic demonology based on the person of Cardinal Ottaviani. It worked the way a good myth should. When Ottaviani stood up in the Council to demand of his brother bishops whether they realized that in the liturgical program they were setting in motion a revolution, the presiding Cardinal Joseph Frings ordered his microphone to be turned off when he exceeded his time limit, a shocking insult to a man of Ottaviani's years, gifts, and service, an act impossible to imagine having happened a year before. The blind old priest failed for a moment to realize what had been done until the exultant cheers of many of his progressive brothers alerted him. The moment remains in the memoirs of radicals like Bishop Remi de Roo as the symbol of the defeat of the old idea of the Church.

History being the propaganda of the victors, the media perception of what happened at the Council has become post-Conciliar truth. Therefore, I recommend Kaiser to anyone planning to set up as a revisionist historian. James Burtchaell, CSC, speaking to the Catholic Press Association in 1981, paid tribute to the great myth-making journalists of Vatican II: "It is arguable that Robert Kaiser, with his soirées throughout the Council and his elaborate columns in *Time*, or Xavier Rynne, in his long retrospective pieces, did as much to render *Pascendi* inoperative as did anyone."[20]

But if you're going to read only one book about the Council, the indispensable work is Father Ralph Wiltgen's *The Rhine Flows into the Tiber*. Wiltgen had access to all the correspondence and documentation of the Rhine Group and was also the director of an independent Council news service. His reporting of the Council's often unedifying manoeuvring turned his account, as Wiltgen ruefully notes, into support for "those who charge that the Council's 16 documents have been vitiated, even invalidated, by pressure groups."[21] The same frankness makes it too close to the knuckle to be palatable to the revolution.

Wiltgen details how at Vatican II, as at all other Councils, a pressure group came to exercise a dominant influence over the Council. In this case the pressure group was formed of liberal bishops and their theological experts (the famous *periti*) from the Rhine countries, Germany, Austria, Holland, Belgium, France, Switzerland. This group was known as the "European Alliance." The following summary account is based in part on Wiltgen's uniquely well-informed work.

From the moment Pope John XXIII announced the Council, preparation began on the texts to be discussed. After consultation with the world's bishops, twelve preparatory commissions under a central preparatory committee headed by the Pope, all with international representation, produced twenty schemas, working drafts, to be discussed at the Council. Despite the wide consultation, the bishops and theologians of the Rhine countries, historically suspicious of Rome, feared that curial control of the drafts would result in defensively orthodox texts that would take no account of the theological and philosophical developments of the twentieth century but which they would be expected to endorse. The Rhine countries had been the leaders in the bold scriptural and liturgical movements set in motion by Pius XII, the fruits of which had already begun to appear in the practices of the Church.

Three months before the Council convened, the central committee sent seven draft schemas to all the bishops. The Dutch bishops met to discuss them, finding them, as their *periti* had foretold, intolerable. They then circulated to all bishops "a devastating criticism"[22] of four of the schemas – *Sources of Relevation*; *Preserving Pure the Deposit of Faith*; *Christian Moral Order*; *Chastity, Matrimony, the Family, and Virginity*. This critical commentary was the work of only one theologian, Edward Schillebeeckx, O.P., the *peritus* of the Dutch bishops and one of the several most influential figures at the Council. The Schillebeeckx commentary rejected the four schemas as being too narrow, representative of "only one school of theological thought."[23] Schillebeeckx approved of only the schema on the liturgy, calling it "an admirable piece of work,"[24] a not surprising endorsement since the Rhine bishops and scholars had dominated the liturgical constitution's preparatory committee and had written their priorities into the schema.

He proposed in the name of the Dutch bishops that the liturgical constitution therefore be discussed first, while the others were subjected to radical revision.

The Dutch action alerted other hierarchies to the possibility of an organized resistance. Before the Council opened, the Rhine Group sought liberal allies in other national hierarchies, meeting with them at the Rome residence of Cardinal Joseph Frings (Cologne) to draw up lists of acceptable candidates for the all-important ten Council commissions which would control what was discussed on the floor and eventually shape the final documents. The "European Alliance" went to the first meeting of the Council ready to reject the curial list of commission members.

When the first session adjourned in less than an hour with no members chosen and curial direction repudiated, one Dutch bishop shouted, "That was our first victory!"[25] Robert Kaiser's jubilant cable from the front has already been noted. In the end, eight out of every ten candidates presented by the European Alliance obtained commission seats, dominated the liturgical commission, and made up half of the most important theological commission (of which Cardinal Ottaviani and Cardinal Bea were co-chairmen).

After this election, the direction and temper of the Council were assured, for good or ill in the long run only God knows. In the short run, at any rate, liberal strategy prevailed. The liturgy schema was, as Schillebeeckx had suggested, the first discussed and promulgated, a fateful concession for the future of the Church. At the early optimistic stage, few of the Council fathers credited Ottaviani's warning that a revolution was being unleashed. Even Archbishop Lefebvre, suspended later for ordaining priests after being forbidden to do so by Pope Paul IV, ratified the *Constitution on the Sacred Liturgy*.

By the end of the Council, their innocence lost, the bishops might have voted differently, or at least insisted on safeguards. But the Council happened the way it did, and Catholics who trust in the Holy Ghost's guidance of the Church must leave the long run to Him Who will be with us till the consummation of the world. In any case, delay would probably have made little difference, as the number of votes against the final forms of the other Conciliar documents did not rise dramatically as the Council wound to its conclusion. Judging by their astonishment and total collapse when the revolution exploded after the Council, most of the bishops never recognized the revolutionary situation. Peter Hebblethwaite's judgement of the Council fathers is probably correct: "Few of [them] were raging liberals – most of them were extremely moderate men, and some of them were sensationally moderate men – they nevertheless all voted, or most of them voted, regularly for moderately progressive measures."[26] The revolution stole up behind them and was in place at the winning post when they awoke from their Conciliar hangover.

They did not recognize the revolution that accompanied the Council because they were themselves wholeheartedly engaged in staging a rebellion of their own against the centralization of power in the Roman curia. But it was rebellion, not revolution; political, not doctrinal. "In the minds of many Council fathers the purpose of the Second Vatican Council was to balance the teaching of the first Vatican Council on the papal primacy by an explicit doctrine on episcopal collegiality."[27] An interesting fact that has recently been made public is that early in the Council, Cardinal Montini, later to become Paul VI, wrote to Pope John XXIII suggesting that the work of Vatican II begin with a formal restatement of papal primacy and infallibility. The language in the *Dogmatic Constitution on the Church* establishes the principle of collegiality in relation to primacy. It deserves to be quoted, given the way in which the concept of collegiality has been distorted by the revolution since the Council:

> Just as in the Gospel, the Lord so disposing, St. Peter and the other apostles constitute one apostolic college, so in a similar way, the Roman Pontiff, the successor of Peter, and the Bishops, the successors of the apostles, are joined together. . . . But the college or body of bishops has no authority unless it is understood together with the Roman Pontiff, the successor of Peter at its head. The pope's power of primacy over all, both pastors and faithful, remains whole and intact. In virtue of his office, that is, as Vicar of Christ and pastor of the whole Church, the Roman Pontiff has full, supreme and universal power over the Church. And he is always free to exercise this power. The order of bishops, which succeeds to the college of apostles and gives this apostolic body continued existence, is also the subject of supreme and full power over the universal Church, provided we understand this body together with its head the Roman Pontiff and never without this head. This power can be exercised only with the consent of the Roman Pontiff. (*Lumen Gentium*, 22)

That is certainly not the language of revolution. (Although Cardinal Ottaviani, always alert to implications, joked that he could find no scriptural basis for the existence of collegial apostolic behaviour except, "And they all fled.")

This dogmatic definition of collegiality, one of the firmest and clearest pronouncements in all the Council's documents, was obtained only after what Wiltgen calls "the most important and dramatic battle which took place at the Second Vatican Council."[28] It was on this point, the juridical authority of the papacy, that the radical *periti* made their biggest and most open push and met their most serious and successful resistance. The theological commission for the *Dogmatic Constitution on the Church* was dominated by radical theologians from the Rhine Group, including Rahner and Ratzinger. It proposed an extreme interpretation of collegiality whereby the Pope could act only as head of the college of bishops in expression of their consensus and never alone.

The radicals on the commission had couched the passages on collegiality in deliberately ambiguous language, in order to win wide Conciliar support; they intended to interpret them after the Council. Edward Schillebeeckx, who held the extreme view of collegiality, had, during the second session, expressed to his friends on the commission his regret that the schema seemed too moderate. In an article published after the Council, Schillebeeckx quoted the reply of one of the *periti*: "We are stating this in a diplomatic manner, but after the Council we shall draw the conclusions implicit in it."[29] Schillebeeckx himself called these tactics "unfair." In the event, they didn't prevail. Pope Paul VI, who for a long time had dismissed warnings from many Council fathers about the intentions of certain elements on the theological commission, was at last convinced by being shown some indiscreet boasting by one of the drafters of the schema about how the ambiguous passages would be used after the Council. (According to Wiltgen, the Pope broke down and wept when he realized how he was being deceived.[30]) He personally intervened with the clarity and decisiveness of which he was capable when stung, and forced the commission to amend the schema to read as it now uncompromisingly stands.

Yet after the Council, in the area of collegiality, as in all other disputed areas, it was the minority, radical, and *officially rejected* view that became the doctrinal norm. On the evidence of their post-Conciliar behaviour, some bishops at least must have thought that they were voting for the wide and optimistic promise of the radical view of collegiality, and they must have returned home determined to put it into practice. This would help to account for the almost total failure of the American and Canadian bishops (as we shall see later) to support the Pope in the first great post-Conciliar test of strength, the birth-control encyclical. The official text on collegiality, as quoted above, doesn't seem to justify, for example, the revolutionary enthusiasm expressed in the following ecstatic memory of Bishop Remi de Roo, who in a recent radio program recalled his greatest moment of victory:

> . . . the working recognition of collegiality in action. When you think of the very harsh debates where a powerful minority generally identified with the curia spoke against collegiality as something dangerous. When you remember a Cardinal Ottaviani, for instance . . . getting up and saying "*Il Papa decide da solo* – the Pope alone makes decisions." Directly counter to this surge of movement for collegial-

ity. And then that electric moment where after several cardinals had gone to the Pope to plead that the question of collegiality be set aside because it wasn't ripe and would divide the Council, divide the Church, when eventually it came to a vote – because other cardinals such as the Suenens and the Montinis and the Frings . . . had prevailed and said that this should be the freedom of the Council, the spirit should speak. And then you had an overwhelming majority in the 90 percent saying that yes, collegiality was the image of the future. And the eruption of applause in Vatican II – you know, you live for those moments – despite all the regulations, the place just exploded. That was a turning point, there's no doubt about it.[31]

This is really an extraordinary reading of what actually happened at the Council. The Council *did* write that "*Il Papa*" is always free to "*decide da solo*," to act alone. Pope Paul VI himself delayed the vote on the schema while a "Preliminary Explanatory Note" to the section on "The Hierarchical Structure of the Church and in Particular on the Episcopate" was added in order to remove any ambiguity. The "several cardinals who had gone to the Pope," a very large group led by the Curial Archbishop Dino Staffa, *did* actually win their point. Much of that applause so life-giving to Bishop de Roo came from the hundreds of Council fathers who felt that the text they were approving had effectively scotched the revolutionary intentions that they had unmasked to the Pope.

Bishop de Roo made clear in his reminiscences of the immediate pre-Conciliar period what he thought he was voting for:

We got very much involved in the whole collegial dimension of the Vatican Council, because the Bishops' Conferences were . . . just getting organized. And we were sent round to visit other representatives of the various Bishops' Conferences that were gradually coalescing and networking in Rome. So I got pitched into the very heart . . . of that dynamic inner circle that was promoting some of the newer ideas. . . . I was given the responsibility of providing the speakers who every Sunday morning gave lectures to the Canadian Bishops. So I was in touch with the Congars and Schillebeeckx and these key men who were delighted to have an audience like the Canadian Bishops. . . . It gave me a personal relationship with a variety of key men.[32]

This naïve account of a revolutionary conversion, from a good man, makes one realize just how delighted Schillebeeckx and Co. must have been "to have an audience like the Canadian Bishops." Bishop de Roo's overripe idea of the doctrine of collegiality is a product of the revolutionary climate at its hottest.

The bishops accepted the help of the radical *periti* in their attempt to wrest the direction of the Council from the curia, and in the drive to enshrine their collegial status in the Council's documents. "Progressive" but orthodox bishops either did not suspect their clerks of revolutionary leanings, or did suspect but felt with the confidence born of long success that they could suppress such urges after the Council was over. At least one such bishop, Cardinal John Heenan of Westminster, had his eyes opened by the bold manoeuvres of the radical theologians. Becoming worried about the influence that certain radical *periti* were exerting on the whole Council through their influence on the European Alliance, he founded during the third session an opposition group of English-speaking bishops called the St. Paul's Alliance, and opposed a move to have a controversial European Alliance "supplement" to the schema on *The Constitution on the Church in the Modern World, Gaudium et Spes* passed without discussion being allowed on it in the Council Hall. Heenan warned: "If we fail to scrutinize both documents [the official schema and the proposed supplement prepared by the *periti*] with great care, the mind of the Council will have to be interpreted to the world by the *periti* who helped the Fathers of the Commission draw up the documents. God forbid that this should happen! I fear *periti* when they are left to explain what the Bishops meant. [Heenan's Latin jibe went: *Timeo peritos et dona ferentes.*] It is of no avail to talk about a college of Bishops if *periti* in articles, books and speeches contradict and pour scorn on what the body of Bishops teaches."[33]

In the struggle between the old theology and the new, the theologians on both sides came into their own. Not all the *periti* were revolutionary in intent. In the light of their post-Conciliar behaviour, we can suggest with some confidence who were. Not, for instance, Father Louis Bouyer, the influential French expert on the commission that drew up the *Constitution on the Sacred Liturgy*; nor Father Joseph Ratzinger, *peritus* to Cardinal Frings and the German bishops, although, like Hans Küng, he had rejoiced in "the strong reaction against the spirit behind the preparatory work" for the Council, the schemas prepared by the curial commissions.[34] Bouyer became a fierce post-Vatican II critic of the liturgical reform, and Ratzinger, ironically, is now the most powerful man in the Church next to the Pope, the activist counter-revolutionary head of the Congregation for the Doctrine of the Faith, successor to Ottaviani and the Holy Office. But it seems reasonable to assume that some of those who became leading post-Conciliar radicals had been of the same mind during the Council; Father Hans Küng, the Swiss *peritus*; Father Edward Schillebeeckx, the very important *peritus* to the Dutch hierarchy; the Canadian *peritus* (at the time Father) Gregory Baum; the English (at the time Father) Charles Davis.

But the role of the most important *peritus* of all, Father Karl Rahner, s.j., remains enigmatic. He is too profound, too original, too complex to be easily categorized, and his output was so prodigious that it will be some time before it can be fully assessed by the Church. He is a contradictory figure; he joined the protest against *Humanae Vitae* yet he publicly supported the papal action against Hans Küng. There is general agreement that he was the most influential theologian at the Council. Wiltgen writes: "Since the position of the German-language bishops was regularly adopted by the European alliance, and since the alliance position was generally adopted by the Council, a single theologian might have his views accepted by the whole Council if they had been accepted by the German-speaking bishops. There was such a theologian: Father Karl Rahner, s.j."[35] Cardinal Frings, one of the ten Council presidents and president of the German episcopal conference at the time of the Council, called Rahner "the greatest theologian of the century" and was guided by him throughout. In the recess between the first and second sessions of the Council, the Rhine Group and the Scandinavians met at Fulda, Germany, to study the Council's schemas as analysed by Rahner. All his suggestions were accepted, and most of them later became Conciliar teaching. Towards the end of the Council, Cardinal Frings and his personal theologian Joseph Ratzinger (who had been a student and enthusiastic disciple of Rahner) began to disagree publicly with him. Several years before Rahner's death, Cardinal Giuseppe Siri, Archbishop of Genoa, himself an eminent theologian and a leading conservative power at the Council, in what looked like the Vatican's opening shot at Rahner, wrote a very serious attack on Rahner's theology and its implications, accusing him of destroying "by a large number of propositions learnedly entangled, the whole truth of the doctrine of the Incarnation of Jesus Christ."[36] Siri accuses the whole contemporary theological movement of which Rahner is the most important figure of being guilty of *historicism* (a classy name for modernism), the belief that the meaning and value of any doctrine or event can be assessed only in terms of what it means and what purpose it serves in any particular historical moment. The final verdict on the Council, when it comes, will depend to a great extent on how the magisterium comes to judge Rahner's work as a whole.

The radical theologians wanted to break the hold of the central authority even more than did the bishops, and they collaborated wholeheartedly in the episcopal drive towards collegiality. They devised provisions that enhanced the concept of an overriding local authority as a means to achieve their own destructuralizing ends. No better example exists of this interaction of rebellious bishops and of reformers orthodox and heterodox than in the moderate-sounding but in the event most revolutionary of all the documents, the only one of the preparatory schemas that Schillebeeckx allowed his bishops to endorse and which he and the Germans managed to have discussed first, the *Constitution on the Sacred Liturgy*. In this document, startling new powers to override the central authority are granted to the local and national hierarchies. Time and time again some traditional feature of the liturgy seems to have been retained, but, as an almost off-hand proviso, made subject to the judgement of "the competent territorial authority."

This provision for liturgical pluralism was a radical departure from the modern tradition. During the Protestant revolution, Mary Tudor and other Catholic rulers had urged Rome to fix the rite of the Mass, since dissident clerics were introducing changes reflective of heretical ideas. The rite now misleadingly known as the "Tridentine," actually the ancient Roman Mass, which dates in its essentials from the end of the sixth century, replaced all local variations as the liturgy of the universal Church. Since Trent, control of the liturgy has been solely the right of the Pope. A price was paid for the ending of organic development of the liturgy. Yet whatever the arguments against it, a fixed liturgy in the Latin language had acted to sustain the idea of a universal Catholicism whose Roman loyalty transcended national loyalties. "The monumental greatness of the Roman Mass," writes Joseph Jungmann, the greatest historian of the Roman Mass, "lies in its antiquity which reaches back to the Church of the martyrs, and in its spread which, with its Latin language, spans many nations. Nowhere else is it so plain that the Church is both apostolic and catholic."[37]

Obviously, to return the liturgy even somewhat to local control would serve greatly to enhance the power of national episcopal conferences, something the bishops, even those most orthodox, were all for. The program of the liberal experts who dominated the various liturgical commissions required the nationalist ambitions of the bishops in order to secure the all-important change from Latin to the vernacular. Not all the liturgical reformers thought this change desirable; Father Louis Bouyer, for instance, did not. Nor is it necessary to postulate ignoble motives for those who did. Joseph Jungmann promoted the vernacular, as did the Germans in general, their post-Reformation Catholicism having developed not only in reaction to Protestant demands but also in a genuine attempt to understand them. During the discussion of the liturgy, Bishop Zauner of Linz, Austria, a leading member of the liturgical commission, explained the principles of the liturgical reform: active participation by all the faithful; direct, increased approach to Scripture; development of a liturgy suitable for catechesis in mission territories and in countries where the Church is forbidden otherwise to catechize; "inculturation," that is, adaptation into the liturgy of tribal or national customs where possible. Fulfilment of these principles depended upon the use of the vernacular and upon local control; in a well-ordered Church, neither need involve a retreat from faith.

The abandonment of Latin and central regulation had implications too radical for most of the bishops to accept readily. It was therefore in the interests of liturgical reformers orthodox and otherwise to smuggle the necessary authorization for the vernacular into the Council document as cautiously and as quickly as possible. One of the key motives of the reformers, ecumenism, the reunification of Christianity by accommodation to Protestant doctrinal and liturgical imperatives, was not allowed into the schema at all, lest it frighten those bishops with long memories of the use the Reformation made of the vernacular. Radical *periti* flattered the bishops, not only those of the European Alliance, with the charming idea of seizing an important power from the curia. The curia for its part, as Wiltgen writes, "correctly surmised that, if it agreed to the principles of local jurisdiction in liturgical matters, a precedent would be established enabling episcopal conferences to gain still wider powers of decision in other areas as well."[38] This, of course, is what has happened; the resultant state of Catholicism at least suggests that the curia was right to oppose local control although it would be insulting to imply that the case from tradition made by great conservatives like Ottaviani was a political exercise intended merely to preserve curial power.

Open-ended sanction of the vernacular made its cautious way past the bishops in this language:

1. Particular law remaining in force, the use of the Latin language is to be preserved in the Latin rites.
2. But since the use of the mother tongue, whether in the Mass, the administration of the sacraments, or other parts of the liturgy, may frequently be of great advantage to the people, the limits of its employment may be extended. This extension will apply in the first place to the readings and directives, and to some of the prayers and chants. . . .
3. It is for competent territorial authority . . . to decide whether, and to what extent, the vernacular language is to be used according to these norms; their decrees are to be approved, that is, confirmed, by the Holy See. And, wherever the procedure seems to be called for, this authority is to consult with bishops of neighbouring regions employing the same language. (*Constitution on the Sacred Liturgy,* 36)

Other sections of the constitution give similar "whether and to what extent" powers about adaptation to local customs, pluralism of rites, and liturgical experimentation to the "competent territorial authority," which in general means the national episcopal conferences. After the liturgical reform was fully in place, a number of bishops said that they and the rest of the Council fathers had never envisaged the total disappearance of Latin from the Mass. Even Paul VI had opposed the idea of a vernacular Canon. But the final vote in favour of the constitution was 2,147 to 4; obviously, most of the bishops were not inflexibly against some wider use of the vernacular and most of them welcomed the expansion of their powers.

Radical reform in the Church, even reform as orthodox as that of Trent, has to centre on the liturgy, in particular on the Mass, for the Mass is, in St. Thomas Aquinas' words, "the central pillar of the Church." Today, as during the Protestant Reformation, "It's the Mass that matters." Nothing could change if the Roman liturgy, symbol *par excellence*, as Jungmann says, of the apostolicity and catholicity of the Church, did not yield to change. An open door to change, secured by the interested collaboration of orthodox reformers, revolutionaries, and bishops, was the major victory of the revolution at the Council.

A legitimate Council of the Catholic Church ratified the *Constitution on the Sacred Liturgy*; therefore, whatever one's liturgical opinions, one may believe that the Holy Ghost would have worked some good from it, if it had been correctly applied. But its implementation is another story.[39] The same can be said of the other Conciliar documents. They support the major doctrines, their failures being of omission rather than commission. They are capable of being interpreted in a traditionally Catholic sense. I believe that eventually they will be. Yet in many places they admit of at least the possibility of a different interpretation. Insertions and qualifications, planted with revolutionary intent, "time bombs," in Archbishop Lefebvre's words, went off with destructive bangs after the Council. Radicals like Küng and Schillebeeckx were willing to pay for their insertion by the acceptance of the downgraded "pastoral" label.

The unedifying behaviour, the ruthlessness of the revolutionary *periti* and their allies among the bishops, the deceits, the vanities, obsessively retailed by the media throughout the Council, seem to devout Catholics very scandalous. Yet it is an historical fact that general councils are often dominated by a single group that manages to get its program accepted, sometimes even as the dogma of the Church, as did the curial group over desperate German and English resistance, with the proclamation of papal infallibility at the First Vatican Council in 1870. German resentment of curial high-handedness had been simmering since then and the high state of preparation by the Rhine Group was intended to prevent a similar happening. The early completeness of German organization made the Council theologically one-sided, and the prominence of their radical *periti* made them dangerous. But there seems no necessity to embrace the conspiracy theory that the Rhine bishops as a group intended the destruction of Catholic doctrine and the Protestantization of the Church. Some of the bishops and theologians (including

Newman) who opposed the Vatican I declaration of papal infallibility did so because, although they themselves accepted the teaching, they thought its promulgation at that particular time inopportune and divisive. I think that they were mistaken in opposing the definition, and that the dogma of papal infallibility has proven to have been prophetic and providential. It is hard to imagine that much would now be left of the Church's inherited teaching without the papal authority exercised during the modernist crisis, and without John Paul II. But the opposition of Newman and Lord Acton did not mean that they were heretics.

The same view can be taken of Karl Rahner's position at Vatican II, which the dominant group as usual adopted, that certain widely held Marian beliefs not yet dogma (Mary as co-Redemptrix, for example) should not be included in the schema on the Blessed Virgin because "unimaginable harm would result from an ecumenical point of view, in relation to both Orientals and Protestants."[40] One may say the same of the Council's decision not to condemn communism, indeed, not even to mention its name in the schema on the *Church in the Modern World*, as the price of Soviet permission for observers from the Russian Orthodox Church to attend the Council. Craven perhaps, shameful even, too optimistic in its expectation of "increased dialogue" that would result in the loosening of communist chains, but not necessarily of evil intent.

General councils throughout the Church's history have often been followed by periods of disorder. But not because of the unclarity, ambiguity, or weakness of Conciliar pronouncements. Rather the opposite. It must be considered the great flaw (from an orthodox point of view) of this best prepared, most representative of all councils, that so many passages or omissions in its documents could be adduced afterwards to support radical departures from doctrine and the almost total destruction of Catholic culture. And though the revolution's victory was in the field of insinuation, of atmosphere, and of ambiguity rather than of explicit rejection of old doctrine or creation of new, it was nevertheless enormous. The Council itself had provided for the revolution a window of opportunity; the double voice in the Council's documents gave the revolution a moment of apparent legitimacy, which it was quick to exploit.

A WEAKENED GOVERNMENT

The third condition necessary for revolution is a weakened government. There had been no weakness or tremor in Pius XII's strong papacy (1939-1958). Its greatest feature had been his prophetic discernment and treatment, decades before they impinged on public consciousness, of issues that would provide the major modern battlegrounds. He spoke authoritatively on the manipulation by science of human life by genetic engineering, *in vitro* fertilization, abortion, euthanasia, artificial insemination, artificial birth control. He liberalized the study of scripture (*Divino Afflante Spiritu*), and arbitrated the claims of evolutionary science (*Humani Generis*). In *Mediator Dei* (1947) he wrote the program for liturgical reform. We forget that a restoration of the liturgy was already well under way by the mid-1950s. Major components, such as evening Mass, restoration to their original splendour and time of the Holy Week services, relaxation of the Eucharistic fast, the dialogue Mass, were all in place years before the Council, and had been enthusiastically received. During his papacy, all the great reconstructive and explanatory liturgical work had been completed, by Pius Parsch, Joseph Jungmann, Odo Casel, Prosper Guéranger, Louis Bouyer. The repudiation of his reform by the post-Conciliar commissions and the embracing instead of every trend he had warned against in *Mediator Dei* must be considered an enormous religious and cultural tragedy. It would have been infinitely more difficult for Catholics to have been led to abandon the *lex credendi*, the rule of belief, if the *lex orandi*, the rule of prayer, had continued to reflect the faith in the glorious way Pius XII intended.

In his later years, his papacy grew increasingly autocratic. He made no confidants and groomed no obvious heirs. He even stopped making new appointments to keep the College of Cardinals up to strength; by the end of his reign, it had dwindled to the lowest number in modern times. During his papacy the centralizing tendency of many centuries reached its culmination in a concentration of rule that could not and probably should not last.

Centring the authority of the Church upon the primacy of Peter has from the beginning served to preserve the purity of Catholic doctrine and discipline. This fact emerges from the earliest records of the Church, from the Acts of the Apostles, and from the letters of Pope Clement to the Church at Corinth at the end of the first century. In later years, people began to appeal to Rome in cases other than doctrinal. Roman justice was more impartial, its decisions less swayed by local pressures. On the other hand, Rome could not hope to have the incumbent bishop's expert knowledge of the local situation nor his pastoral sensitivity. As Rome's very virtues led to routine appeals over the bishops' heads, the machinery for even minor dispensations came to be located in Rome and the legitimate powers of local bishops were much circumscribed. By the end of Pius XII's papacy, resentment among the bishops, especially those from the Rhine countries, had grown very bitter.

Pius XII, although genuinely reform-minded, was committed to a gradual reform guided by a powerful papacy. He had decided against convening a Council and was not interested in broadening the definition of collegiality outside one. Therefore, at the time of his death in 1958, it did not take a prophet to predict that his successor would be a bishop much older, much simpler, and much more malleable. Angelo Roncalli, John XXIII, became at once the darling of Catholic liberals and the secular media. They found his gregarious personality a welcome change after the austere manners of Pius XII, and his surprise announcement of an ecumenical Council "to bring the Church up to date" earned their warm approval.

There is no hint in his life or words that the "Good Pope John" who touched off the revolution had anything more in mind by *aggiornamento* than a modernization and simplification of procedures and disciplines, a kind of cheerful spring-cleaning of all the Church's treasures to make them more attractive to expected guests. The idea of calling a Council seems to have been his own; at least, no one has taken credit for putting it in his mind. He thought the whole thing would be over in a few months, and he seems not to have understood the new meaning the word "ecumenism" had taken on. His own idea of ecumenism, expressed in his opening speech, was that all the separated brethren should return to the Catholic Church forthwith.

Born in a peasant family, separated from it in childhood to the service of the Church, a man of simple piety and conservative politics, he expected from his Council only a deepening of fidelity and a renewed energy for service. When, during the rebellious first session of the Council, he realized that the papacy had lost control of the process, he attempted, as Cardinal John Heenan of Westminster later revealed, to organize a group of bishops to try to force it to an end.[41] Before the second session opened he had died.

By the time his successor, Giovanni Battista Montini, reconvened the Council, the old government of the Church had already been triumphantly routed by the united opposition of several national hierarchies. The Council continued on their terms. Paul VI was not the man to offer them any resistance even if he disagreed with their direction. Orthodox in doctrine, liberal in inclination, indecisive by temperament, he was the weakest Pope of the past century. His style of government liberated the revolutionaries and demoralized the faithful. He would, to give an example of his disastrous style, issue a firm, lucid, orthodox pronouncement, such as the *Credo of the People of God* or *Mysterium Fidei*, the encyclical on Holy Communion aimed at abuses in Holland, or *Humanae Vitae*, against artificial contraception, and then proceed to tolerate, almost, it seemed, to encourage open, universal disobedience. Sometimes his schizophrenic approach to government appeared within a single document. *Memoriale Domini* (May 29, 1969), on the manner of receiving Holy Communion, begins by explaining why reception by mouth is the best, most respectful way, concluding that "In view of the overall contemporary situation of the Church, this manner of distributing communion must be retained." It proceeds with statistics showing that the bishops of the world had recently expressed themselves as overwhelmingly against a change in the manner of reception. It then, astonishingly, says that because the "contrary procedure," reception by hand, at the time illicit, had become established in places, the abuse must be permitted, becoming an equal option with the licit practice. Not only traditionalist Catholics were appalled by this virtual invitation to disorder.

This became the pattern of his government. He repeatedly expressed distress at the condition of the Church and the errors that were gaining ground, yet he never moved against those responsible. The only bishop to be publicly rebuked and suspended was traditionalist Archbishop Marcel Lefebvre, who refused to accept the liturgical changes coming out of Vatican II. The Pope said that Lefebvre's disobedience had been the event that wounded him most in his papacy, this from a chief pastor who had signed with his own hand the laicization papers for over thirty thousand priests and who had expressed "satisfaction" at the Canadian bishops' dissent from *Humanae Vitae*. He alienated the papacy's natural supporters, traditionalists and conservatives who accepted the Council but objected to features of its implementation; yet he also, because of his doctrinal intransigence, angered liberals and radicals who had hoped for more from his undoubted liberalism.

Orthodox Catholics had been spoiled by the long peace. They had built up no tolerance for the kind of confusion at the top that had been more the norm than the exception until the great reform of Trent. Paul VI's contradictory behaviour so unnerved certain traditionalist Catholics that they believed and circulated the story that he was being kept a prisoner in the Vatican while an impostor took his place. (I was shown pictures of his ears to prove the charge.) But for most orthodox Catholics, Paul VI's troubled papacy was a textbook demonstration of the accuracy of the model of the Church as She and It, with the Holy Ghost maintaining the integrity of faith and charity of the spotless Bride of Christ amid the unholy mess the visible structure and its governors had fallen into. When, against all expectations, against his own inclinations, against pressure from eminent churchmen like Canada's Cardinal Léger and from the lay experts on the commission he himself appointed, Paul VI at last reluctantly reiterated the Church's historic teaching on the transmission of human life, the possibility of an orthodox schism disappeared. It is difficult to imagine how Pope Paul VI could have behaved more unwisely both before and after the promulgation of *Humanae Vitae*. Yet the teaching Church had authoritatively once again located itself. The appearance of *Humanae Vitae* was, in fact, the turning point of the revolution, on the one side the throwing off of the pretence of moderation and legitimate development, on the other the birth of the counter-revolution.

Humanae Vitae, to someone who accepts the Church's understanding of the natural moral law, is a wonderful teaching, beautiful and true to human nature, prophetic, compassionate, and, given the pressures, extraordinarily serene and timeless. It earned Paul VI the forgiveness and gratitude of orthodox Catholics and an unexpected tribute of respect from a famous unbeliever, Malcolm Muggeridge, who wrote to the *London Times* to praise and defend it.

Yet it did nothing to stay the revolution. On the contrary. Pope Paul's tolerance of open dissent during his years of delay before the promulgation of *Humanae Vitae*, the consequent resentment of Catholics who had assumed the law was about to change, his failure to rebuke the concerted defiance of the Church's leading theologians after the encyclical's appearance or to require adherence from bishops and clergy did enormous, irreparable damage to the idea of Catholic authority. (I shall discuss Pope Paul's uncertain handling of the birth-control issue at more length in the following chapter.)

The confusions of Paul VI's reign, paramount among them his conduct during the birth-control crisis, served all the purposes of the revolution, not the least of which was the discrediting of the papacy itself. In his book *The Pope's Divisions*, Peter Nichols quotes Hans Küng: "After the Council, Küng remarked to me at his home in Tubingen that he thought Paul VI made a good pope because the need was to demythologize the papacy and, just by being there, Paul VI did so."[42] It is difficult to quarrel with Küng's assessment of the effect of Pope Paul's tenure. Under his weak and contradictory government, the revolution realized that it was loosed and safe.

FIVE

The Triggering Incident

The release of *Humanae Vitae* on July 29, 1968, touched off the full public emergence of the present revolution in the Catholic Church. In this chapter and the next I will try to show why the revolution chose to concentrate all its forces in opposition to this particular doctrine and why the doctrine remains today the bitter crux of the Catholic quarrel and the feature of Catholicism that most irritates the secular world.

As I said earlier, *Humanae Vitae* provides the sharpest defining line of one's Catholic political-religious allegiance: all "conservatives" accept it; all "liberals" reject it. This is true of no other Catholic issue. Orthodox Catholics are sharply divided over the liturgical reform, for example; probably a majority prefers the new vernacular liturgy to the older Latin rite. *Humanae Vitae* is the touchstone of orthodoxy, just as it is the symbol of rebellion. The encyclical acted as the catalyst for the revolution because it identified with shattering clarity that the real subject matter of the struggle going on in the Church was the basic religious and political question of moral authority: Whose? If the Church's account of its authority was correct, then it would not find itself in a position in which it had to change a teaching consistently and authoritatively put forward since its foundation. If the Church were to accept a different account of authority, that of the autonomous and authoritative individual conscience, it would have to vacate its claim to have been divinely inspired and appointed to interpret both the Scriptures and the natural moral law.

Since the story of the birth-control crisis is long and involved, I have tried to make it clearer by discussing it under four headings. In this chapter I will look at (1) the history of the doctrine on contraception until 1963, and (2) the attack on the doctrine made by the emerging revolution, 1963-1968. In chapter 6, I will consider (3) the events surrounding the issuing of *Humanae Vitae*, and (4) what the dispute over *Humanae Vitae* was really about.

HISTORY OF THE DOCTRINE TO 1963

The history of the doctrine until 1963 was one of complete agreement. In 1965, John Noonan, later to be a dissenter from *Humanae Vitae*, in his authoritative history of the doctrine on contraception in the Church, described the theological consensus thus: "The propositions constituting a condemnation of contraception are . . . recurrent. Since the first clear mention of contraception by a Christian theologian, when a harsh third-century moralist accused a pope of encouraging it, the articulated judgment has been the same. . . . The teachers of the Church have taught without hesitation or variation that certain acts of preventing procreation are gravely sinful. No Catholic theologian has ever taught, 'Contraception is a good act.' The teaching on contraception is clear and apparently fixed forever."[1]

The magisterium of the Church made periodic reaffirmations of the teaching. Pius XI's encyclical *Casti Connubii* (December 31, 1930) reiterated the Church's teaching in the wake of the abandonment by the Church of England at that year's Lambeth Conference of the traditional Christian doctrine. Pius XII's October 29, 1951, *Allocution to Midwives* again asserted the teaching, developing it in the light of recent medical discoveries to allow the use of the infertile period in the female cycle for the limitation of families.

These earlier papal pronouncements had caused no surprise and no obvious resentment. On the contrary. Throughout the 1950s and into the 1960s, lay groups such as the Christian Family Movement had apostolically promoted the Church's teaching and the new class of academic and professional Catholics and socially prominent Catholic families like the Kennedys and the Buckleys made themselves an example, "a sign of contradiction," to the secularized, anti-Catholic society into which they had moved, by conspicuous fidelity to the Church's teaching. Maurice Moore, a University of Chicago sociologist, in his study *Death of a Dogma* discovered how conspicuous and how conscious their fidelity was. He found that the Catholic population of the United States "has in the past provided an interesting exception" to the general rule that educated people have smaller families than uneducated people: Catholics with higher levels of education not only had larger families than non-Catholics of similar education, but they had larger families than other Catholics with less education, a pattern not true for other major religious groups. "It is not education but devotion that accounts for differences among Catholics,"[2] Moore concluded, a judgement that still applies. The big family and the material and spiritual sacrifices required for it were incarnational ways of repudiating the Manichaeism and materialism of modern western society.

The same instinct has surfaced today among Catholics active in the anti-abortion movement, where there exists a gallant and amusing rivalry over who will have more children, and among the ex-liberals who now make up the conservative wing of the charismatic movement. The anti-materialist, pro-incarnational urge also survives in the affection and sympathy left-wing Catholics feel for the poor, fecund societies of the Third World. Many children are a proof of one's trust in God, love of creation, hope for mankind. The Pope's invitation to spouses to "conform their activity to the creative intention of God, expressed in the very nature of marriage and of its acts, and manifested by the teaching of the Church" (*Humanae Vitae*, 10) would have fallen more seasonably upon the Catholic ear of the early 1960s, when there was still a large uncorrupted community of believers able to testify from their own practice to the great joy and sweetness and permanence which the carrying of this particular part of the Cross of Christ brings to marriage.

Maurice Moore summarizes the behaviour of the laity into the Council years: "For all practical purposes, no one, not even the individual layman regardless of what his personal practice may have been, raised his voice in opposition to official teaching even into the 1960s."[3]

As for the theologians, they were equally loyal. The move within secular society during the early 1960s to dismantle civil laws against the advertisement and sale of contraceptives encountered determined opposition from Catholic theologians. Extraordinary as it may seem to readers of the magazine today, the Jesuit publication *America* was editorializing in 1961 against the first big ad campaign by Ortho Pharmaceuticals for contraceptives: "It indicates a willingness to risk public outcry from Catholics. . . . Perhaps the most alarming aspect of the new advertisement is that it indicates a lowering of the standards of the magazines which have accepted it."[4] *America* later noted approvingly that its influence had led to the termination of the ad campaign. In 1962 *America* objected to the use of government money for population control research, and to the handing out of free contraceptives to Negroes and Puerto Ricans by drug companies.[5] In 1963 *America* ran a major attack on the theories of Dr. John Rock, the Catholic developer of the birth-control pill, rejecting his position that "motivation justifies use of any contraceptive means"; the magazine quoted approvingly another critic who said, "Dr. Rock has made the tragic mistake of underestimating the intelligence of his own religious leaders. The Roman Catholic Church will recognize sugar-coating and reject it as artifice"; it also pointed out that Dr. Rock was enthusiastically pro-abortion.[6]

Also in 1963, two of the leading theologians in America, Jesuits John Ford and Gerald Kelly, taught in their widely used theological textbook *Contemporary Moral Theology* that "The Church is so irrevocably committed to the doctrine that contraception is intrinsically and gravely immoral that no substantial change in this teaching is possible. It is irrevocable." On the question of its dogmatic status, they wrote that it was "at least definable doctrine and it is very likely already taught infallibly" by the ordinary magisterium.[7] In 1963, the sociologist Father Andrew Greeley, now so apostolic in his desire to link the massive defection of the laity since the mid-1960s with the Church's teaching on birth control, reported that American Catholics accepted and followed the Church's traditional teaching.[8]

THE DOCTRINE UNDER ATTACK, 1963-1968

And then something happened to that united and untroubled front. Fidelity to the Church's teaching on marriage disappeared within a very short period, beginning in 1963. The first important break in the theological front was made by Edward Schillebeeckx, who argued in a Dutch Catholic weekly magazine that openness to procreation applies to the whole of marriage rather than to each act. He and several other European theologians wrote that the newly invented anovulant pills were acceptable to Christian ethics. As noted earlier, *America* disagreed. Meanwhile, Schillebeeckx and other like-minded European *periti* had the Council talking about the possibility of changing the teaching. The excitement spread quickly. Donald Thorman, publisher of the radical newspaper *National Catholic Reporter*, which since its beginning has been the organ of the revolution, recalled the atmosphere at the time in a 1977 memoir:

> I remember back in early 1963 at a symposium at which some of the speakers were having a hotel room rump session. One well-known and respected observer just returned from the council indicated the changing mood among those of us who had large families and who had made great personal sacrifices to observe the church's teachings. We simply could not believe the theologians would ever take a contrary position. Not long after, I was at supper in a rectory with the pastor . . . and I asked for his reaction to this information. 'My God', he said with anguish, 'I can't believe it when I think of all the marriages and lives I've helped ruin because of this teaching [against contraception].'[9]

It seems to be a fact that not even sophisticated, educated Catholic intellectuals like Donald Thorman, or like Patrick and Patricia Crowley, the influential laypeople who headed the Christian Family Movement in the United States, entertained the possibility of serious change in the Catholic doctrine on contraception, or in any other area of Catholic sexual ethics, until some revisionist theologian got hold of them. The Crowleys are a case in point: under them until 1963 CFM was utterly loyal and energetically apostolic. When my husband and I moved to a large Canadian city in the early 1960s, a CFM couple knocked on our door, invited themselves in to talk to us about Catholic marriage and its supports in our diocese, urged us to join the movement and asked us to dinner. Never before had I, a cradle Catholic, experienced this kind of one-to-one lay proselytizing so familiar to evangelical Protestants. We lazy Catholics were impressed.

The Crowleys were early members of the commission appointed by Pope John XXIII in 1963 to study the subject of birth control. Paul VI continued its mandate. The group's original instinct seems to have been to find modern arguments to supplement the traditional case for the Church's ancient teaching. Then in April 1964, the noted German Redemptorist theologian and Council *peritus*, Bernard Häring, addressed the commission and persuaded it to drop the whole argument from the natural law upon which the Church's teaching on contraception was largely based. In a recent book on the birth-control crisis, Robert Kaiser, the influential *Time* correspondent at Vatican II, calls Häring's intervention "a turning point for the commission."[10] From that time, the emphasis in the commission's discussion of marriage shifted from the objective, social, and eternal dimensions of marriage to the subjective, personal, and temporal. By 1968, the Crowleys were eager to sign their names to the first Catholic dissent from *Humanae Vitae*.

During the Council's third session, the revisionist theology of Häring and Schillebeeckx surfaced in the discussion of the section of *Gaudium et Spes*, *The Church in the Modern World* that deals with marriage and the family. On October 29, 1964, the Canadian cardinal Paul Emile Léger, the Belgian cardinal Leo Suenens, and the Melkite Patriarch of Antioch, Maximos IV Saigh, all spoke for a new understanding of marriage that would make the sexual union of the couple legitimate in itself without reference to procreation. They wanted the retirement of the teaching that there was a hierarchy of ends in marriage, with procreation being considered the primary purpose of marriage and the other values of marriage being considered secondary. "Primary" and "secondary" are not comfortable words to our anti-hierarchical age, but the bishops made it clear that it was Catholic morality, not philosophical language, that they wanted changed. Patriarch Maximos, not very politely, attributed the historic Roman Catholic teaching to "the celibate psychosis" of the western church.

Gregory Baum wrote in 1964 of the revolutionary impact of these interventions: "The impression of these speeches in Rome, on the same day, cannot be exaggerated. The reaction of the theologians on the American bishops' press panel went through the world press: 'This is a turning point, this is a watershed – we are free to examine the meaning of sexuality in married life according to God's plan of salvation.' "[11]

Pope Paul was so upset by Cardinal Suenens' speech in particular that he had a private meeting with him. On November 7, Suenens publicly denied on the Council floor that he had meant to question the Church's authentic teaching on marriage. On November 25, Pope Paul sent four compulsory amendments on the marriage section to the Conciliar commission that was finishing the revision of the text. He left the commission free only to determine the phrasing of the amendments. After a bitter battle, the final text voted upon by the fathers contained Paul VI's sentences which repeated the traditional teaching that procreation is the primary natural and supernatural purpose of marriage: "Marriage and conjugal love are by their nature ordained toward the begetting and educating of children. Children are really the supreme gift of marriage and contribute substantially to the welfare of their parents" (*Gaudium et Spes*, 50). By another of the Pope's amendments, the word "also" was removed from the theologians' original version of the first sentence quoted above, which had read: "Marriage and conjugal love are by their nature *also* ordained toward the begetting and educating of children." The second sentence quoted above was inserted at the Pope's express command.

The battle would seem to have been won by the tradition. However, in true Pauline fashion, a later formulation in the very same article (50) seems to contradict the sentences above, which the Pope fought so hard to obtain: "Hence, *while not making the other purposes of matrimony of less account* [my italics], the true practice of conjugal love, and the whole meaning of the family life which results from it, have this aim; that the couple be ready with stout hearts to cooperate with the love of the Creator and the Savior, Who through them will enlarge and enrich His own family day by day." The italicized passage seems to cancel the earlier teaching that the *primary, supreme* purpose of marriage is procreation. Does not the Council seem to be saying that (a) procreation is the supreme purpose of marriage, *and* (b) that this supreme purpose has a host of equals? Having inserted this "formulation of a modern tendency" asserting the equality of ends in marriage, the next section of the document cancels it in its turn:

> This council realizes that certain modern conditions often keep couples from arranging their married lives harmoniously, and that they find themselves in circumstances where at least temporarily the size of their families should not be increased. As a result, the faithful exercise of love and the full intimacy of their lives is hard to maintain. To these problems there are those who presume to offer dishonorable solutions indeed . . . but the Church issues the reminder

that a true contradiction cannot exist between the divine laws pertaining to the transmission of human life and those pertaining to authentic conjugal love. . . . Hence when there is question of harmonizing conjugal love with responsible transmission of life, *the moral aspect of any procedure does not depend solely on sincere intentions or on an evaluation of motives, but must be determined by objective standards.* Relying on these principles, sons of the Church may not undertake methods of birth control which are found blameworthy by the teaching authority of the Church in its unfolding of the divine law. . . .

[I]n their manner of acting, spouses should be aware that they cannot proceed arbitrarily, but must always be governed according to a conscience dutifully conformed to divine law itself and should be submissive toward the Church's teaching office which authentically interprets that law in the light of the Gospel. (*Gaudium et Spes*, 51. My italics)

The double voice of the Council is very evident in article 50 of the *Gaudium et Spes, Pastoral Constitution on the Church in the Modern World*. Radical theologians interpreted it after the Council to mean that the apparent downgrading of procreation to a position of equality not only admitted the use of contraceptives but actually required such use in order that the non-procreative values of marriage might be enhanced. They had succeeded, at least to some extent, in having the Council adopt the romantic, subjective western perception of marriage. This perception, as a Third World bishop, Adrianus Djajasepoetra of Djakarta, pointed out, is not a universal truth; in much of the world continuance of a particular social group is the primary intention of marriage, and arranged marriages the principal means to this end.[12]

In December 1964, Pope Paul VI added forty-six more members to the original thirteen on the commission studying the birth-control issue. By this time, the climate of Catholic opinion, at least at the level of the white western intellectuals, religious and lay, who held most of the seats on the commission, had been changed by the Council's explosive debates on marriage and by the growing public dissent of well-known theologians. In 1964, Gregory Baum, a *peritus* to the Canadian bishops, wrote a series of articles in the secular press taking issue with the traditional doctrine. Archbishop Philip Pocock of Toronto, whose adviser he was, did nothing. Baum went on teaching at St. Michael's College in the University of Toronto, where he remains to this day, even though he left the priesthood and married without waiting for laicization. He is also an instructor of future priests at the Toronto School of Theology. This episcopal pattern of turning a blind eye to blatant clerical dissent was repeated in many countries and it quickly became clear that no action would be taken against radicals. The few bishops who tried to take action were hounded and isolated.

The efforts of several bishops to have the matter of contraception opened to the Council failed. Paul VI reserved the decision to himself; but by an intense educational effort certain theologians convinced a good number of bishops that the pressure from the laity for relaxation in this area was so intense that it could not any longer be resisted and was so pure, unselfish, and reasonable that it should not be resisted. The bishops took these statements largely on faith, since few of them still heard confessions, the forum where the disgruntled laity were supposed to have revealed their unanswerable objections. It is open to question how many theologians like Baum and Schillebeeckx heard confessions either, but the plight of agonized confessors was continually urged as a reason for not waiting for an official ruling. The expectation was generated that the official teaching would change because it must, in the light of new scientific and psychological discoveries. Even before the encyclical appeared, some bishops (including, as was widely known here in Canada at the time, the then Bishop of London, Emmett Carter, and Toronto's Archbishop Pocock) instructed their priests to be lenient in confession in this area.

The revolution was wise to choose sexual freedom as its issue. The sexual revolution under way in secular society ensured for the dissenters the sympathetic support of the secular media, which from the beginning enthusiastically co-operated in the strategy of isolating that part of the government of the Church that stuck to the traditional morality.[13] Radical theologians had, too, the support of some progressive bishops and the wishful thinking, if not open support, of many other bishops who quailed at the prospect of maintaining the unpopular teaching and hoped it might be changed. In this matter, there is no question of bishops having mistaken the revolutionary intent of the dissenters. Opposition to *Humanae Vitae* is one position on which progressive, non-revolutionary bishops like Toronto's Cardinal Carter have not reneged, even though some of the theologians who signed the famous protests against the encyclical have publicly recanted. (At the 1980 synod on marriage and the family, Cardinal Carter supported the calls of the Cardinal of Westminster, Basil Hume, and the American Archbishop John Quinn for a re-evaluation of the teaching on contraception.)

And if the revolutionaries were wise in their choice of issue, they were lucky in their Pope. Paul VI has been blamed by orthodox Catholics for the long delay before he issued *Humanae Vitae*, during which time the revolution irreparably undermined obedience to the traditional doctrine. In his favour, however, several points should be counted. As noted earlier, he pushed Cardinal Suenens into a formal denial that the Cardinal had intended to question the truth of the Church's teaching on marriage and an admission that the decision depended upon the Pope's supreme authority alone. And also as earlier noted, he insisted that four amendments written by himself be included in the section on marriage (*Gaudium et Spes*, Ch. I), clarifications intended to preserve the teaching about a hierarchy of purposes, to retain the prohibition of artificial contraception, and to reaffirm the teaching of *Casti Connubii* and the *Allocution to Midwives*. Moreover, to try to forestall propaganda that the teaching was about to be changed, he warned in a report to the College of Cardinals in June 1964 that his commission had as yet found no grounds for abandoning the traditional teaching; therefore, "no one, for the present, should take it upon himself to make any pronouncement at variance with the norm in force." And of course, in the end, whatever his own hopes of finding a legitimate way to relax the teaching, he ruled that the Church's ancient and modern interpretation of the natural moral law in the matter of the transmission of human life remained correct and could not be changed.

It should also be remembered to the credit of this timid and liberal man that he made his ruling despite the fact that an overwhelming majority on his birth-control commission were against it. Early in 1966, he had added seven cardinals and nine bishops (including Karol Wojtyla) to the commission, but even then the commission's final vote was 64 to 4 in favour of removing the ban on artificial contraception. He rejected the majority report because it had relied on "certain criteria of solutions . . . which departed from the moral teaching on marriage proposed with constant firmness by the teaching authority of the Church" (*Humanae Vitae*, 6). The four theologians who continued to use the Church's objective criteria for truth delivered their own minority report, and Paul VI was guided by it.

Yet for all his ultimate brave orthodoxy, his handling of this crucial issue was a disaster for the Church. The contradictions in his character were never more fatally active. He came down on the side of constant teaching, thus earning the hatred of dissenters; yet, by making no effort to enforce the teaching or to discipline prestigious bishops and theologians who publicly dissented, he earned the rooted distrust of the still numerous obedient faithful who would otherwise have rallied to his support. He undercut what early attempts were made to reinforce the teaching, thus giving aid and comfort to the dissenters while alienating and dividing the loyalists. He temporized, nursing the vain hope that dedicated revolutionaries could be talked into returning to orthodoxy. Determined not to resort to the measures employed by the Church in the first modernist crisis, he refused to employ any of the disciplinary measures available to him.

Throughout the birth-control controversy Paul VI's behaviour supported the suspicion in some quarters that he lacked confidence in the rightness of his ultimate decision. He wrote in *Humanae Vitae* (12) that the Church's historic teaching, now reaffirmed by himself, "is founded upon the inseparable connection, willed by God and unable to be broken by man on his own initiative, between the two meanings of the conjugal act: the unitive meaning and the procreative meaning." Yet, when he issued the encyclical, he welcomed "the lively debate" he hoped would ensue. But if contraception is indeed, as *Humanae Vitae* says, "in contradiction with the design constitutive of marriage and with the will of the Author of life," what can be left to debate? He claimed in *Humanae Vitae* that "the teaching authority" of the Church was exercising the power given it by Christ to interpret authentically and authoritatively not only the Gospel but also the natural moral law. Yet he instructed the spokesman for the Vatican at the press conference held upon the publication of the encyclical to answer to the question upon the status of *Humanae Vitae* that the encyclical was not to be considered an infallible teaching.

A few days later, the revolution was to ground its first major attempt to delegitimize the authority of the magisterium of the Church precisely on the argument that there already existed the right, even the duty, of theologians to dissent from "authoritative, non-infallible" teaching, such as the Pope had just admitted *Humanae Vitae* to be. One wonders if the revolution's thrust might not have been blunted or even defeated if Paul VI has trusted the logic of his own firm argument in *Humanae Vitae* and defended his encyclical more decisively.

But perhaps by the time *Humanae Vitae* appeared, it was already too late to save the Church's teaching on marriage. Maurice Moore's *Death of a Dogma* quotes a variety of sociological studies that trace the dramatic effect on Catholic belief and practice of the theological assault on the doctrine on birth control during the mid-1960s. The number of American Catholic women aged eighteen to thirty-nine who used birth control rose from 30 per cent in 1955 to 53 per cent in 1968; in 1967 a *Newsweek* study of U.S. Catholics showed that 73 per cent of adult Catholics favoured a change in the Church's teaching, even more so among the young college educated; a 1968 Gallup Report for the American Institute of Public Opinion showed that 58 per cent of American Catholics said that "good Catholics" could ignore the Pope's teaching on contraception.[14] Moore, writing in 1973, confirmed what we didn't really need a sociologist to tell us: that since about 1963 there had taken place "an intramural departure from official Catholic teaching that has no parallel in modern times – at least not since 1517 when Martin Luther posted his 95 theses on the castle church in Wittenberg and declared that man is saved by faith alone."[15]

~~

SIX

THE CONSEQUENCES OF HUMANAE VITAE

~~

Humanae Vitae was chosen by the revolution to figure as the insult too gross to be borne, the issue that showed to the world that the hierarchy of the Church was deaf to the pleas of the faithful for justice and compassion. The magisterium, weakened by Vatican II and subverted after it, rudderless under Paul VI's uncertain leadership, was unable to exert its customary moral authority. Dissenting theologians, not the papacy, nor two thousand years of consistent Christian teaching and practice, determined episcopal response. In this first great post-Conciliar trial of strength, the revolution performed brilliantly and decisively. It now reaped the fruits of its crucial support-role during the Council. Bishops had naturally installed their Conciliar allies in all the key posts of the huge new local bureaucracies and now these trusted staffers wrote and stage-managed the response to *Humanae Vitae*.

THE EVENTS SURROUNDING THE ISSUING OF HUMANAE VITAE

On July 25, 1968, Pope Paul VI promulgated and on July 29 he publicly released his encyclical letter *Humanae Vitae, On the Transmission of Human Life*. His accompanying statement couched his decision to stay with the historic dogma in apologetic terms: "We had to assess, out of obligation to but also with the freedom of our apostolic duty, a doctrinal tradition which is not only centuries old but also recent, the tradition of our three immediate predecessors. We were obliged to make our own the teachings of the Council which we ourselves promulgated. . . . Our labor was accompanied by the hope that this document will be accepted for its truth." He made his usual plaintive bid for sympathy: "Never as at this point have we felt the burden of our office" or "the inadequacy of our humble person for the formidable apostolic obligation of having to pronounce on the matter." The Vatican official who handled the press conference called upon the release of the encyclical, Monsignor Ferdinando Lambruschini of Rome's Lateran University, answered the question about the document's status thus: "It is not infallible but does not leave the questions concerning birth regulation in a condition of vague problematics. The assent of theological faith is due only to the definitions properly so called infallible but there is owed also loyal and full assent, interior and not only exterior to an authentic pronouncement of the magisterium."

The Vatican, of course, is not to blame for the fact that the world's press quoted the first part of this theologically precise answer and not the second. " 'Not infallible' says Vatican's spokesman," cheered the *National Catholic Reporter*. But things would have been considerably easier for non-revolutionized Catholics if Pope Paul had for once put aside his tendency towards over-qualification and said something like the following:

> Yes, it is infallible. It is an infallible exercise of the ordinary magisterium of the universal Church. The fact that it has not been formally defined as infallible by an *ex cathedra* exercise of the extraordinary magisterium in no way detracts from its status. No other moral teaching has been defined *ex cathedra* either. The teaching in *Humanae Vitae* fulfils every criterion of authenticity: it has been taught from the beginning, always, everywhere and by everyone; it has lately been ratified by two Popes and an ecumenical Council. It therefore requires that "religious submission of mind and will" which, as the Second Vatican Council dogmatically declared, "must be shown in a special way to the authentic magisterium of the Roman Pontiff even when he is not speaking *ex cathedra*." This means, dearest brethren, that you must believe it and make your best shot at practising it.[1]

That, more or less, is how Rome's statements would have been translated to the world in a better, non-revolutionary time by the orthodox equivalents of *National Catholic Reporter* and Robert Kaiser.

From the moment that it was known that Paul VI was about to issue an encyclical against contraception, the gloves were off. In the United States, several powerful bishops, notably Cardinals Patrick O'Boyle (Washington) and James Francis McIntyre (Los Angeles), resisting pressure from prominent American theologians, committed the U.S. bishops to an assenting response to the encyclical. The theologians' revolution had not yet quite managed to become solidly enough established to force the fiery O'Boyle to allow them to draft the U.S. bishops' official statement. In anticipation of the impending reiteration by Rome of the disputed teaching, there was a savage, unedifying struggle over the nature of the American answer, which the dissenters narrowly lost. On July 29, the U.S. hierarchy accepted the unchanged teaching and the Pope's right to so teach. Moreover, they made it clear that they expected compliance. Cardinal O'Boyle called on his priests to transmit the teaching "without equivocation, ambiguity or simulation,"[2] and suspended those who publicly disobeyed.

This particular united front of the U.S. bishops was not at all what the radicals had expected from the spirit of collegiality. When it became clear that the American bishops would endorse *Humanae Vitae*, the revolution decided to go public before the bishops could. Confident that they had little to fear, the radicals planned a bold and insulting move. Father Charles Curran, a theologian at Catholic University of America, managed to obtain a copy of the encyclical from sympathizers in the Vatican before it was released. During the night before the encyclical was released, Curran got on the phone to members of his long-established radical network, alerted them to the contents of the forthcoming papal letter, and by morning had secured eighty-seven signatures, Bernard Häring being the prize catch. (Curran's avowal that "I nearly fell off my chair when Häring agreed" may be taken with a grain of salt, given that Curran had been his student.)

On July 30, at a press conference in the Mayflower Hotel in Washington, Curran countered the Pope's statement with that of the theologians. In a nicely ironic touch, considering their own end-run around their bishops, the dissenters rebuked the Pope for bypassing collegiality and for ignoring the new collegial model of the Church. They took aim at the encyclical's account of authority: "The encyclical assumes that the church is identical with the hierarchical office. . . . It betrays a narrow and positivistic notion of papal authority as illustrated by the rejection of the majority view presented by the commission established to consider the question as well as by the rejection of the international Catholic theological community." The statement charged that the encyclical was based not on Scripture but on "an inadequate concept of natural law," and amounted to no more than "mere repetition of past teaching."[3] The theologians' declaration of independence concluded with a ringing insertion of the Protestant principle into Catholic ethics: "As Roman Catholic theologians, conscious of our duty and limitations, we conclude that spouses may responsibly decide according to their conscience that artificial contraception in some circumstances is permissible and indeed necessary to preserve and foster the values and sacredness of marriage."

In 1975, in a breathtakingly frank account of the incident and his leading role in it, essential reading for the student of the Catholic revolution, Charles Curran gave the authoritative version of the great coup and the steps leading up to it.[4] Under the influence of Bernard Häring, his teacher, Curran had become discontented with the older approaches to moral theology. But like Alfred Loisy, the earlier modernist, he had to be careful. He adopted Loisy's tactics: "Teaching a new approach to moral theology in a pre-Vatican II seminary environment was an exhilarating experience – especially since my approach was different from that of all the other theological professors." But another key figure in the coming revolution, Francis X. Murphy, a Redemptorist patristic theologian (and the ultra-liberal "Xavier Rynne" who reported Vatican II for the *New Yorker* and in several influential books) at the time a professor at the Redemptorist College in Rome where Curran was studying, advised him on strategy: "Murphy encouraged me to go slow and not make too many waves. . . . He suggested that I begin by teaching my classes in Latin . . . so that first attention would not focus on the newer approaches I was teaching. The strategy worked quite well."

Until the summer of 1964, Curran supported the traditional teaching on contraception. Writing sympathetically of those who advocated change, Curran nevertheless concluded that their arguments were insufficiently probable to be followed in good conscience.[5] Yet, by what process he does not describe, "shortly thereafter I became convinced of the need to change the teaching . . . and before the year was out wrote an article to explain my views and gave addresses on the topic." He began to teach the right to dissent from "authoritative, non-infallible" Church teaching, recognizing that "the possibility of dissent was seen as extending to all other specific moral questions." In July 1965, the diocese of Rochester, alarmed by his teaching, dismissed him from St. Bernard's seminary, but permitted him to accept a post in the School of Theology at Catholic University of America. In April 1967, amid rumours of pressure from Rome, he was fired.

Immediately, a large and emotional public rally of faculty and students protested his firing and demanded that he be rehired. Petitions circulated. The press headlined the story. Led by the theology department, the whole university struck in sympathy: "We cannot and will not function unless and until Father Curran is reinstated." Curran recalls those heady days: "Demonstrations and rallies continued. My room was turned into 'strike headquarters,' but the whole operation was truly collegial with many people working together who had never even known one another before. The media continued to give immense coverage to the strike both in daily papers and on evening television news programs. The pressure was building." Negotiations began and the university administration buckled. The chancellor, Archbishop Patrick O'Boyle, announced to a crowd assembled in front of the library on April 24 that Curran would be rehired and promoted.

This successful rehearsal for the main performance "set the stage for a future development," as Curran admits. The hierarchy was divided, having allowed itself to be sidetracked from the real doctrinal points at issue by the question of academic freedom. It collapsed with indignity. Meanwhile, the revolution had perfected its techniques:

Throughout the strike we purposely made every effort to keep the basic issue as narrow as possible – proper academic procedure was violated because the trustees fired me without giving reasons or a hearing despite the unanimous decision of my peers that I be promoted. This was the formal reason, but everyone knew that the real reason was my teaching, especially in the areas of contraception and also masturbation. In the final victory our tone was also purposely restrained – we had now been given not an ultimate victory but an opportunity and a mandate to continue our efforts on behalf of Catholic University, scholarship, and Catholic theological investigation.

Curran's choice of the word *mandate* is revealing and instructive, for it accurately describes the revolutionary shift of authority that could now be seen to have occurred. Authority from now on was to be vested in the dissenting academy, not in the traditional magisterium of the Church. The "ultimate victory" could not be far off. Since Curran's description of how it was attained is essential documentation for the revolution, I will quote it at length:

As 1968 dawned there were signs that perhaps Pope Paul would not take the recommendations of the majority of his commission studying the question of birth control who called for a change in the teaching of the Church. . . . In July rumors began to fly that an encyclical condemning artificial contraception was imminent. I was in frequent contact with colleagues at Catholic University and throughout the country. The strike at Catholic University the year before had the effect of catapulting me into a very prominent leadership role on this question of artificial contraception and the Roman Catholic Church. We tried in vain to raise enough publicity to prevent the issuance of any encyclical. It was my judgment that an encyclical at that time reaffirming the older teaching would be catastrophic. Many people would think that they could no longer be loyal Roman Catholics because of their decision to practice artificial contraception. Priests would be searching for guidance and would also be thrown into great crises of conscience. I was convinced that most Catholics and priests did not even know about the right to dissent from authoritative, non-infallible teaching, hierarchical teaching. Plans then began to take shape to formulate a response to the encyclical. . . . On Sunday evening, July 28th, it was reliably reported on radio and television that an encyclical would be issued on Monday, July 29th. The encyclical was released in Rome on that Monday morning (at 4:30 A.M. New York time). I already had contingency reservations to fly back to Washington about noon on Monday. After numerous phone calls Sunday evening and Monday morning, a meeting was set for Caldwell Hall (my residence) at Catholic University that afternoon for a group of theologians to assemble and discuss a response to the encyclical. Copies of the encyclical were promised to us at that time. Other calls were made to theologians around the country telling them that a statement would be forthcoming and asking them to be prepared for a phone call later that evening asking them to sign the statement. A group of about ten theologians met in Caldwell Hall, read the encyclical, and discussed a response. I insisted that the statement could not hedge, but would have to meet head on the question of dissent. After a fruitful discussion I typed out the final draft on my typewriter with help from Dan Maguire, but the whole enterprise had been the fruit of the contributions of those present at the meeting. It was agreed to hold a press conference Tuesday morning to announce the statement, and in the meantime we telephoned the other theologians. The number later swelled to over 600 signatures of people qualified in the sacred sciences as a result of a mailing to members of various professional organizations. Naturally this response became headline news throughout the United States and in all the television media. In fact we were able to hold subsequent press conferences in the next few days in an attempt to obtain as much coverage as possible. Our quick, forceful response supported by so many theologians accomplished its purpose. The day after the encyclical was promulgated American Catholics could read in their morning papers about their right to dissent and the fact that Catholics could in theory and practice disagree with the papal teaching and still be loyal Roman Catholics. Other theologians around the world joined in and also even individual bishops and later some conferences of bishops. But our response as a quick, well-organized, collegial effort was unique. This, I hope, solved some problems for many Catholics, although I am sure that it also created problems for many other Catholics, those who could not understand this type of dissent.

The magisterial serenity emanating from this passage exactly reflects the amazing confidence, competence, and strength of the revolution in its first concerted challenge to the central authority. Such blazing self-confidence spurred a rush of powerful figures to the revolutionary standard. Bernard Häring, having taken the plunge by signing Curran's manifesto, issued a separate statement urging the Pope to employ collegiality in order to reach a broad consensus of the Christian community.[6] The prominent moral theologian Father David Tracy in a speech to fifteen hundred people at Catholic University of America uttered a ringing defiance: "I cannot in conscience accept and I will neither in the classroom nor in my confessional practice follow the teaching of the encyclical on birth control."[7] The American theologians' statement spawned imitations in Canada, Britain, and Europe. Big guns like Hans Küng and Karl Rahner added their names. The noise attracted academics of smaller calibre from the lesser seminaries and provincial universities, from St. Francis Xavier in Nova Scotia, for instance, and from St. Michael's, the Catholic college within the University of Toronto.

The hierarchy, sensing defeat, was reluctant to take up the dare implied in Father Tracy's speech or in the *National Catholic Reporter*'s satisfied note that "by the week's end no hierarchical disciplining was reported taken against priests who had defied the Pope."[8] The revolution, on the other hand, was eager for the confrontation. Radicals knew that few of the bishops would move against them, partly because, having divorced themselves from the Vatican, the bishops had become dependent upon and intimidated by the modernist skills of their revolutionary *periti*, and, more importantly, because certain bishops, those in the fore of the collegiality drive, also wanted a relaxation of the traditional teaching on birth control. They had been the first converts of the proselytizing *periti*. Only one bishop – James P. Shannon, auxiliary bishop of St. Paul-Minneapolis – resigned on the grounds that he could not agree with the historic teaching (his subsequent marriage to Mrs. Ruth Church Wilkinson taking the shine off his nobility perhaps a little). Shannon's departure was mourned by Robert Hoyt, editor of the *National Catholic Reporter*: "He has been the bishop who has made life tolerable for liberal Catholics in this country."[9] But the revolution had no need to feel abandoned. Those few bishops still possessing the resolve to move against priests publicly dissenting were the ones who were not only abandoned but actively undercut by their brothers in collegiality. For example: when Father Thomas Dailey, a moral theologian at St. John Vianney Seminary in Buffalo, New York, was dismissed by his bishop, James McNulty, for signing a public statement against *Humanae Vitae*, he was immediately hired by Toronto's Archbishop Philip Pocock to teach theology at St. Augustine's, the major English-speaking Canadian seminary. Archbishop Pocock's personal *peritus* during and after the Council was Gregory Baum. Pocock and Baum were leading movers in the Canadian bishops' dissenting response to *Humanae Vitae*.

To take a further example of the failure of episcopal solidarity: Washington's intrepid Cardinal Patrick O'Boyle had made a determined effort to enforce the encyclical. He ordered over fifty priests to stop exercising some or all of their priestly faculties because of their public defiance. Moreover, he not only wrote a pastoral letter urging Catholics in his diocese to be faithful to *Humanae Vitae* and to make every effort to win back dissenters, he also had the courage to defend the encyclical himself from various pulpits. He got a standing ovation in one congregation, but there were also two hundred walk-outs, an amazing insult to a bishop.

When the Canadian bishops issued their own different answer to *Humanae Vitae* in late September 1968 in Winnipeg, two other Canadian bishops made it clear where their collegial loyalties lay. After the Winnipeg meeting, the *Catholic Register* questioned Bishops Remi de Roo (Victoria) and Emmett Carter (London), leading progressives, about the difference between the Canadian bishops' statements and actions and those of Cardinal O'Boyle. Like the American theologians they sounded the collegial note. Bishop de Roo, head of the theological commission that had drafted the *Winnipeg Statement*, as the Canadian bishops' official response to *Humanae Vitae* was called, said he was not following Cardinal O'Boyle's line or anyone else's line: "If there is a line that we are following, it is the line of the Canadian hierarchy. We have our own collegial responsibility for the people of God in Canada." And Bishop Emmett Carter added: "You can't put into the same category what one bishop does in his diocese and what a national conference of bishops teaches. Cardinal O'Boyle has made his own interpretation of the encyclical."[10]

The idea put forward here – that the authority of national episcopal conferences overrides that of the Pope alone, of the Pope and bishops in unity, and of the individual bishop in his own diocese – was not a creation of the Council, whose uncompromising language on the limits of collegiality I quoted earlier. Obviously, some radical post-Conciliar development of the concept of collegiality had to have taken place for national hierarchies or individual bishops to feel able to repudiate the consistent, united teaching of the ordinary magisterium throughout Catholic history in favour of the interpretative authority claimed by the young (thirty-four-year-old), only recently defected theologian, Charles Curran.

But whatever some bishops' dreams were, the fact was that the only collective action that now mattered came from the revolution. The revolution's "quick, well-organized, collegial effort" has since its anti-*Humanae Vitae* coup been the *de facto* if not yet *de jure* government of the Church on the local and national levels. For, having divided the bishops from Rome, the revolution proceeded with contemptuous ease to conquer them.

In the United States, as I have described above, the radical theologians, by the exercise of their own awesome collegial strength, simply out-flanked the shaky front momentarily maintained by the force of Cardinal O'Boyle's conviction. By the time the encyclical appeared, dissenters held all the key posts in the new national bureaucracies and had long enjoyed the admiring support of the press, secular and religious, through which they propagandized untiringly, unrebuked by authority, for the revolution. When the U.S. bishops met in November 1968 to discuss their response to *Humanae Vitae*, 150 priests sat in, in a drench of approving publicity, outside the rooms where the bishops were meeting. Large rallies of clerics, religious, academics, and students were staged to support the priests whom Cardinal O'Boyle had disciplined. Influential Catholic lay professionals from outside the academy intervened threateningly on the side of Curran and his fellow dissenters. When Cardinal James Francis McIntyre, a trustee (along with all U.S. archbishops) of Catholic University, introduced the motion that "the utterances of Father Curran, his followers, and associates with regard to the encyclical *Humanae Vitae* constitutes a breach of contract that admits of no other consideration than termination,"[11] a Catholic law firm in New York donated its services in the successful year-long effort to defend Curran and company. Curran is still at Catholic University.

After the initial triumph over the bishops on the appearance of the encyclical, revolutionary fervour spread quickly. Other theologians rushed to make the point that sexual morality was not the only area under fire. When Cardinal O'Boyle refused to endorse the August 19-22 National Liturgical Week because of its invitation to Herbert Aptheker, director of the American Institute of Marxist Studies and member of the U.S. Communist Party, to give the keynote speech on "Revolution: Christian Responses," the seven-thousand-member liturgical conference announced that it did not seek and did not need "permission from the local bishop."[12] It was no coincidence that two of the conference's most radical liturgists, Gerald Sigler and Robert Hovda, were among the priests whom Cardinal O'Boyle had suspended.[13]

The revolution picked up support. At St. Louis University five hundred laymen, religious, and priests signed a statement supporting Curran's original group. The newly formed National Association of Laymen began a country-wide campaign to collect signatures supporting the dissenting priests. The liturgical conference and the National Association of Laymen sent invitations to one hundred thousand Catholics to come to Washington to show solidarity with the suspended priests and to put pressure on the bishops' meeting that was to decide the official response to *Humanae Vitae*.[14] The week before the U.S. bishops met to consider their official response to *Humanae Vitae*, *National Catholic Reporter* editorialized: "The principal tool the council fashioned to translate aspiration into reality was an idea which was given the name 'collegiality'. Technically, it meant that all the bishops share by right in the responsibility for governing the church. So explained, that obviously wasn't a dynamic idea. But it implied much more: the final dethronement of the papal curia's career functionaries, the recognition of pluralism within the walls, the encouragement of initiatives from below, the demythologization of the papacy. But the council did not enact collegiality. It only praised it."

Now, said *NCR*, the time had come to enact true collegiality. It advertised for the day before the bishops' meeting a massive "Unity Day Rally in support of the valiant efforts of the 54 Washington, D.C., priests to affirm and defend 'freedom of conscience' in the church." The full-page ad was headed "November 10 is the time for uprooting."[15]

On November 10, four thousand revolutionaries gathered in the Mayflower Hotel in Washington around the new collegium, the dissenting theologians who were in the process of establishing themselves as what one of the most influential of them, Richard McCormick, S.J., calls "the second magisterium." After the rally, 150 priests marched on the hotel where the bishops were meeting and sat in the lobby to the accompaniment of vast publicity. By this stage of the revolution, after several months of fierce argument over *Humanae Vitae*, everyone was clear about the principle at stake: "Do we as Catholics want a system of objective morality or one of situation ethics?" as one U.S. bishop put it during the bishops' discussion on their answer to the encyclical.[16] At least one of the original signers of Curran's July 30 manifesto would have agreed with the bishop. Father Robert Faricy, head of the religious education department of Catholic University of America, claimed that "the theological issue of birth control had turned into a political issue of Church authority," and withdrew his name from the list of dissenters.[17]

Nevertheless, in spite of an intensity of pressure they had never before faced from their own flock, the U.S. bishops held firm, at least on paper. In an eleven-thousand-word pastoral letter, the bishops accepted *Humanae Vitae* as not only "authoritative" but "obligatory," since it was based, they said, on principles "not ecclesiastical but divine." They refused to modify Catholic teaching on conscience. As with other sins, circumstances might often act to reduce moral guilt, but "no man following the teaching of the Church can deny the objective evil of contraception itself."[18]

But the bishops' declaration did not mean that the war was over; the revolution had only just begun to fight. Having failed to influence or frighten the bishops into submission, it simply ignored them from that time and settled down to run the Catholic Church in America without them. Since 1968, with only scattered rebellions from individual bishops, the "parallel hierarchy" has written and enforced policy in every area – liturgy, catechetics, seminaries, sex education, social justice, political involvement. "I'll tell them to stop and they say they will, but they won't," one U.S. bishop admitted after a Vatican attempt to halt widespread liturgical abuses. "What do the Pope and Knox expect me to do? Fire half the priests in my diocese?"[19] Not until 1983, well into John Paul II's papacy and several years after his visit to the United States, did faint signs of an episcopal revival of nerve appear.

I shall return in a later chapter of this book to the revolutionary events in the United States surrounding the appearance of *Humanae Vitae*. At this point, I wish to deal with the response of the Canadian hierarchy to the encyclical. I wrote about it in an earlier book[20] but I return to it here because of the fact that the revolution scored in Canada the major success that escaped it in the United States. In Canada the hierarchical magisterium officially surrendered. It established the Protestant principle as the norm that Canadian Catholics might follow in their practice of sexual ethics.

It is usual in Canada to say that Canada is far less radical than the United States. In fact, the opposite is true when it comes to the ease with which radical social change can be brought about. The Catholic revolution hit Canadian Catholicism, via Quebec and France, years before it affected the United States. While English-speaking North America remained virtually untroubled, French Canadian Catholicism, by far the largest and most influential part of the Church in Canada, had been radicalized at the level of the academy a decade before the Council, through its close contact with the radical Catholic left in France. During the 1950s, French Canadian Catholic intellectuals (many of them, like Pierre Elliott Trudeau and René Lévesque, students of the enormously influential Dominican, Georges-Henri Lévesque, founder of the University of Laval's School of Social Sciences) engineered the so-called "quiet revolution" within Quebec society, whereby the Church voluntarily disengaged itself from its hitherto almost total authority over education, social welfare, unions, and cultural life, in an amazingly rapid secularization. By the time the post-Conciliar revolution was loosed upon the rest of Catholic North America, the Church in Quebec was prostrate. The collapse of Catholicism in French Canada was extremely important for Canadian society in general, since it gave the green light to government liberalization of laws on contraception, divorce, and abortion, which the large Catholic representation from Quebec had hitherto blocked in the Canadian Parliament. French Canadian intellectuals, notably Pierre Trudeau, introduced into Canadian political philosophy the idea that legality need not reflect morality, and that a Catholic could be "personally opposed, but . . ." on moral issues like abortion. By exploiting the nationalist loyalty of Quebec Catholics, Trudeau introduced as justice minister and as prime minister legislated liberal abortion laws, several years before the United States managed to accomplish the same thing.

But even by 1968, except among Quebec intellectuals and the staffers of the new bureaucracies, the revolution had not penetrated very deeply into Canadian Catholic consciousness. Therefore, in Canada initial lay response was loyal. The largest English Catholic newspaper, the *Catholic Register*, in early editorials, welcomed the encyclical: "Undoubtedly, the Holy Father's authoritative statement, even if not dogmatic, requires of the loyal Catholic full religious assent";[21] "It remains only for us as loyal Catholics to accept his ruling, coming as it does from the supreme teaching authority."[22] The largest lay organization, the Catholic Women's League, agreed, and even the liberal *Western Catholic Reporter* declared that "unless we acknowledge the right of the Pope to teach this way and the duty of Catholics to follow his teaching . . . we forfeit the primacy of the Pope, a primacy which Christ instituted in his selection of Peter."[23]

But, as Charles Curran noted, the successful coup of the American theologians set off a chain reaction in other countries. The *Catholic Register* changed its mind: "The encyclical, quite frankly, disappointed me," wrote P.A.G. McKay in an unusual signed editorial.[24] The Canadian leaders of the Christian Family Movement, until then so apostolically committed to the traditional teaching, signed a protest about *Humanae Vitae* addressed to Toronto's Archbishop Pocock. A group of academics called Catholics in Dialogue, based in St. Michael's College in the University of Toronto, similar groups in Nova Scotia and Ottawa, and a large group from the Western Conference for Priests signed public dissenting statements.

As in the United States, conscience was suddenly big news in Catholic circles. The notes of conscience and its connection with the Catholic teaching authority were repeatedly struck. Catholics in Dialogue ran this poll in Toronto newspapers: "Q: Do you think that the recent papal encyclical has settled the question of contraception for all faithful Catholics? Q: Do you think it is possible for a Catholic to practise contraception in good conscience? Q: Are you satisfied with the way in which the Church's teaching authority has been used in dealing with the question of contraception?" A spokesman for the group underlined their point: "The main concern of our group was the possibility that people and priests might accept without question the view of the *Register* editorial that the papal encyclical deserved complete and unquestioning obedience."[25]

The Western Priests' statement, over the signature of Father Ora McManus, urged that the Canadian bishops' forthcoming statement recognize the right to dissent from the teaching of the encyclical.

McManus's action was a particularly offensive pressure tactic, given that he was to be a consultant for the bishops' own statement. The influential Société canadienne de théologie voted (52 to 14) for the "effective recognition of the right of all Christians, including the poor and ignorant, to know the doubts of the Church on the question of contraception."[26] Actually, it was the doubts of the *theologians* that McManus and Andre Naud, both *periti* for the *Winnipeg Statement*, wanted to convey to the poor and ignorant; they had already conveyed them successfully to the rich and educated.[27]

From the beginning of the fall 1968 assembly of the Canadian Catholic Conference of Bishops, the deck was stacked against those who wished to accept the traditional position. Canada's leading progressive bishops, in particular Remi de Roo, head of the theological commission, and Alexander Carter, then president of the CCCB, obtained a consensus of sorts on the *Winnipeg Statement*, the official episcopal response to *Humanae Vitae*. Fathers McManus and Naud were theological consultants. Father Edward Sheridan, S.J., also a consultant, was permitted to circulate a translation of Karl Rahner's rebuttal of *Humanae Vitae*[28] while canonist Monsignor Vincent Foy's criticism of Rahner's position, also sent to the meeting, was suppressed by Archbishop Pocock. Archbishop Pocock's consultant for the meeting was Gregory Baum, also an early dissenter to *Humanae Vitae*. Bernard Daly, the layman who headed the family life bureau of the CCCB, and a public dissenter from the encyclical, was permitted to be present and to speak at all the bishops' closed-door sessions on the response to *Humanae Vitae*. There is a full, approving account of the meeting in the *Western Catholic Reporter*, which was loud in its praise of Bishop Alexander Carter's cynical "collegial" tactics: "The progressive nature of the statement would not have been possible without the strong chairmanship of Bishop Alexander Carter . . . who is steeped in the meaning and process of the conciliar life. As late as Friday morning, when a bishop made a last-ditch effort on the floor to water down the statement, Bishop Carter firmly ruled him out of order."[29]

Even so, the revolution's victory was narrowly achieved. Bishop André Ouellette, co-chairman of the theological commission, put up a strong fight with the support of certain theologians like Father (now Cardinal and president of the Pontifical Council for the Family) Edouard Gagnon. Ouellette at one point procured a commission majority against de Roo's position that the statement should read simply that Catholics were free to follow their conscience, and proposed this draft declaration: "We are as one with the Holy Father in his teaching and pastoral concern about conjugal life and responsible parenthood." At this point, Edward Sheridan, Ora McManus, Bernard Daly, Andre Naud, and other dissenting theologians united to present an ultimatum to the bishops, warning of dreadful consequences if Bishop de Roo's prescription were not accepted. Their position carried by one vote; the revised statement withholds agreement from the encyclical, merely saying non-committally: "We are in accord with the teaching of the Holy Father concerning the dignity of married life, and the necessity of a truly Christian relationship between conjugal love and responsible parenthood." Several bishops have said to me, "This was the best we could get. You should have seen what they first proposed." Yes, we should have; as it is, this formulation is a piece of sophistry. It conveys the dissenting position of the revolution with complete accuracy, but in terms vague enough to allow the bishops to argue, as Cardinal Carter does to this day, that the *Winnipeg Statement* received an incredible misreading.

The most famous and controversial phrase in the *Winnipeg Statement* is: "Whoever honestly chooses that course which seems right to him does so in good conscience." This formulation is a radical departure from the Church's constant teaching on "good conscience," or "right conscience" as Vatican II calls it. Maurice Moore, listing the factors leading to the collapse of the authority of the magisterium of the Church, remarks:

> A notable development in the moral thinking of American priests is the importance attached to individual conscience. It has always been a commonplace of Catholic moral theology that the individual conscience is the final arbiter for a person's actions and that a person must follow the dictates of his conscience. But conscience was the norm to be followed at the moment of decision-making and action. Conscience itself was to be formed according to principles which hopefully were understood and accepted on their own terms, but which also derived validity from the fact that they were taught with the authority of the Church. . . . The Protestant reformers reversed the order of importance in moral judgment, and this line of thought appears to be taking hold among the Catholic clergy.[30]

The Canadian bishops, like the Protestant reformers, reversed the order of importance in moral judgement, that is, they put the private, subjective elements of morality before the universal and objective. They said that a man acts "in good conscience" when he does what "*seems*" right to him, whether or not it *is* right in the objective order. Surely this teaching questions the existence of any "objective," outside, moral order. Did the bishops know what they were implying when they so faithfully reflected the position held by leading radical theologians like Richard McCormick, s.j., and Charles Curran? Did they realize that they were saying that there could be no moral absolutes?

Edward Sheridan, s.j., who was a dissenter from *Humanae Vitae* and consultant for the *Winnipeg Statement*, wrote in his insider's account for *America* that "The [Winnipeg] Statement contained no general profession of assent to the whole teaching of *Human Life*, and nothing that could be interpreted as adding the local authority of the Canadian hierarchy to that of the encyclical in general. . . . It sidestepped the thorny question of the right of a Catholic to refuse internal or external assent and to reduce such refusal to practice."[31] Father Sheridan modestly refrained from mentioning his own crucial part in having the Canadian Catholic Conference of Bishops commit itself to the Protestant principle of autonomous inner direction.

The revolution was jubilant over the Canadian step. The *National Catholic Reporter*, at that time putting intense effort into influencing the U.S. bishops' upcoming assembly, headlined on October 2: "Canada: Yes On Conscience," and on October 9 adorned their front-page story with a maple leaf and the headline: "A Canadian Credo." In his *America* report, Father Sheridan quoted a Canadian bishop on the significance of the statement: "It was something of an identity crisis. . . . We had to recognize our own magisterial role. . . . I think we gained new appreciation of our collegial role and responsibility." The *Catholic Register* picked up the collegial theme: "Collegiality of bishops has been advanced four or five years," and quoted one bishop who thought the *Register*'s estimate too modest: "It had put the whole church ahead from 20 to 100 years." The *Register* story (by Michael O'Meara) understood the revolutionary import of the Winnipeg action: "The issues, of course, are much more than birth control. That's only the tip of the iceberg. What is involved are the principles and practices of authority, the principles and legitimate grounds for dissent, the role of national conferences of bishops in modern society, the role of priests, in particular, and of laymen and religious in the church, the fact of more than one moral code in our society."[32] The same issue of the *Register* ran an editorial headed "We Are A Truly Canadian Church":

> It will take weeks, perhaps months, for Canadians to appreciate and really believe what happened at Winnipeg last week. It has not happened in the Church – anywhere – for centuries. And in Canada perhaps for the first time in our history. We can now become a truly Canadian Church in the deepest sense of the word. . . . No matter what one's opinion may be on birth control . . . every Catholic, and perhaps every citizen, must say: "God bless the Canadian Bishops" for their courage and maturity. . . . Their statement is making waves throughout the world and we are exceedingly proud of them. . . . They have a free hand to build a Canadian Church that will truly serve the needs of our time.

Everyone who commented on the birth-control dispute seems to have understood its implications. Everyone, that is, except the wave-making bishops. For though they allowed their radical *periti* to write their lines, the logical consequences of their new permission for the exercise of individual conscience divorced from the Church's objective teaching in the matter of birth control seem to have escaped them. They did not see that by abandoning the teaching against contraception to the private conscience they were destroying the whole inner logic of the Church's account of sexual morality. For if in marriage it is sometimes permissible to divorce the sexual act from its natural purpose, procreation, in the name of other values – love, charity, support, fidelity, health – why should it be wrong to divorce it from its purpose in cases where the same values might be felt to obtain – in masturbation, homosexuality, adultery, fornication, bestiality, artificial insemination, the sale of sperm, surrogate motherhood?

The English philosopher Elizabeth Anscombe, speaking at St. Michael's College, Toronto, shortly before the encyclical on birth control appeared, brilliantly stated the philosophical grounds for the traditional Catholic argument, concluding: "The rationale of the old objection [is] as follows: in contraceptive intercourse the intentional action is deliberately altered from being a generative kind of action to being an act of attaining sexual climax. If it is indeed all right to do this for good ends, then it is excessively difficult to see *why* after all the act need closely resemble a normal complete act of copulation."[33] St. Mike's Catholics in Dialogue had taken the point, but the bishops, judging from their post-Winnipeg flounderings, had not. The *Winnipeg Statement*'s conscience provision granted permission for a divorce between sex and procreation which the Vatican Council had eventually refused to countenance. Yet several weeks after they met in Winnipeg, the bishops took the *Catholic Register* to task for its story headed "Let your conscience be your guide." The bishops scolded the *Register* and the press in general for misreading the statement. The *Register* retorted with a sharp set of awkward questions about the *Winnipeg Statement*:

> If this is the overall impression of skilled journalists and it is wrong, what must be the interpretation taken by the average newspaper reader, even Catholic? . . . Among points that seem to require emphasis are: Whether or not the bishops accept the papal teaching that "each and every marriage act must remain open to the transmission of life"? What is the relationship between the authority exercised by the Pope in this instance and that of the bishops? Is there a difference between freedom of conscience with regard to civil authority and freedom of conscience with regard to God? Why do the learned have the right to reject "some point" of papal argument while being obliged to accept the conclusions? In choosing love without procreation, may married couples resort to abortion and sterilization, as well as contraception? What is the difference between the conflict of

values situation of married couples and that of habitual masturbators, fornicators and adulterers? Finally, in ecumenical approaches to these problems, is the present trend of following the Protestant ethic encouraged?[34]

Excellent questions, which must have occurred to a roomful of bishops and theologians. The fact that they were not addressed cannot be considered accidental. The more one ponders the Winnipeg performance, the more angered and shamed one is by its sophistry, its deceitfulness, its sly winks, its destruction of Catholic truth. Most intolerable of all is the claim to be acting in pastoral "solidarity with the faithful." "With shepherds like these," as Hamish Fraser remarks, "wolves become superfluous."

Six months after the Winnipeg meeting, the bishops issued a "clarifying statement," insisting that they had not meant that Catholics could employ the Protestant ethic. Five years later (December 12, 1973), they issued another, on the formation of conscience, which concluded that "To follow one's conscience and to *remain a Catholic* one must take into account first and foremost the teaching of the magisterium. When doubt arises due to a conflict of 'my' view and those of the magisterium the presumption of truth lies on the part of the magisterium" (the bishops' italics). This statement has not caused a roll-back of the revolution, for the bishops did nothing to repair the damage. They did not preach the doctrine, or try to restrain the by now almost universal theological dissent, or require confessors and priests who run the obligatory marriage preparation courses to direct Catholic consciences in line with Catholic teaching, or support Catholic couples who try to follow Catholic sexual morality. It is clear that many bishops must believe that the historic teaching of the Church in this matter has been wrong. They cannot, for various reasons starting with ambition and cowardice, bring themselves to say this publicly, yet by letting the teaching fall so pointedly into abeyance, they tacitly admit their inner loss of faith.

This episcopal behaviour has been more destructive of Catholic faith than the worst that revolutionaries could do. It has resulted in the well-documented situation Charles Curran thus describes: "There is no doubt that many people in the Catholic Church today disagree in theory and in practice with hierarchical church teachings on a number of specific moral issues. . . . A *modus vivendi* seems to have been reached in matters of birth control, divorce and even homosexuality. Although official teaching has not changed, in actuality the church has changed, for many people acting contrary to official teaching fully participate in its life. That *modus vivendi* seems to have provided a climate in which diversity exists without threatening the official teaching of the church." But even this leading revolutionary finds this situation intolerable: "However, I strongly insist that the present situation should not continue.

The hierarchical teaching office cannot have it both ways. The present situation in which the official teaching and the accepted practice are different cannot continue. . . . Although achieving a kind of peace, the present situation also involves some glaring problems and inconsistencies which call for it to be changed." Curran, naturally, wants the situation changed in a radical direction: "The Pope and the bishops must be willing to publicly admit that the previous teaching is wrong [or] at the very least . . . to acknowledge publicly the legitimacy of dissent on this question and the ramifications of dissent in the entire life of the church."[35]

One must agree with Curran about the absolute necessity for honesty in the Church situation today. The prescription for any counter-revolution must go further: the bishops must *either* publicly say that they think the previous teaching on sexual morality was wrong, *or* publicly repudiate the *Winnipeg Statement* in Canada and their equivocal behaviour everywhere. Until the present dishonest situation is resolved, the Church can only continue to sink deeper into confusion and irrelevance. The most a hopeful counter-revolutionary can say at the moment is that since Curran wrote his retrospective in 1978, the possibility of the Pope's joining the revolution according to Curran's prescription has faded into fantasy, John Paul II having, by his worldwide missionary enthusiasm for the cornerstone teaching on sexual morality, signalled the official beginning of the counter-revolution.

"Our quick, forceful response supported by so many theologians accomplished its purpose," was Curran's accurate judgement of the revolution's actions in response to *Humanae Vitae*. That purpose had been the separation of the mass of the governed from its allegiance to the government. The revolution did this by using the issue of birth control to divide the bishops from the Pope and the laity from both.

The radical theologians carried out their presumptive strike against the highest level of Church authority before the bishops had time to reflect. By exploiting the Vatican's anxious over-precision during the issuing of *Humanae Vitae*, the radicals were able to plant solidly the idea that the teaching had no claim to infallible status. It was merely part of the body of what Curran called "authoritative, non-infallible" teaching, to which there already existed, so they said, a well-recognized "right to dissent." They made it seem as if the decision about whether or not to have children was on the same level as the decision about what schools to send them to, a matter in which the Church could be said to have a legitimate interest, but not power to bind under pain of sin. Thus they were able to separate the Church's teaching on sexual morality within marriage from the rest of the solemn ancient deposit of Catholic moral doctrine and practice. The revolution's case against the Church's competence to teach with binding force in the matter of contraception could be applied in the same way against every other "non-defined" Catholic moral teaching and very soon it would be, but not while the revolution needed the support of the many non-revolutionized Catholics to whom the theologians' partial case seemed at first glance modest and orthodox. By the time the carefully laid smokescreen cleared, the battle had been won. The citadel had been betrayed, the dogma was dead, and open season had been declared on every Catholic moral and doctrinal proposition.

WHAT THE DISPUTE OVER HUMANAE VITAE WAS REALLY ABOUT

It is clear today, well into the second decade of the Catholic revolution, that what inspired this carefully planned departure from the consistent teaching of the "authentic magisterium" of the papacy was the passionate desire and vital necessity of the revolutionary clerisy to destroy the idea that the hierarchical magisterium possessed supreme authority in the Catholic Church, authority unavailable to any other segment of that community. The most committed on both sides of the revolution always recognized that the battle over birth control was not primarily over sexual morality but about the nature of authority in the Roman Catholic Church. An interesting finding of Maurice Moore's study which tends to confirm the genuinely revolutionary springs of the dissent from *Humanae Vitae* was that major superiors of male religious orders were several times more liberal on the issue than bishops of the same age and education, position in the authority structure being the crucial variable.

The authority of authority derives from its claim to *know*. The Church has always claimed to *know* what is intrinsically right and wrong in the matter of covenanted marriage. To reject the Church's claim to know in this moral issue is to reject its claim to know anything as universal and absolute. To reject it is to say that there are no moral *givens*, to admit the "absolute relativity" of the "truths" of Revelation and the "law" of nature. It is to reject the very concepts of "Revelation" and "natural law." So the quarrel over *Humanae Vitae* was not just about sex; it was about creation and God's plan for it, about Revelation and the natural law, about the nature of authority in general, and about the nature of the Church and of authority within it. The hierarchical magisterium of the Church, the teaching office centred upon the successor of Peter, had for two thousand years cherished, refined, elaborated, and defended the unique world view we call Catholicism. If the revolution wished to succeed in replacing the ancient Catholic explanation of existence with its own radically different cosmology, it had first to undermine the magisterium's claim to know infallibly. This logic did not dawn upon the progressive bishops until it had crippled them.

In 1978 in an anniversary reflection on *Humanae Vitae*, Charles Curran wrote: "Those who argued against the acceptance of artificial contraception in the Roman Catholic Church in the 1960s recognized the more radical nature of the problem. As mentioned in the so-called minority report of the papal commission on birth control the primary reason for not changing the teaching was the necessity of admitting that the previous teaching had been wrong. One must honestly recognize that 'the conservatives' saw much more clearly than 'the liberals' of the day that a change in the teaching on artificial contraception had to recognize that the previous teaching was wrong,"[36] with all that that implied for the idea of authority in the Church. If Curran was among those who in 1968 did not recognize the consequences of his arrogantly proposed right of dissent, he does now recognize it: "The acceptance of the possibility of dissent within the Roman Catholic Church calls for a changed understanding at least in the minds of many Catholics of the role of the hierarchical magisterium. If the hierarchical magisterium can be wrong in non-infallible matters (there has never been an infallible teaching on a specific moral question so it is not necessary here to enter into the debate over infallibility), then it follows that the hierarchical magisterium cannot be the only way in which the church teaches. . . . There are many *magisteria* in the church – papal and episcopal *magisteria*, the authentic magisterium of the laity and the magisterium of theologians."[37]

It is startling to note in how casual a way Curran now dismisses the subject of infallibility, considering that the core of the argument he had mounted against *Humanae Vitae* was that the teaching did not require the assent of faith because it had not been proposed *infallibly*, that is, by specific solemn definition, as, for example, the dogmas of the Trinity or of the Immaculate Conception. This extremely narrow definition of "an infallible teaching" would exclude almost everything Catholics believe, including the Ten Commandments. Of course, the Church operates under a much broader notion of infallibility. It has always believed, and still professes in the documents of Vatican II, that the teaching authority vested in the successors of the Apostles is competent to interpret authoritatively not only the Scriptures but also the natural moral law, and that this infallibility in matters of faith and morals is vested in a special way in the primacy of the successor of Peter.

It was this age-old idea of Catholic authority that Pope Paul VI threw down like a gauntlet in *Humanae Vitae*: "No believer will wish to deny that the teaching authority of the Chuch is competent to interpret even the natural moral law. It is, in fact, indisputable" (*Humanae Vitae*, 5). A most accurate and economical definition of the scope and demands of the Church's authority, but obviously not one calculated to disarm an emerging revolution making its bid to become the paramount magisterium.

In 1960, the majority of Catholics were *believers* in the full sense in which Pope Paul used the word: they gave to the Church the presumption of truth in sexual morality as in all moral law because of the idea they held of the authority of the Church. And the presumption of truth bound them to obedience. Catholics accepted this, approaching the difficult teaching on marriage with varying degrees of heroism. Being sinners, they probably disobeyed it at least as often as they disobeyed the other natural moral laws. But even when they were totally disobedient, they continued to accept the Church's competence to teach it as true. Disobedient Catholics, knowing they had no firm purpose of amendment, absented themselves from the sacraments until such time as grace or circumstances enabled them to be once again in communion.

But by 1968, Pope Paul's definition of *believer* no longer applied to many of those who still called themselves "Catholics"; it applies to even fewer today. Within a very short period, a significant number of Catholics had stopped believing that the teaching authority of the Church had the competence and right, given to it by Christ, to interpret infallibly the natural moral law. That massive loss of belief was a direct consequence of the way the revolution used the issue of contraception to reintroduce the Protestant principle of authority into the Church with the intention of deposing the authority of the magisterium.

The men who made the Catholic revolution during Vatican II understood what was at stake. Towards the end of the Council, Hans Küng, Edward Schillebeeckx, Karl Rahner, Gregory Baum, and other radical theologians started a journal to advance their interpretation of the Council's meanings and intentions. It was, significantly, called *Concilium*, and it remains the front-line expositor of "progressive" theology. The very first issue, dedicated to exploring the "implications of collegiality in the age of renewal," carried an article by Michael Novak, the American who had produced the earliest attack in English on the Catholic doctrine on contraception. In his "Diversity of Structures and Freedom within Structures," Novak described the post-Conciliar attitude to authority this way: "To a great extent we must embrace the 'Protestant principle': reliance on the fidelity of the individual conscience, assisted by the Holy Spirit, for the ability of Catholics to take their due place in the secular world."[38] The revolutionary intent was not often stated so frankly at that early stage (1964); Novak had, and retains (he is now on the neo-liberal bandwagon), the knack of exactly expressing the hidden agenda of whatever ideology he considered the coming power.

Charles Curran, too, understood what was being proposed by the revolution: "An acceptance of the possibility of dissent calls for significant changes in the understanding of the church . . . whether or not one should dissent from a particular hierarchical teaching rests with the decision of conscience after a thoughtful and prayerful reflection on the aspects involved. As a very first step the Catholic Church will have to learn to live with greater pluralism on specific moral issues."[39]

The appearance of *Humanae Vitae* produced a flood of statements making it clear that the real focus of the revolution was not sexual ethics but the magisterium's claim to supreme moral authority. Jesuit sociologist John Thomas said of the encyclical: "This puts the question of what the magisterium is right on the line."[40] The chairman of the theology department at Notre Dame, Indiana, Holy Cross Father James Burtchaell, in a speech to four thousand people, mostly students, described the encyclical as "grossly inadequate and largely fallacious," called for "a reevaluation of authority in the church," and termed the Pope's call to obedience "graceless and unfair," "blackmail."[41] Jesuit moral theologian Richard McCormick wrote in the *National Catholic Reporter*: "If the encyclical does not clearly answer all the questions, it does raise the one which is probably at the heart of the matter: the relationship of theological reflection and analysis to the magisterium, and more generally, the nature of the magisterium in the contemporary world."[42] Later, in his very influential regular column in *Theological Studies*, he wrote that before the publication of *Humanae Vitae*, a good number of theologians had reached the conclusion that the traditional teaching on contraception was "genuinely doubtful" and that there were "serious and positive reasons" for questioning it. In this situation, *Humanae Vitae* was merely "another authoritative voice." Therefore, "If other theologians, after meticulous research and sober reflection, share this opinion in sufficient numbers, if bishops and competent married couples would arrive at the same conclusion, it is difficult to see how the teaching would not lose the presumption of certainty ordinarily enjoyed by authoritative utterances."[43] In a book entitled *The Magisterium and Morality*, which he edited with Charles Curran, McCormick described the theologian's role as "to precede and prepare the opinions of the magisterium."[44]

In *Humanae Vitae* (28), Paul VI called believers to the "internal and external obedience" required by Vatican II in *Lumen Gentium (25)* to "the authentic magisterium of the Roman Pontiff, even when he is not speaking *ex cathedra*." McCormick dealt summarily with this Conciliar pronouncement: "Appeal is made repeatedly to n.25 of *Lumen Gentium*, but it is widely, even if quietly, admitted in the theological community that this paragraph represents a dated and very discussable notion of the Church's teaching office."[45] So much for the Council's theological expertise.

McCormick does not admit that even all theologians are worthy to share the "true authority" of the theological magisterium. He distrusts the many non-revolutionized theologians whom the Vatican's curial congregations employ to formulate its official statements. Since Vatican statements – for example, the 1984 *Instruction on Certain Aspects of the "Theology of Liberation,"* or the 1976 *Declaration on the Question of the Admission of Women to the Ministerial Priesthood* (both from the Congregation for the Doctrine of the Faith) – generally contradict basic radical positions, it is not surprising that McCormick wants to put the Vatican's theologians out of business. He writes, insultingly: "More radically, one can wonder whether congregations as such should be involved in doing theology. The temptation is almost irresistible for such groups to support the theological views of the office holders whom they serve."[46]

McCormick wants a new "communal" model of magisterium different from the hierarchical model of traditional theology. This new communal magisterium would draw its authority from the lived experience of the whole Christian community (minus, that is, the Council fathers and the Vatican and orthodox theologians). This idea, that magisterial authority derives from the experience of the community, is now widespread. "We are Church!" is the slogan of every dissident group.

The revolution's assault on the authority of the supreme magisterium succeeded. In the period of the birth-control argument, a revolutionary displacement took place and one idea of authority was replaced by another. One authority had been deposed and another had usurped its place. If one follows Max Weber's definition of authority as "the probability that certain specific commands (or all commands) from a given source will be obeyed by a given group of persons,"[47] then it has to be admitted that if the "given group of persons" is taken to mean Catholic society at large the probability of any general obedience to the hierarchical magisterium is now so low that the magisterium may be said to have lost its authority. Of course, the Catholic who continues to accept that the Church is divinely commissioned to teach and interpret the moral law to the individual conscience will insist that this is not the whole story since the Church is more than a social organization. But that temporal part of the Church that is a social organization is engaged in an ideological struggle in which a revolutionary ideology has the upper hand. For although the magisterium continues to hold and repeat its moral teaching, it sees it everywhere repudiated, and lacks or feels it lacks the support necessary for a counter-offensive.

The revolution reintroduced the Protestant principle into the Church through the "conscience provision" offered to the laity in the theologians' dissent from *Humanae Vitae*. Through the choice of the birth-control issue as its first battleground, the revolution was able to broaden its base of support rapidly among the previously unreachable laity who were now seduced at their most vulnerable point, the complex heart of marriage. Many accepted the bribe but then left forever. Those who stayed but practised the sanctioned disobedience had in self-justification to throw in their lot with the revolutionary ideology. Having accepted the dissenting position on contraception, the revolution's converts moved logically to embrace the whole conscience argument for sexual libertinism. If a Catholic feels free to go to Holy Communion while disobeying the Church in a matter he has previously believed to be a serious sin, why stop there? As indeed many Catholics have not. Andrew Greeley documents the extent of the triumph of the Protestant principle of authority among the Catholic laity: during the years from 1963 to 1974, opposition to contraception declined from 52 to 13 per cent; to divorce, from 46 to 25 per cent; to premarital sex, from 75 to 35 per cent. The figures were particularly striking for weekly communicants: opposition to contraception fell in that period from 82 to 24 per cent; to divorce, from 80 to 46 per cent; to premarital sex, from 87 to 48 per cent. These were people who were unlikely to commit these sins themselves, but who had come to believe that it was all right for those who thought it was all right. After all, if this sort of thinking is okay for the Canadian bishops – "they may be safely assured that whoever honestly chooses that course which seems right to him does so in good conscience" – then it's okay for us.

At three different times, in 1963, in 1974, and in 1979, Greeley looked at Catholics in their twenties. Among this group, opposition to contraception fell in that time span from about 50 per cent to 4 per cent; to divorce, from 41 to 11 per cent; to premarital sex, from 70 to 17 per cent. In the area of authority, by 1979 only 10 per cent of those under thirty accepted that the Pope was infallible in matters of faith and morals. Greeley summarized: "Church leadership had the moral power to obtain consent from a large number of U.S. Catholics as recently as 15 years ago. It no longer has that moral power."[48]

Maurice Moore, reflecting on "the breakup of old sets of self-evident truths and unquestioned religious attitudes," wrote that "someone" (not of course an unbiased social scientist) "may even want to argue that reliance on inner direction rather than compulsion from without is the more religious stance."[49] Moore knows as well as the rest of us who were adult Catholics before the Council that there was no "compulsion," other than the moral necessity exerted upon one by principles to which one had given inner assent. The unfavourable comparison of so-called "Catholic compulsion" with Protestant or secular "inner direction" is an old insult.

Catholics are not "told what to think." Catholicism offers to human reason a coherent body of truth, a world hypothesis based on divinely revealed truths and on universal moral principles accessible to unaided reason. Once the individual conscience has accepted the Church's teaching as true, it is under an obligation to obey it. Shocking as it may seem to people influenced by the latitudinarian "spirit of Vatican II," the Second Vatican Council repeated the hard teaching about the extent to which this obligation binds: "Whoever, therefore, knowing that the Catholic Church was made necessary by Christ, would refuse to enter it or to remain in it, could not be saved" (*Lumen Gentium*, 14). And the same Council repeated another basic Catholic teaching: that man is free to reject the Church's account of truth: "God calls men to serve Him in spirit and in truth, hence they are bound in conscience but they stand under no compulsion" (*Dignitatis Humanae*, 11).

Catholicism, which knows everything about human nature, is realistic about what "inner direction" too often means. No conscience can be entirely autonomous; it can be influenced by argument; it chooses authorities to justify its choices; it is uncomfortable if it cannot resort to the argument from authority; it is seduced by the demands of the flesh. In fact, the Catholic appeal to external universal principles, far from amounting to "compulsion," has the effect of freeing the conscience from the pressures of society and the domination of the passions. The conscience may choose to reject the Church's account of universal morality or to reject altogether the very idea of absolutes. In which case it is no longer a "Catholic" conscience; it is indeed truly on its own.

The two principles of authority cannot long coexist within a church. Those Protestant bodies that have survived as recognizably Christian did so by sternly repressing the exercise of the Protestant principle within them, falling back on a more-or-less-disguised hierarchical magisterium with large powers of interpretation and expulsion. The successful Protestant body might be said to have exercised the Protestant principle once only, in its section from its parent communion. The Catholic Church has never attempted to allow and never will allow the two ideas of authority to coexist within it. Not even to survive will the highest authority of the Church permit itself to be reduced to the position of constitutional monarch in a modern state, a figurehead who functions merely to legitimate the actions of the actual government. Yet the magisterium came perilously close to accepting that position in the immediate post-Conciliar years, as Pope Paul helplessly ratified the decrees of the predominantly radical commissions set up after the Council to implement the Conciliar reform. Many of these decrees, particularly in the area of the liturgy, where the revolution has been most completely successful, will have to be revoked.

"In a sense," Charles Curran wrote ten years later, "*Humanae Vitae* has become symbolic. If the hierarchical church refuses to change here, there will probably be no change on other issues," such as "divorce and remarriage, women priests, and clerical celibacy."[50] Many bishops may have failed to grasp the symbolic significance of the conflict over *Humanae Vitae* but the revolution always understood. I wrote at the beginning of my anatomy of the revolution that it might seem to secularized moderns too extravagant to go back to the Book of Genesis for the real cause of the present rebellion against objective authority, the principle of insubordination that resides in every human heart. Yet in the end this is where one must go for understanding, for Genesis is the source of the religious archetypes that shape the Judeo-Christian moral imagination.

In a true revolution, the empowering symbols of the existing order of authority are dragged from their usual integrated subliminal existence into the raucous ideological public square. That is what happened during the battle over *Humanae Vitae*. Everything in Catholicism, from its teaching on procreation to its teaching that only men can be priests, derives faithfully from its understanding of Genesis. Which is why, at its moment of truth, the revolution called that moment "the time of uprooting." The phrase called forth every theme and archetype that created and nurtured the Catholic world view – the Garden of Eden and the original unity of man and woman before the Fall; the temptation to power and man's first disobedience over possession of the tree of life and the tree of the knowledge of good and evil; exile from the presence of God; the tree of knowledge and its fruit, sin; the tree of Jesse and and its fruit, Christ; the tree of the Cross and its fruit, Redemption. The revolution's choice of image showed that it had a deep understanding that it was striking at the very roots of the existing religious order of Catholicism.

Perhaps the middle-aged, Roman-collared, jowly, predominantly Irish bishops gathered in the Washington Hilton to deal with *Humanae Vitae* did not look to most observers much like the cherubim with flaming swords set by God to keep guard in Eden over the tree of life and the tree of the knowledge of good and evil, but the revolutionary priests and their supporters sitting-in around the bishops' meeting understood the symbolic resonances. The radicals wanted the guard removed from the tree of life; they were already in exile from their priestly mysteries; they even had their own Eve to tempt them to disobedience, a student whose trip to Washington to sing to them was paid for by her Catholic college. She sang to them a ribald song about the Holy Father, the Pope, "Are You Sure That's What God Said?" At its jeering refrain, "Go out and multiply!" they applauded and yelled, "One more time!"[51]

The revolution indeed knew what it was about, the overthrowing not of a government but of a cosmology.

e~o

THE PHASES OF THE
REVOLUTION

e~o

The periodization of history is always arbitrary, because it is so often ideologically inspired. The Dark Ages, the Middle Ages, the Renaissance, the Enlightenment, the Modern Period, are polemical, not scientific, descriptions; they are propaganda triumphs of earlier modernists anxious to show a steady progress from barbarism and superstition to civilization and reason. "Modernism" itself is a polemical term, and modernists object to its use. Father Dan Donovan, professor of systematic theology at St. Michael's College and Toronto School of Theology, recently complained: "An unfortunate development in recent inner-Catholic polemics has been the resurgence of the term 'modernist.' Historically, it distorts what was an extremely complex and in many ways tragic moment in the recent life of the Church, and in relation to the present it lends itself to wide-sweeping allegations that undermine understanding and dialogue."[1]

THE MODERATE AND RADICAL PHASES

It is, of course, impossible to bracket periods of human history as neatly as historians seem to do. And, as I noted earlier, the phases of a revolution overlap each other. At least until the end of the Council, the revolution remained if not moderate, at least cautious. During the Council, the radical intent of the leaders of the theological and cultural revolution was hidden. Obviously, if theologians like Küng and Schillebeeckx had said then what they say now about Christology, the Eucharist, and the priesthood, there would have been an uproar resulting in their expulsion. It was imperative not to alarm the bishops, whose interests and grievances the radicals had so assiduously supported. An attempt was about to be made in the name of collegiality to break down the universal Church into self-interested committees. The reformers had to get control of these organs of implementation of the Conciliar decrees, in Rome for the creation of universal norms, and at home in the departures from these allowed to local ordinaries.

Towards the end of the Council, the radicals were growing careless enough about their cover to worry the most important Rhine liberal, Cardinal Frings; together with his *peritus*, Joseph Ratzinger, he began to distance himself from Karl Rahner. Also, Paul VI, alarmed by the outburst of radical liturgical experimentation that took place immediately upon the promulgation of the *Constitution on the Sacred Liturgy* early in the Council, issued in 1965 his encyclical on the Eucharist, *Mysterium Fidei*, to supply doctrine that had been omitted, for whatever reason, from the *Constitution on the Sacred Liturgy* and to condemn heretical ideas then in circulation. This encyclical was assumed to have been directed at the Dutch, in particular at Edward Schillebeeckx, who was not, however, named.

In 1964, in the hiatus between the end of the Council and the revolution's institutionalized interpretations of it, the revolutionaries' cover was still so intact that a leading orthodox liturgical *peritus*, Louis Bouyer, and the radical Hans Küng could each write a book, jubilant, all hopes fulfilled, about the *Constitution on the Sacred Liturgy*.[2] As it turned out, Küng was right in his prognostications; Bouyer was wrong. By 1968 Bouyer was writing in angry dismay of "the decomposition of Catholicism," with particular reference to the newly implemented liturgical reform, which he now called "a denial and imposture."[3]

At the end of 1965 the bishops and their *periti* came home from "the new Pentecost" spirit-filled, as they kept telling us. The bishops, revelling in their new feelings of independence, grouped themselves into national and regional conferences, and proceeded to set up dozens of commissions and subcommissions with wide powers to write and administer the policies of the national churches, an exceedingly important step for the future success of the revolution. In Canada, the bishops and their administrative arms are united into a complex organization called the Canadian Conference of Catholic Bishops, the CCCB, or Concacan Inc., as it is affectionately addressed by its correspondents. The CCCB has a general secretariat and thirteen episcopal commissions, for liturgy, social justice, education, and so on. Each department consists of several bishops and a number of full-time staffers. It is the professional Catholic bureaucrats, mostly lay people, who are the real power. For instance, Bernard Daly, in 1968 the head of the CCCB's Family Life Bureau, was a *peritus* for the *Winnipeg Statement*, and the only layman allowed to address the bishops concerning *Humanae Vitae*; in 1984 he was a member of the all-important Pastoral Team for Study and Action and assistant general secretary to the CCCB.

The United States Catholic Conference (USCC) is the administrative arm of the National Conference of Catholic Bishops (NCCB). As in Canada, the episcopal conference and its administrative bodies are closely combined. The USCC/NCCB, in which the tail notoriously wags the dog, has its headquarters in Washington, D.C., with a staff of over three hundred and a budget (in 1983) of $22.5 million.[4] It is no exaggeration to call Father J. Bryan Hehir, secretary of the powerful Department of Social Development and World Peace of the USCC, the most important ecclesiastic in the Roman Catholic Church in the United States. Hehir masterminded, for instance, the U.S. bishops' news-making pastorals on nuclear war and capitalism, for which he then acted as spokesman to the press, to Congress, and to the Church. In effect, the new bureaucracies of the national conferences have become parallel hierarchies, home-grown curias which run the national churches. Ironically, collegiality, in its spirit of Vatican II application, has destroyed the once very great pre-Conciliar authority of the individual bishop on his own turf. Today bishops who are not ambitious politicians find themselves reduced to silence in a coerced consensus, which, as the revolution gains strength, serves to guarantee the legitimacy of the parallel hierarchy.

Cardinal Emmett Carter, once a leading mover in the struggle to wrest power from the Roman curia and now side-lined by the powerful leftist Canadian social-justice organizations, recently complained publicly about the situation. The occasion was the release by the Social Affairs Commission (headed by Bishop Remi de Roo) on December 29, 1982, of a controversial statement titled *Ethical Reflections on the Economic Crisis*, for which Gregory Baum had once again acted as consultant. The eight bishops and the lay staffers of the commission had issued the statement without consultation with the rest of the Canadian bishops. Cardinal Carter complained:

> Mr. Baum, as some may not know, was a peritus . . . at the Second Vatican Council. He was present at the important and vital debates on collegiality . . . and he even appeared to have absorbed some understanding and sympathy with the prevailing view. We were leading the Church on a new – or renewed – road to decentralization. . . . Alas, where are the snows of yesteryear? . . . Collegiality? Don't make me laugh. . . . The Canadian bishops were not only not consulted, they were not even informed. . . . For Mr. Baum, apparently, the only important aspect was that the statement maintained "the shift to the left." Many of us feel strongly that we have no intention of exchanging a new bureaucracy centred on CCCB headquarters in Ottawa in place of a much more sensitive and universal one in Rome.[5]

113

It is awfully difficult for those of us who have long been clear on Mr. Baum's priorities to summon up any sympathy for Cardinal Carter and the rest of the deserted Canadian bishops.

The Cardinal speaks from hindsight, for in the period 1965 to 1975, during the feverish building of a nationalist Canadian Church, collaboration between Cardinal Carter (then Bishop of London) and a handful of other Canadian bishops with the large reformist bureaucracy they created was warm and exclusive. Most of the bishops and all of the laity became strictly outsiders. The usurpation of legitimacy was far smoother and went longer unchallenged in Canada than in the United States, perhaps because of the more oligarchic nature of Canadian society. An episcopal oligarchy – Cardinal Carter and his brother, Bishop Alexander Carter, Cardinal Flahiff, Archbishop Plourde, Archbishop MacNeil, Bishop de Roo, Bishop Power, one or two others – was enthusiastically at one with its *periti* in their pursuit of the same progressive goals. The Canadian bishops, for example, were the first hierarchy to install the revised liturgy. By the end of the Council they had also begun to introduce their compulsory *Canadian Catechism*, a series that can best be described as only residually Catholic. Under the presidency of Bishop Alexander Carter, they began in 1971 to press for a married clergy. Thus, although the Conciliar "time-bombs" may have been armed by the radical theologians, they could not have been detonated without the empowering sanction of the ruling group of progressive nationalist bishops.

I am inclined to argue that the moderate phase of the revolution ended with the Council, at the end of 1965, though some measure of discretion was called for, as noted above, while the *periti* were jockeying for the key post-Conciliar gun-turrets. Also, for a short time during the destruction of the Roman liturgy, the revolution's first large-scale encounter with the laity, there was some small political attempt to justify the brutalities by claiming that all that was involved was a return to the purity of the origins, to the way the pilgrim people of God worshipped before they were trammelled by Roman – or Byzantine, or Baroque, or post-Tridentine – accretions. This attempt had to be based on fictions – that Jesus had worshipped in the vernacular, that the Mass in primitive times was celebrated facing the people, that the Mass used before 1963 dated only from the Trent reform in the late sixteenth century – claims angrily repudiated by scholars with no axe to grind. However, the argument from antiquity was dropped so quickly not because it had been refuted but rather because the completeness of their hold over the liturgical reform rendered it unnecessary to the revolutionaries. The liturgical reform had been radical from the moment it emerged from its cautious cover in the early Council.

The April 1967 strike at Catholic University was, as Charles Curran

114

noted, a dress rehearsal for the main event. July 30, 1968, the day on which Curran and the other dissenting theologians declared their independence from the hierarchical magisterium at the Mayflower Hotel in Washington, was the point at which the revolution broke in fully fledged radicalism upon the public consciousness. But between the return from the Council and the July Revolution, the psychological ground for revolt had been prepared by the staging of those fascinating public spectacles which Peter Shaw, in his recent book on the subject, calls "the rituals of revolution." These rituals are designed to diminish the power of existing authority by destroying its mystique during a process in which the symbols that inspire awe are mocked and degraded in "reversed ceremonies of legitimacy." The mocking reversal of sacred symbols serves as psychological preparation for a transference of allegiance.

Rituals of revolution function as rites of passage; the public defiance they allow makes acceptable hitherto private desires and defiances, and coalesces nebulous, unassociated discontents. The psychological effect of ritual preparation on previously obedient observers helps to explain the most unnerving feature of the early years of the revolution for the Catholic who has remained non-revolutionized. That feature was the dramatic and seemingly overnight reversal of confident orthodox positions by the very people who had taught one obedience to those positions. My friend (may he rest in peace) James Daly, a Canadian scholar, recounted this example: "Cardinal Flahiff turned me down for the Medieval Institute because I had only two years' Latin; the next time I met him he was backing women's ordination!" It is fairly safe to assume that before the emergence of the revolution, neither Cardinal Flahiff nor most of the other people now advocating it had any desire, suppressed or otherwise, to ordain women to the Catholic priesthood. Likewise, every priest I have asked admitted that before the Council no parishioner had ever expressed a desire to get rid of Latin or to receive Communion by hand.

True to type, the Catholic revolution's preparatory rituals involved class mockery, mockery of the empowering symbols, dressing-up, role reversal, use of the crowd for intimidation, parody, and charades. The best continuing source for examples of these is any issue of the *National Catholic Reporter* during those years (and now), but many of them also made it into the secular press. As in the Protestant revolution, the main target was the Mass, the focal point of Catholicism. Nothing could change as long as this great symbol-complex did not. Therefore, parodies of the old Mass became frequent among liturgists, most of them priests, during the introduction of the early liturgical changes. In one local instance, a late-middle-aged priest hitherto notably pious bent exaggeratedly over the Mass book on the altar gabbling nonsense "Latin" as a prelude to his sermon on how much more sensible the new way was than "the way we used to do it."

Since the authority figure in the Catholic cult is already in ritual attire, parodic dressing-up meant *not* dressing-up. Priests at university and group Masses wore ordinary clothes, more casual, if anything, than the norm; the age of the orange clerical turtleneck dawned. In their particular application of ritual disguise, priests and religious put aside religious dress altogether except when involved in some public protest against religious or civil authority, where it served at the same time as a usurpation of legitimate authority to make a point with onlookers and as a mocker of legitimacy.

Ritual postures were reversed. At small group-Masses, priests sat with the congregation around a table instead of standing at an altar; congregations were forced to stand at times when they had previously had to kneel. The altar itself was displaced, and replaced by a table, though no Vatican II or post-Conciliar directive required this. The "clown Mass" became popular, priests climbing into motley on every possible occasion. The Catholic chaplaincy at the University of Buffalo staged a Hallowe'en "Mass" with both celebrant and congregation in costume. On Hallowe'en, several priests at the high school my children attend came to school in "costumes," their long-discarded religious cassocks. A priest at the big Montreal college Mariopolis celebrated Mass in clown costume, obligingly posing for the press. The chaplaincy for the Catholic community at the University of Toronto dressed as clowns, addressed the congregation through hand-puppets, and danced at student Masses.

Priests and laity reversed roles. Nuns began to "celebrate Mass" at Catholic universities; this is now almost standard at gatherings of feminists and nuns. At Notre Dame, Indiana, a congregation of seated students, each holding a piece of bread and a paper cup of wine, "consecrated" along with the priest. There were numerous accounts of the substitution of chicken and coffee, cookies and soft drinks, pizza and beer, for the bread and wine. The official Canadian liturgy bulletin, beginning its campaign against the stylized round Mass hosts, sneeringly referred to them as "host chips."

The attack on Church authority was combined symbolically with the current attack on the legitimacy of the civil power: two Jesuits, students at Fordham University, denied the altar at St. Patrick's Cathedral to put forward their anti-war views, hijacked the Church's sacramental symbols and said a Mass in white vestments to symbolize peace on the steps outside. Masses on the steps of St. Patrick's became a trademark ritual of the revolution. Continuing the double theme of religious and political revolt, six students from the Jesuit University of Marquette, in Milwaukee, Wisconsin, walked to the altar during Mass in

St. Boniface's Church, Milwaukee, burnt their draft cards over a candle, deposited the ashes in a bowl on the altar as if they were incense, and commandeered the pulpit to proclaim their defiance.

The reversed ceremonies of legitimacy reached their climax in Washington around the week-long meeting of the legitimate episcopal authority in November 1968, during which the official response to *Humanae Vitae* was to be drafted. Here the *turba divina*, the divine crowd of a revolution, was used in an attempt to terrorize authority into abdication. I have described how it was summoned to "the time of uprooting" by a mock pastoral letter published in the *National Catholic Reporter*. In a parody of the NCCB assembly, three hundred priests from thirty-three states met collegially in the Mayflower Hotel. The suspended priests were ceremonially exalted by personages like Senator Eugene McCarthy, who recited his own (dreadful) poetry in lieu of psalms. The crowd stood in ovation as Catholics do in Mass for the Gospel. The mock liturgy ended with a "litany" in which Father John Corrigan, one of the suspended priests and head of the new pressure group, the Washington Association of Priests, intoned the revolution's demands to the crowd's chanted agreement. In a further parody, this time of a religious procession, the rebellious priests and their supporters marched on the bishops' meeting. Once at the Hilton Hotel, the priests, every one of them wearing clerical dress (many for the last time), ritually reversed the traditional role of priesthood. They sat humbly on the floor, faces upturned to a young woman who preached to them a sermon mocking the two sources of Catholic authority: the Scriptures and the infallible magisterium centred in the Pope. They, too, responded antiphonally to her jeering hymn. After the bishops had made their statement supporting the encyclical, the rebellious priests and their supporters took over the same pulpit to issue their own anti-authoritarian declaration.[6]

It might seem that the revolution had lost the decisive battle over who is the magisterium, since Rome, the American bishops, and the national hierarchies, with a few exceptions such as Canada, had not given way and formally denied their principle of authority. Yet, though the revolution lost that battle, it won the war. The magisterium refused to abdicate, but it was everywhere driven into exile. The Pope and those bishops who tried to support the unpopular teachings of the Catholic tradition were made to look like those pathetic governments in exile from successful revolutions that set up poverty-stricken and quarrelsome shop in tolerant host countries and issue justifications of their position that nobody reads. Non-revolutionized Catholics began to behave like exiles, distrusting each other and the refugee government. This remained the situation until several years into the papacy of John Paul II.

CONSOLIDATION AND INSTITUTIONALIZATION

I described earlier how the radical theologians got control of the post-Vatican II national and Roman bureaucracies and how they were thus able to write policy and administer it. The smoothness and rapidity of the take-over surprised even the revolutionaries themselves. One way to document the progress of the revolution towards institutionalization is to allow the revolutionaries to give their own assessments of their progress at different stages of the revolution.

Several weeks before the climactic November 1968 week in Washington, Rosemary Ruether, a lay theologian then and now on the radical front of the revolution, wrote an article in the *National Catholic Reporter* entitled "On the New Reformation: Creating a New Kind of Religious Community."[7] At that time, it still seemed a possibility that the magisterium would pull itself together and expel the revolution:

> The Catholic reform movement is in a dilemma as to whether it should create a new community to express its new self-understanding, if it becomes clear that it cannot shape the whole of the old Roman Catholic Church to express this new understanding. . . . I would propose that discussions for the formation of an autonomous reformed Church that would express the most advanced insights of contemporary Catholicism might be due to begin. Priests and laymen's councils might begin to gather commissions of theologians, church historians, ecumenical experts and the like to discuss the nature of such a reformed church, its understanding of its substance and structure.

According to Ruether, such a reformed church would have "functional rather than 'state-of-life' understanding of ordination," clusters of small communities to replace the diocese, and elected pastors. After this preliminary organization, a national council of communities would be called: "The present Catholic hierarchy would be asked to step down or to attend as fellow Christians. Needless to say, this would probably be refused by most bishops, but the offer should be made. This reformed Catholic church should declare itself in communion with all men of good will, and specifically with all branches of the Catholic church throughout the world, including the See of Rome."

Ruether's proposal followed hard on the heels of a demand by the bishop of the diocese of Kansas City-St. Joseph that the Kansas City-based newspaper *National Catholic Reporter* remove the word *Catholic* from its masthead on the grounds that the word did not describe the paper's orientation. Bishop Helmsing cited Ruether by name along with other regular *NCR* contributors who were not in his judgement in communion with the Church. In an open letter to the bishop in *NCR*, Ruether charged that it was Helmsing, not she, who was out of communion with the Church and invited him "to break bread and share the cup of salvation with me and my family in my house."[8]

Several weeks after the November confrontation in Washington things looked brighter. Theologian Daniel Callahan disagreed with Ruether's conviction that a new Church was necessary. He took issue with reformers who had left the Church:

> It is hard to see why they do. Unless they are in particularly backward areas they could find underground liturgies if liturgy is their bugaboo. Why lust for "official sanction"? Who needs it? If contraception is their problem, they can find plenty of Catholic support for a conviction that contraception is not only acceptable but on occasion morally good and required. If authority is their obsession there are any number of books – by Catholic authors – they can read now which will provide them with a rationale for as much dissent as any but the most neurotically rebellious conscience could want.[9]

Ruether, who in any case, as she later revealed,[10] had as long ago as her first year of college abandoned Catholic belief for a kind of paganism, quickly came to agree with Callahan. By 1973 she was writing:

> I would not feel any difficulty in speaking of one aspect of Vatican II aggiornamento as a protestantisation of the Roman Catholic Church. It seems to me that any modern Roman Catholic theologian has absorbed and indeed taken for granted the achievements of Protestantism, especially its theological and biblical developments. Catholic reform thus started in the Vatican Council with people who were already disciples of Protestant crisis theology. Catholic theology today in its increasing approximation to the curriculum of the Protestant seminary and often in its movement actually to amalgamate with such seminaries shows its need to absorb the work of Protestantism.

And as for the "bugaboos" Callahan mentioned – they no longer mattered enough to leave over:

> Even the practices that once would have marked a "Roman Catholic" from one who had "left the Church" have largely collapsed. Many of those who are most intimately concerned with developing new thought forms and community groupings may never see the inside of a parish church from one year to the next, have abandoned practices like confession some years ago, many practise birth control, and either be or be associated with married priests, and nevertheless with good conscience identify themselves as Roman Catholics. . . . The new consciousness of the Council has effected a sweeping take over of all the structures of catechetics and religious formation in the Church on every level. The general tone of the material . . . is

clearly ecumenical, universalistic and humanistic in a way that breaks the moulds of much of what one used to think of as religious let alone Roman Catholic. . . . There is simply no need to create a new church in order to have a different point of view from the bishop or the Pope. One has only to create a discussion group, a new school or a publication or simply talk with friends. . . . Pluralism of the most rampant sort has come. The episcopal leadership can ignore it, resist it or wall itself off from it, but it has become powerless to expel it.[11]

That was the revolution's correct perception of its institutionalized solidity at and just after its public debut. Ruether was not in any way exaggerating "the sweeping take over" of Catholic teaching structures and materials, as any Catholic like myself with children at several levels of Catholic education can swear to.

Now let us move forward to the present, for the revolution's own assessment of the extent to which it has managed to become institutionally grounded. In June of 1984 the *New York Review of Books* published a review of Hans Küng's latest work, *Eternal Life?* The review, entitled "Revolution in the Church," by Thomas Sheehan, professor of philosophy at the Jesuit University of Loyola in Chicago, was in effect a state of the disunion report to the New Class intellectuals who read *NYRB*. Sheehan wrote:

> The dismantling of traditional Roman Catholic theology, by Catholics themselves, is by now a *fait accompli*. . . . Catholic theologians and exegetes . . . in scarcely two decades have marshaled the most advanced scriptural scholarship – until recently the work mainly of Protestants – and put it at the service of a radical rethinking of their faith. . . . In Roman Catholic seminaries, for example, it is now common teaching that Jesus of Nazareth did not assert any of the divine or messianic claims the Gospels attribute to him and that he died without believing he was Christ or the Son of God, not to mention the founder of a new religion. . . . The surprising thing today is that the scholars who are advancing the reevaluation of Jesus are neither atheists . . . nor liberal Protestants. . . . Rather, these scholars are Roman Catholic exegetes and theologians, most of them priests, faithfully ensconced at the heart of their faith. . . . The new approach that Catholic scholars are taking to Jesus and the scriptures I shall call, by way of shorthand, the "liberal consensus." By that I mean the scientific methods employed and the conclusions generated by Catholic exegetes and theologians internationally recognized in their fields, the ones who hold the chairs, get the grants, publish the books, and define the limits of scientific exegesis and theology in the Catholic Church today. This liberal consensus reflects the presuppositions and procedures that Catholic scholars like Rudolf Schnackenburg,

Raymond E. Brown, Roland Murphy, Pierre Benoit, John P. Meier, J.A. Fitzmeyer, David M. Stanley, Rudolf Pesch, Walter Kasper, David Tracy, Edward Schillebeeckx, Hans Küng, and hundreds of others use when they do research. . . . Scholars who continue to employ the older methods find themselves pushed to the margins of scholarly discourse. . . . Many of the conclusions of the "liberal consensus" conflict sharply with traditional Catholic doctrine.[12]

Today, Sheehan contends, "one would be hard pressed" to find a Catholic biblical scholar who maintains that Jesus was the divine Son of God, or who believes in the doctrines of the Trinity, the virginity of Mary, the miracles, the founding of the Church by Jesus, the Resurrection, or immortal life.

Sheehan's review caused something of a stir, but it is hard to see why. Küng's liberal Protestantism (Karl Rahner's judgement) is hardly news. Küng's new book reduces the Resurrection to some kind of revelatory experience, now unreconstructible, on the part of the Apostles. Belief in the Resurrection of Christ and as a consequence our own resurrection to immortal life are data "existentially meaningful" only, not rationally provable; reductionist conclusions familiar since nineteenth-century liberal Protestantism and Catholic modernism. Moreover, everyone knows that Sheehan's "liberal consensus," the parallel magisterium, has for nearly two decades had a stranglehold on the teaching apparatus of the Church. Everyone knows that while the "official teaching" of the Church is still on the books and is forcefully maintained by the papal magisterium, the *actual teaching* at all levels is the radically different doctrine of the theological revolution. Sheehan is correct that "a new and revolutionary approach dominates Catholic theology today, even if the folk religion of most practicing Catholics still lives on the prerevolutionary fare that generally is served up from their local pulpits and especially from the one currently occupied by the conservative Pope John Paul II."[13]

Everybody knows this, but it has not been considered good form to admit it. At least not in front of the children and the domestics. The bishops are painfully aware of what Charles Curran describes as a situation "in which the official teaching and the accepted practice are different." Yet since they cannot bring themselves to do anything about it, they pretend that it isn't there, or that it is a figment of the imagination of the left, as represented by the *National Catholic Reporter*, or of the right, as represented by *The Wanderer* or *The Remnant*. At the behest of Raymond Brown and company, they occasionally berate "the right." When I wrote for a large secular newspaper an article about the bishops' subordination to the parallel magisterium, no less a personage than the president of the CCCB, Archbishop J.N. MacNeil, wrote to the paper calling me an hysterical liar, and the CCCB's trouble-shooter, Monsignor Dennis J. Murphy, was later trundled out to rescue the Archbishop from the ensuing unpleasantness.[14] Big guns indeed for such an unimportant target. Lonely counter-revolutionaries (counter-revolutionaries are *very* lonely in Canada) are the only safe targets left for bishops to shoot at.

Given the example of the bishops' concerted blindness towards the revolution, Sheehan's – and Curran's and Ruether's – frankness seems brave and admirable, but it merely reveals the confidence of a revolution that has not been seriously challenged since 1968. Sheehan, like other dissenters, ritually invokes the theologians' folk-memory of persecution: "He [Küng] has consistently risked his own career in order to unmask the ideological power structures that inform so much of the Roman ecclesiastical order." Sure he has, as a glance at the best-seller lists or the schedules of his speaking appearances will prove. But this invocation is just nostalgia; even Sheehan can't maintain it: "A few of them, like Hans Küng, have had their wrists slapped. In 1979 the Pope removed him from his chair of Catholic theology at Tübingen but he was not excommunicated and continues to teach there."[15] And to travel from one Catholic university to another, drawing large crowds, huge fees, standing ovations, and emotional welcomes like that of Notre Dame's Richard McBrien, who embraced him as "our fellow Catholic theologian."

This, therefore, is the confident state of the revolution now. Dissent has become orthodoxy. The revolution has become the legitimate government at all levels below the papacy. The empowering symbols of legitimacy are in the possession of the revolution. The hierarchical magisterium has been forced to tolerate the working separation of faith from practice. The Pope is the leader of a rump Church only.

EIGHT

෧~෨

THE BATTLEFRONTS

෧~෨

Thomas Sheehan's review of the work of an early and constant revolutionary embodied the widespread conviction on both sides in the Church that the revolution was home and safe, and that the possibility of counter-revolution could be discounted. Before I proceed to discuss the question of a counter-revolution, I will review the situation on the principal battlefronts. Also, several new offensives have been mounted since 1968 and some old ones abandoned. Someone whom I was interviewing for this section said to me with cheerful grimness, "You're doing a body count!" That's been done already by the revolution's sociologists, some of whose findings I have quoted above. There is no disputing their basic finding of a mass departure on an historically unprecedented scale from Catholic practice, although I am prepared to dispute the reasons they adduce for it. It is important to be honest about just how fundamental and solid the revolution's gains are and about the magnitude of the task faced by any group within the Church that intends to have a shot at restoring Catholic faith and order.

THE DOCTRINAL FRONT

On paper the doctrinal front has been held, but on paper only. The great, perhaps the only, achievement of Vatican II was the retention and reassertion of the body of Catholic dogma. Despite all their weaknesses, the documents as they stand admit of a perfectly orthodox Catholic reading. That not inconsiderable feat achieved, the magisterium collapsed, exhausted. Of course, it has to be considered of enormous importance for any future Catholic restoration that the Church's very grounds of existence do not have to be fought back on to the law books, but at present there is no value left in pretending that these teachings animate the lives of more than a minority of even practising Catholics. The authority of the Church is no longer authoritative. It has been delegitimized.

The revolution was unable to bring about an official doctrinal revolution, yet the doctrinal situation in the Church is today as Curran, Sheehan, Greeley, Ruether, and I describe it. How did this happen? It happened because the revolution, through its majority control of the bodies appointed to implement Vatican II, was able to bring to pass a sweeping cultural revolution that radically altered the Catholic cosmology.

THE CULTURAL FRONT

Catholicism is a cosmological religion, that is, one that integrates all the phenomena of space and time into a sacred order in which divine and human existence are continuous. This cosmology locates and explains man's existence. For the Catholic, therefore, religion is not private and autonomous but communitarian and cosmic. Every aspect of existence is explained as part of an eternal benevolent continuity. For the Catholic, suffering is rescued from absurdity by being seen as a valuable co-operation with the suffering of the Son of God on the Cross, and Christ's suffering in turn is seen as the Atonement only the Son of God made man could offer for the original sin of Adam. The marriage act is ennobled to an act of co-operation with the Creator in His loving design for the universe.

The Catholic Church at Vatican II permeated all its documents with this cosmological understanding of existence. The chapter on the laity in the *Dogmatic Constitution on the Church, Lumen Gentium* urges us "to learn the deepest meaning and value of all creation, as well as its role in the harmonious praise of God" and quoted St. Paul: "All things are yours, and you are Christ's and Christ is God's." Rather unexpectedly, the *Pastoral Constitution on the Church in the Modern World, Gaudium et Spes* even more eloquently puts the Catholic cosmological vision in its first chapter, "On the Dignity of the Human Person." Man, according to Vatican II, "is created to the image of God . . . capable of knowing and loving his Creator . . . master of all earthly creatures . . . little less than the angels." Male and female companionship is to be seen as "the primary form of interpersonal communion." Original sin, committed "at the urging of the Evil One," was responsible for the disruption of man's "proper relationship to his own ultimate goal as well as his whole relationship towards himself and all created things." And so on, through the ancient Christian and Catholic account of things, to the conclusion that "the root reason for human dignity lies in man's call to communion with God."

Human actions, then, have eternal consequences. But how is one guided to "do this, shun that"? In his "rightly formed conscience," "man detects a law which he does not impose upon himself but which holds him to obedience." This law "written by God" binds universally to "objective norms of morality." Like Protestantism, Catholicism derives these norms from Scripture; Catholicism, however, has another seat of appeal. The particular Catholic genius lies in its synthesis whereby the truths of Revelation are corroborated by extra-biblical findings from a "natural law" available to all men even if they have no knowledge of Revelation. "What divine revelation makes known to us agrees with experience," *Gaudium et Spes* remarks during its summary of the biblical account of the consequences of original sin. Man can derive the moral virtues and even the existence of a Creator from the observed nature of things, a concept both comforting and democratic. Catholic natural-law philosophy made explicit what was implicit in the Bible. The universalizing instinct of Catholicism extended to all mankind the gift of the knowledge of natural revelation.

The Catholic resource of natural law saved it from the fate of a large part of Protestantism. Protestantism divorced itself from any mediating link between God and the believer except the Bible. When this source seemed to be discredited by the rise of science and the researches of modernism, much of Protestantism fell into infidelity or fundamentalism. Catholics fell back upon the natural law and upon other cosmological concepts that Protestantism had rejected.

There are no empty spaces in the Catholic universe. God has not disappeared as He did in Protestantism into radical transcendence to dwell unknowable, arbitrary, unapproachable. Catholicism has a universe of symbolic discourse, of mediating and communicating signs and structures through which one can remain in touch with the sacred. Among these are the institutional Church and its magisterium; the sacraments and the rituals through which they are administered; the sacrifice of the Mass; the sacrificial priesthood; the reserved Eucharistic Species; sacramentals: holy water, holy oils, blessed candles, blessed ashes, the Sign of the Cross, relics, innumerable blessings attached to physical things – to boats, cars, houses, churches, rosaries, medals, wedding rings; transtemporal concepts: Purgatory, the Mystical Body of Christ, the Communion of Saints; friendly intermediaries: the Blessed Virgin Mary ("Our Lady"), guardian angels, a plethora of patron saints for individuals and places and occupations; body language: genuflection, making the Sign of the Cross upon oneself, beating the breast, bowing, standing for the Gospel, kneeling for Communion, prostration during ordination, incensing of the priest and congregation. The Catholic universe is full to its limits and rich with meaning and affection.

In a cosmological religion, the central act of worship embodies in symbols the community's understanding of the nature of God and of existence. Both the religious symbols of Catholicism and the social behaviour of Catholics are outward signs of inner beliefs, the high altar and the large family equally eloquent about one's world view. The cult informs the culture and is inseparable from it. The Catholic perception of the liturgy was summed up long ago in the Latin saying, *Lex orandi, lex credendi* – you can deduce what people believe from observing the way they pray. This is as true as it always was. In Catholic liturgy and therefore in Catholic life, there is no such thing as "a mere external."

The Church has had periodic liturgical reform – the early shift from the Jewish liturgy, the move to Latin at the end of the fourth century, the great Gregorian reform at the beginning of the seventh, the definitive reform of the Council of Trent which sacrificed national variations for the sake of doctrinal unity as an initial counter-revolutionary move against the Protestant Reformation, the popular and effective pre-Vatican II reforms of Pius XII, and the early liturgical movement. It was not, therefore, inevitable that the latest liturgical reform should end in disaster. Orthodox defenders of the Council, myself among them, argue (as we more or less have to do unless we want to repudiate the Council altogether) that the liturgical movement need not have ended this way and that the reform we got was not the one actually intended by the Council. This is the argument made by the undeniably orthodox Louis Bouyer, one of the leaders of the liturgical movement before the Council and a member of the Council's liturgy commission. In 1964, Bouyer described the *Constitution on the Sacred Liturgy*, which he had helped to write, as "an irreformable statement of what the Church's belief is. . . . It will never be superseded as the Church's fundamental teaching concerning what she does in her worship."[1] But in 1968 he wrote: "We must speak plainly: there is practically no liturgy worthy of the name today in the Catholic Church. . . . Perhaps in no other area is there a greater distance (and even formal opposition) between what the Council worked out and what we actually have. . . . I now have the impression, and I am not alone, that those who took it upon themselves to apply (?) the Council's directives . . . have turned their backs deliberately on what Beauduin, Casel and Pius Parsch [great figures of the liturgical movement] had set out to do."[2] (The question mark is Bouyer's.) Whatever was officially intended, it was Küng's and Schillebeeckx' reform that was implemented, not Bouyer's, largely because – there is no avoiding it – ultimate responsibility for its quality fell upon Paul VI instead of upon Pius XII. For it is not fair to call Monsignor Annibale Bugnini and his Consilium, which devised and enforced the new liturgy, "those who took it upon themselves to apply (?) the Council's directives." They did not take it upon themselves; they were appointed, defended, and obeyed by Paul VI. That unfathomable ruler enforced their most revolutionary innovations over the anguished protests of the most faithful of the Catholic laity, all the while issuing his

126

own stream of anguished complaint against doctrinal errors arising from proliferating liturgical abuses. Even though he at last dismissed Bugnini in disgrace (upon well-founded accusations of his secret membership in the Masonic Order), Paul VI did not even then rescind any of Bugnini's directives. In sober truth, by empowering the liturgical radicals to do their worst, Paul VI, wittingly or unwittingly, empowered the revolution.

In the past, liturgical reform was always in the direction of an intensification of the Catholic idea of the sacred. Every external, from the language of the liturgy to the music that accompanied it, to the shape and illumination of the churches that housed it, served to elucidate the Catholic world view. The revolution understood the psychology of religious belief far better than did the many orthodox bishops and priests who blithely pressed radical change upon their congregations. The liturgy is the most important public repository of the truths of the Catholic religion and the symbols that teach those truths; it is "the summit toward which the activity of the Church is directed [and] the font from which all her power flows" (*Constitution on the Sacred Liturgy,* 10). The radical shift in Catholic consciousness that the revolution proposed could not be accomplished unless and until the liturgy was radically altered. The *Constitution on the Sacred Liturgy* noted that "the liturgy is made up of immutable elements divinely instituted and of elements subject to change" and proposed "to undertake with great care" a "restoration" of "texts and rites . . . so that they express more clearly the holy things which they signify." It warned that "there must be no innovations unless the good of the Church genuinely and certainly requires them; and care must be taken that any new forms adopted should in some way grow organically from forms already existing" (*Constitution on the Sacred Liturgy,* 21; 23).

The sincere and dedicated men who made the revolution really believed that the good of the Church genuinely and certainly required the secularization of Catholic consciousness. Increasingly agnostic about God and eternal life, the reformers passionately believed that the only hope for mankind lay in a shift of emphasis from the sacred to the secular span of human life, to global community, to the quest for social justice and peace. For them, Christ's prayer "Thy Kingdom come" was a hope meant to be realized and capable of realization here and now, if the spiritual energies of the Catholic Church were redirected to that end instead of being squandered on myths and dreams. A truncated cosmology, a human community, was "the holy thing" that the revolution intended that the new liturgy should convey.

From before the Council, the revolution had its hands on the future of the cult. Always present in force throughout the long liturgical movement, the radicals were, immediately upon the passage of the cautious language of the *Constitution on the Sacred Liturgy,* in the majority on the commissions which implemented it. They understood that there was no need to make a frontal assault upon "the immutable elements divinely instituted" in order to destroy belief in them; that could be done even more effectively under cover of orthodoxy by a radical transformation of "the elements subject to change," the "mere" externals. By wholesale replacement of these, they demystified and broke the cult, thereby desperately weakening the authority over the religious imagination of the doctrine it had enshrined and destroying the culture to which it had given form and meaning. The "immutable elements" could not, in the early stages of the revolution, be got rid of entirely. They remain, but surrounded by a symbolism that acts to contradict them. The present liturgical reform is indeed, as Bouyer charges, a "denial and imposture," presenting as it does at every public act of the Church's worship an unbearable tension between two opposing world views, the "immutable elements" affirming and the new external symbols denying the traditional Catholic cosmological view of order.

Externals were reversed in order to reverse the concepts for which they were icons. Representations of Christ's sacrifice, the Crucifix and stations of the Cross, disappeared. Where the Crucifix remained, the Figure was that of the risen not the crucified Christ, a representation with sound Catholic antecedents but now used in the service of a different theology. In the Church I usually attend, the cross has disappeared entirely; a golden, stripped Christ hovers, arms raised, head high, toes pointed, several inches from the wall. (This image, I regret to say, is known among us as The Diver Who Dived for Our Sins.) The altar of sacrifice was replaced by a table for a community meal. The tabernacle disappeared from it, to be replaced by a microphone, modern symbol of human-to-human communication. The priest was officially designated "president of the assembly" and conducted much of the Mass from a chair at one side of the table. When he was at the table, the direction of communication was reversed. He faced the people, instead of, as leader, facing with them towards God. The liturgical language special to the Mass disappeared, to be replaced by the vernacular. The vernacular itself, at least the English vernacular, fell victim to disgracefully revisionist translation by the extremely radical International Commission on English in the Liturgy (ICEL), which translation, as Richard Toporoski writes, "represents and will inculcate a different understanding of God's relation to man and of man's response to God in the salvific scheme than has been held and taught heretofore in the Catholic Church."[3]

Ubiquitous microphones made the dubious vernacular a communication with an audience rather than with God. Every word must now be loud and clear, a performance, and priests began to commentate, joke, ad lib, show off. Religious decorum was lost; priests were instructed to smile, make frequent eye contact, read with liveliness. (The Toronto Pastoral Centre for Liturgy issued these instructions: "The presider will endeavour to speak well, sing well. . . . He will also be aware of the importance of body language. . . . The essential prayer gesture of the *orans* must be wide, graceful and relaxed; the hallowing gesture at the invocation of the Spirit should be imposing and majestic; the showing of the elements at the institution narrative should be done ostensibly but with some restraint. . . . The priest should also have a facial expression that is open and inviting . . . that says: 'Here we are together praising, remembering, and offering.' . . . The priest's countenance should never appear forbidding or fretful. His face should express reverence, joy and concern for all."[4] Note the revisionist terms, *presider* for *priest*, *institution narrative* for *consecration*. Poor wretches, no wonder they behave in such an antic way.)

Sacred music was replaced by secular, and Catholic hymns by Protestant, which, though often beautiful and grave, expressed a different theology. The feeling of the sacred place was destroyed wherever possible. Altar rails were removed, destroying the idea of a sanctuary, a holy of holies. Externals that enhanced the mystery of the enduring Real Presence in the Blessed Sacrament were done away with: the tabernacle removed to one side or even to a cupboard in the sacristy or a room in the basement; Benediction was discontinued; kneeling for Holy Communion was forbidden. A Nova Scotian parish actually had several people who knelt arrested: the bishop of Antigonish, Bishop William Power, appeared in court to testify against them. (The bishop testified thus: "Well, naturally if you perceive a mystery in a different way than what you perceived it before, it stands to reason that you begin to express yourself in relationship to that mystery in a little different way. . . . It seems now more suitable in relationship to the way we perceive the . . . eucharist, that we stand. Previously it seemed the most suitable way . . . to receive communion kneeling. Now, the custom has come the other way and I have approved of it.")[5]

The option of Communion in the hand was made the rule through bullying and mockery (the pastor of St. Bartholemew's in Toronto stuck out his tongue and mugged at those of his parishioners who wanted to receive by mouth). Standing even during the Consecration was promoted "in honour of the Resurrection" (the above-mentioned priest had all the kneelers pulled out of his Church, presumably to give the doctrine of the Resurrection a boost). Large numbers of lay people, men and women, were appointed "extraordinary ministers" who, contrary to Church legislation, distributed Holy Communion while priests deliberately sat idle in the sanctuary. (Priests at a church I used to attend did this for a considerable time after the introduction, much resisted, of lay ministers, in order to break down the religious sensibilities of communicants who had been changing lines in order to receive from a priest.) Genuflections were reduced and the ringing of bells at the Consecration stopped; many priests stopped elevating the consecrated elements. Distractions proliferated; the newly introduced "sign of peace" after the Consecration became a prolonged bout of hand-shaking, kissing, and talking. It became usual for the priest to shake his way down through the whole church.

It was made impossible for even the most determined adherent of the traditional Catholic view of the sacred to keep it in mind during Mass. We are not talking here of wild private Masses but of the usual Mass in the parish church. The sanctuary was filled with distracting junk, banners, trees, movie screens to carry the words of hymns and for media help with the sermon. (St. Joseph's, the Church of the English-speaking Oblates in Ottawa, has in its sanctuary an organ, a movie screen, and a large kidney-shaped pool with, at last count, twenty goldfish in it. Honest. "Judging from the 'homilies' I sometimes hear," says a parishioner, "I think they are directed to these particular parishioners.") Folk groups with guitars and bad manners fill the sanctuary, they and the various lectors logging much more air-time than the priest and the Mass actions. Applause from the congregation is often encouraged after baptisms, marriages, religious professions, anniversaries; couples write their own marriage vows and nuns their vows of commitment. Old sacred vessels and sacred furnishings went to pawnshops. (I have a collection of sad pictures of such sacred discards given me by a man who devotes his time to rescuing them – "17th century French chalice, sold by auction, $35." Several restaurants in Toronto sport monstrances and tabernacles among their decor; one uses an altar with tabernacle as a bar.) Meanwhile, the historic Mass, which had for fifteen centuries protected and conveyed a particular idea of the sacred, was everywhere proscribed; priests who celebrated it were suspended and persecuted, and people who attended it were told that they were not fulfilling their Sunday obligation.

No significant change can be made in a rite without endangering the belief the rite expresses. Actually, that formulation is backwards: no significant change *is* made in a rite unless the men making it have experienced a serious change of belief in what the rite formerly expressed to them. This is certainly the case with the men who made the present liturgical reform, many of whom are on record as not believing in the Real Presence, the divinity of Christ, the natural law – the whole, intricate Catholic structure of belief. Reacting to Sheehan's article, writers in the *National Catholic Reporter*, which has since 1964 propagandized for a radical liturgy that would symbolize "the new model of Church," expressed their relief about the institutionalization of the revolution in belief. One wrote: "I'm honestly relieved to hear that the virgin conception and birth are highly suspect . . . as for infallibility, they ought to put it wherever they put indulgences," and another "would be relieved if the church would quietly drop the creed from the Sunday liturgy to make more room for the faithful doubter."[6] Indeed, as Bouyer said, let us speak plainly. We may not, as he charges, have the liturgy intended for us by the Council fathers, but we do have "a liturgy worthy of the name," a revolutionary liturgy that could hardly convey with more clarity the secular world view its makers intended it to convey. Catholic liturgy today, both in its official version and its far more usual unofficial versions, is in rapid progress towards Sheehan's prescription of abandoning apocalypse altogether in favour of post-apocalyptic concerns: moral, social, and political. The "immutable elements," in chief the Consecration and the Gospel, look increasingly embarrassed and subservient amid the ruthlessly secular symbolism. Even "immutable elements" can be denatured, the Consecration by small, sacrilegious manipulations such as I have described above – simply, for instance, by calling it the "institution narrative"; the Gospel by relegating it to an exemplary hook on which to hang sermons on radical concerns.

I shall give two examples, one Canadian, one American, of the secularization process in full force.

On September 12, 1976, in a room at the Church of St. Peter the Apostle, Montreal, a "Marxist Mass" was "concelebrated" by several priests including the then minister of labour in the Parti Québécois government, Father Jacques Couture, and a Protestant minister. All wore lay clothes. All the prayers of the Mass were replaced by political readings and protest songs. On a movie screen beside the uncovered desk that served as an altar was projected a film about Salvador Allende, the "martyred" Marxist president of Chile. Published pictures show the preparation of the elements: Father Anselmo Leonelli pours from a bottle of wine into six handleless Chinese teacups and places a large round loaf on the table; and the consecration: three of the priests, including Couture, hold a cup in one hand and read from a script in the other; and the communion: the congregation helps itself to the broken loaf and the cups of wine scattered over the desk top among the pens and papers.[7]

And the American example: the seventh annual National Clown, Mime, Puppet and Dance Ministry Workshop Week, July 29 to August 4, 1984, on the campus of St. Mary's College (Notre Dame), Indiana, as juicily described in the slashing new counter-revolutionary magazine *Fidelity*.[8] Father Dave Mura's workshop, "Jesus Christ, King of Kings, Lord of Lords and Clown of Clowns," was actually a three-hour clown liturgy, during which Mura "simultaneously put on clown make-up and retold the gospel stories in a humorous . . . vein," celebrated Mass in full clown costume, mimed instead of said the Consecration, and issued this invitation to the mixed congregation: "You are invited to receive the Eucharist to whatever degree is consistent with your faith." When asked about the theological implications of the clown ministry, another leader answered revealingly, "It has to do with reversal."

These examples, though exotic, are not untypical. Any issue of the *National Catholic Reporter* or of official national liturgy bulletins, any dip into parish or university liturgy (the local cathedral brought Santa Claus into the sanctuary for the early Christmas Eve Mass last year), will provide thousands of others. The bitter truth is that the public worship of the Catholic Church has become an institutionalized ritual of revolution. Father Patrick Byrne, the radical liturgist officially in charge of interpreting the liturgical reform for the Catholic Church in Canada, claims that Vatican II gave us a new Christology, anthropology, and ecclesiology, which the new liturgy is trying to make manifest over the opposition of "prophets of doom" and "some mandarins . . . with . . . windows to close" in the Roman curia.[9] Byrne's conviction that Vatican II brought about what Jesuit John O'Malley calls "a major paradigm shift" involving not only changes in law and ritual but "a new frame of reference . . . that had an across-the-board impact"[10] is the mainspring of revolutionary action.

In the new paradigm or model, the horizontal this-wordly dimension of Christianity has crowded out the vertical dimension. All that remains is the social gospel, practised in the kind of noble agnosticism flavoured by admiration for the man Jesus which Küng and Sheehan express – "As far as one can know, when you're dead, you're dead – and the same holds for Jesus. Rather than hoping him out of the tomb, leave him there and try to lead the kind of life that got him to his grave. The rest, whatever it may be, is out of our hands."[11] God melts into radical immanence, to be encountered only in our neighbour and revealed only in "the signs of the times." Salvation is of this world, redemption means political liberation. The "locus of revelation" shifts from Scripture to experience.

The liturgy offered the most available opportunity for conveying this paradigm shift to the consciousness of the Catholic laity; first, because the bulk of the laity is unreachable by the revolution in any other way; second, because of the way the liturgy communicates, on an immediate, intuitive level, to the stomach before the head. Radical change in the cult at once conveyed the signal that everything might be considered subject to change. Thus, orthodox commentators who pointed out from the beginning that Vatican II had actually produced no doctrinal changes were ignored. I once, during a confrontation on CBC Radio with Father Jim Roberts (a Vancouver priest suspended from public exercise of his faculties by Vancouver's Archbishop Carney), challenged him to support his claims that Vatican II had changed everything. He laughed.

You only had to go into any Catholic Church, he said unanswerably, to see that everything had changed. The Catholic imagination has found this logic irresistible. A cosmology doesn't come to pieces bit by bit. It explodes. "If the sun and moon should doubt, they'd immediately go out." They did, and they have, for millions of Catholics, leaving their religious universe empty. It is often pointed out that millions of devout Catholics prefer the new liturgy. But these Catholics also, according to sociologists, are now tolerant of contraception, abortion, divorce, and so on. I argue that this incredible change is very much the result of the new liturgy whose symbolic externals never reproach humanist secularist morality; its people-centred emphasis makes it easier to accept the secular community's libertine values even if one does not yet live by them.

This feeling of an exploded cosmology, with its baggage of guilt and anger, is the theme of much popular fiction. It is present in a trashy thriller I read not long ago: "Out of nowhere, Denny remembered the joke he had made when they first started doing the Mass in English: 'If that's all the whole thing is about, I never would have started in the first place.' Was he to be punished for that harmless joke? God, dear God, I didn't mean it."[12] Or in *Catholics*, Brian Moore's prophetic novel about the necessary connection between revolution and the destruction of the old Mass. In *Catholics*, set in the near future after Vatican IV, the restructured Roman curia sends the young Father Kinsella in the name of the World Ecumen Council to a monastery in Ireland to stop the last remaining Tridentine rite Mass, to which people are flocking from all over the world. The Abbot addresses Kinsella:

"What is the Mass to you?"
[Kinsella answers:] "I suppose the Mass to me, as to most Catholics in the world today, is a symbolic act. I do not believe that the bread and wine on the altar is changed into the body and blood of Christ, except in a purely symbolic manner. Therefore, I do not, in the old sense, think of God as actually being present, there in the tabernacle . . ."
"Isn't that remarkable," the Abbot said. "And yet you seem to be what I would call a very *dedicated* young man."
"In what way is it remarkable, Father Abott? It's the standard belief, in this day and age."
"Or lack of belief," the Abbot said. "I think I was born before my time. A man doesn't have to have such a big dose of faith anymore, does he?"
Kinsella smiled. "Perhaps not." He had been about to add that today's best thinking saw the disappearance of the Church building as a place of worship in favor of a more generalized community con-

cept, a group gathered in a meeting to celebrate God-in-others. But decided that, perhaps, the Abbot was not ready for that step.

"Yes," the Abbot said. "I see now why the old Mass is *non grata*. And why you're here to tell us to cease and desist."[13]

Brian Moore is a lapsed Catholic but his instructed imagination remembers what it all meant and he has the great artist's understanding of symbol. Explaining why he wrote *Catholics*, he offered the inimitably Irish explanation that after a long absence he went to Mass and found that the thing he had stopped believing in was no longer there. I think that even the most faithful Catholic, if he were truly honest, would admit to experiencing something like that at the beginning of the liturgical revolution, a sudden, desolating feeling that there is no longer Anybody there, a moment of panic as the stomach reacts before the reason kicks in. It happened to my father and he left the Church. It happened to me years ago, at a late afternoon Mass in a church I used to attend. There were only a few people in the church. The young priest behaved in a particularly wild and frivolous manner (he was, as it turned out, just about to leave the priesthood under unsavoury circumstances). He and a couple of jean-clad girls dashed about the sanctuary. In an attempt to light the altar candles he extinguished the sanctuary lamp that burns always before the tabernacle to show that Christ is sacramentally present; it seemed to me a symbolic accident. Mass proceeded between unlit candles. There is no need to recount all the mocking details. Halfway through the Mass, I went out and sat on a wall outside the church and wept in rage, panic, and despair. I sat there for a long time and then I went home. If I had been asked at that moment what happens at a Catholic Mass, I might very well have answered like Moore's Father Kinsella, or I might have echoed what Hans Küng is reported to have said: "Nothing."

I've been to many worse Masses since then, but on that day my other Catholic resources had not yet been summoned to the aid of my faith. The impact of the revolutionary shock had been prior to this cushioned by our older parish priest, whose unquestionable piety and orthodoxy had lulled our suspicions and whose judicious editing then (and still) makes the liturgy barely tolerable. Thankful as one is for a decent place to go to Mass, this situation is destructive not only because of its necessary impermanence, but also because it has led to a revival of Donatism, whereby one finds onself sitting out Holy Communion if one has doubts about the validity of the Mass in progress, and judging the validity of the Mass by the way the priest says it. This is dreadful. One is forced to fall back upon Catholic legislation worked out long ago to deal with situations like this, though it seems to lead in a circle. The Mass is valid if said according to the mind of the Church. But how does one know if the priest is actually saying it according to the Church's understanding? In general, the outward sign of inward accord is adherence to the Church's rule of worship. But what if the priest departs significantly from the prescribed form in the wide extra-legal fashion tolerated by most bishops? And far more serious, what if the Church's legal form of worship is theologically divided against itself? Catholics had to face this early on in the revolution.

I wrote years ago that the new liturgy was devised by ideologues and installed by dupes. Do I still stand by this harsh judgement? Yes, I do. I also wrote that I categorically assert the validity of the new liturgy when it is celebrated according to the mind of the Church. Do I still assert this validity? Yes, I do. I think that the paradigm shift attempted by the revolution is nowhere more clearly or dangerously taught than in the reformed liturgy, but I also believe, as I must if I wish to remain Catholic, that the Holy Ghost has not allowed His Church on earth to lose its power to make present perpetually the Sacrifice of the Cross. Therefore, I go to the new Mass, although I recognize that attendance is an act of passive acceptance of the revolution's world view, to the extent that it has managed to present itself in the new liturgy, and although I know from experience that attendance demands a constant struggle to maintain the Catholic world view against the current liturgical expression of it. It is difficult to imagine a more ironic religious predicament.

Catholicism resisted the forces of secularization hundreds of years longer than did mainline Protestantism because of the immense scope it gave to the sacred and because of the adequacy of the supports, symbolic and philosophic, that it developed and maintained for its view of reality. Into the twentieth century, when Protestantism had become almost completely secularized, Catholicism's world view remained remarkably durable. Catholics were able to coexist with the modern forces of secularism without accepting secular premises. Catholic religious consciousness had proven itself immune to significant modification from without. It remains to be seen whether it can survive the present determined attempt at conversion from within, particularly since the revolutionary consciousness has already become institutionalized and internalized to a disheartening extent.

Every world view has a central cultic object that its culture translates into behavioural terms. Catholic worship and life used to reflect a cosmic order centred on God. The cultic centre of the secular world view is the self, the autonomous human personality; this is the logical point of arrival for the Protestant principle. And as Father Roberts correctly sensed, you only have to go into most Catholic churches to verify the change of vital centre. The impression that the public worship of the Church now conveys is that the congregation is worshipping itself. There is a new air of complacency, of self-congratulation, of self-sufficient communitarianism:

"Good morning, everyone . . . Good morning, Father . . . Thank you for making such a great effort to celebrate with the worshipping community of St. Martin Luther King's on this rainy (hot, snowy, beautiful) day. . . . I hope you noticed the great new air-conditioning (carpet, windows, banners, choir robes) that the parish council (RENEW, building committee, liturgy team) have provided. . . . My name is. . . . My colleagues are. . . . The eucharistic ministers are. . . . I'd like you to welcome Ms —— , the new pastoral assistant. I'd like to welcome visitors to the parish. I'd like to remind you that baby-sitting is provided in the parish hall. . . . What does this Gospel have to say to us in our own context (peace, strike, election)? . . . I would like to read the wonderful insights of the Grade IV class on the meaning of Thanksgiving (Christmas, Easter, peace, war, God, caring, sharing) . . . You will notice their wonderful interpretations of these themes on the walls behind the altar. They have so much to teach us all. . . . Would anyone care to add their own petitions to the prayers of the faithful? . . . Any further petitions? . . . Would —— stand up on this occasion of their baptism (confirmation, wedding anniversary, death) for a well-deserved round of applause? . . . Now we will all sing. . . . Everyone try to sing this one. . . . Well, we didn't do very well with that one. Let's all try harder next time. Ms —— will practise with you for a few moments before each song. . . . Don't be afraid to sing. God doesn't mind if you don't have a great voice . . . Surely we can all do better than that. . . . The collection today is for the struggle for justice and peace in El Salvador (Nicaragua, Guatemala, Brazil). Sister —— who has just returned from three days of living among the poor in Central America (Tanzania, the Philippines) will say a few words about it and show a short film. . . . Here comes the Sunday school class. . . . They will place their representations of today's readings around the altar in the offertory procession. . . . Now let us offer each other a sign of peace. . . . Peace, Anne . . . John . . . George . . . Joe. . . . Nice to see you . . . The Peace of Christ . . . Hi . . . Hi . . . Hi . . . When you come to Holy Communion follow the ushers' directions so the lines to the various ministers will be equal . . . Body of Christ, Anne . . . Body of Christ, George . . . Oh, this must be the new baby. . . . Please be seated for some further announcements. . . . I would like to welcome the Sunday school (first communion, confirmation) class. . . . The leaders of RENEW will now speak on this week's theme. . . . Thank you for celebrating with us. . . . Come again. . . . Pick up a bulletin (RENEW pledge, Global Village Voice, Development and Peace Report) at the back. . . . Peace pledge at the back if anyone would care to sign. . . . Coffee and doughnuts in the parish hall. . . . Go in peace to love and serve each other and have a good day."

But for all its folksiness, the new regime turns nasty if crossed, as witness this announcement in a local parish bulletin: *"Extraordinary Ministers of the Eucharist*: Six members of the parish will start training this week for this ministry. My choice of these six must be accepted by all. Sin will be committed by those who question or criticize my selection."[14]

The bigger and more public the occasion, the more the secular aspect is stressed at the expense of the sacred; by this point in the revolution, most priests, very often orthodox men with the best possible intentions, emphasize the secular to the virtual extinction of the sacred. This past Christmas the nice young priest called all the children in the church up to stand around the altar during the Consecration – "Christmas is a time for children" – and then sent them tumbling back at the sign of peace to "give your parents a big hug!" Sunday Masses are worse than those on weekdays, and public spectacles, such as Masses during papal visits when the liturgy committees are in full flight, are the worst of all. I offer as evidence the televised Masses during Pope John Paul II's Canadian visit in September 1984. Hours of speeches from interested groups – natives, blacks, women, people with mental and physical handicaps – and of parading and posturing in national costume, compared to minutes of the essential "immutable elements" of the Mass. Only at the moment of Consecration, which this Pope performs with a transfixing faith and solemnity, did the sacred emerge from the secular. But even at that moment, at the most ideological of all the Masses, in Montreal, hundreds of costumed dancers, chosen for their youth and beauty, postured and pirouetted around the altar (in "liturgical dance," at present forbidden) with a prominence that would have distracted seraphim from the poignant moment of sacrifice.

During his recent condemnation of liberation theology, Cardinal Ratzinger pointed out how that method uses "an inversion of symbols" in the liturgy to promote its revolutionary view of reality: "The eucharist is no longer to be understood as the real sacramental presence of the reconciling sacrifice, and as the gift of the Body and Blood of Christ. It becomes a celebration of the people in their struggle. As a consequence, the unity of the Church is radically denied. Unity, reconciliation and communion in love are no longer seen as a gift we receive from Christ. It is the historical class of the poor who by means of their struggle will build unity. For them, the struggle of the classes is the way to unity. The Eucharist thus becomes the Eucharist for the class."[15] This is rather more serious than clapping for Sunday school kids, yet it is only a difference of degree.

At long last, Rome has admitted the hidden agenda of certain aspects of the new liturgy. Not that it was ever very hidden. Rosemary Ruether described in 1973 a gathering at the French Canadian seminary of Cap Rouge, Quebec, of laity, priests, and theologians from Canada, the

United States, France, Latin America, and Vietnam: "Their working theology was that of the Christian-Marxist theology of liberation . . . and none of the dogmatic and institutional concerns that so task the energies of a Hans Küng even so much as entered their discussions . . . except by way of occasional humor. A Latin American bishop celebrated an agape with Protestant clergy, a Black Muslim, a Buddhist monk and North Vietnamese priests in somewhat uncertain standing with the Vatican, and it was evident that the sacrament that was being transubstantiated was that of human revolutionary transformation."[16]

The revolution's inversion of symbols in the liturgy has been the means of separating the tens of thousands of "base communities" from the institutional Church in Central and South America, and the same process is now under way in North America. A revolutionary passion for the political liberation of the masses is unlikely to penetrate very deeply into many Catholic breasts. The type of liberation that the secularized spirit of the reformed liturgy signalled to affluent western civilization was liberation from the constraints of Catholic sexual morality. A humanist liturgy acted as psychological preparation for the revolutionary freedom offered to the laity by theologians in the organized dissent from *Humanae Vitae*. People who would never have encountered a carefully reasoned dissenting argument were converted by the inversion of religious symbols at the only point at which their lives ritually encountered the teaching Church.

Hammering home the point of the paradigm shift, the liturgical reform quickly removed all the symbols of Catholic culture that had signified mortification of the flesh, of dying to the world for the sake of the kingdom of heaven, practices distinguishing the difference of the Catholic world view from the secular. Fast and abstinence on Friday and in Lent and Advent disappeared, as did Holy Days of Obligation, religious dress, confession boxes. Psychology took over from religion. Confession was replaced by counselling; the confessional by "reconciliation rooms" (priests were issued with plans for these, with the positions of chairs and potted plants indicated); penance was replaced by therapy; silent retreats by group encounters. Programs for "finding oneself" proliferated. Sex-education crowded out catechism: nine years of programs like *Becoming A Person* for grade-schoolers; *Search* for teenagers, "to put you in touch with your own sexuality"; Engaged Encounter for those contemplating marriage, and Marriage Encounter "to make a good marriage better," both based on encounter therapies, both rigidly excluding any discussion of the Church's teaching on contraception. Wide psychological grounds were used to nullify tens of thousands of Catholic marriages, so many that the Pope called the new scandal "divorce under another name." The Canadian Association of Separated, Divorced and Widowed Catholics was officially chaplained and sponsored even after it publicly professed its disagreement with Church teaching.

It is not my intention to lay every revolutionary manifestation in the post-Conciliar Church at the door of the liturgical reform. Nevertheless, I believe that it is not possible to exaggerate the effect of the reform on the psychological and cultural heart of the Catholic religion. The revolution would probably have taken place even if the liturgy had remained unchanged. Catholics were bound to be affected by the moral and cultural revolution then taking place in the West. But an unchanged liturgy, which continued to assert that Christ's Kingdom is not of this world, would have served as a key point of resistance to the revolution and have helped to contain the damage. As it was, the liturgy acted as the key point of communication and dissemination of revolutionary consciousness.

To take one serious cultural area only, let us look at the questions raised by Catholic feminism. The reduction of the liturgy to an expression of contemporary secular aspirations made it a platform for feminism, the "liberation theology" that combines the sexual and political revolutions into a radical cosmology. Feminism swept the orders of religious women after the total collapse of the mystical vision they had lived by. Many nuns who didn't leave turned resentfully upon the male hierarchy of the Church and the male God in whose name they believed they had been deluded and used. Nuns spearhead the movements for the removal of "sexism" from Church language and structures and for the ordination of women to the priesthood. In the area of symbolic language, they have been amazingly successful, largely because the membership of the International Commission for English in the Liturgy and of all the multitudinous liturgical conferences are committed revolutionaries. In a daring incursion which showed their power, feminists actually managed to have the language of the words of Consecration adapted (from "for all men" to "for all"; the second change in the words of Consecration – so much for "immutable elements"). In Canada, they pressured the bishops to revise their official *Catholic Book of Worship* (paid for out of parish funds by congregations who use it) to bowdlerize traditional Christmas carols.[17]

The Catholic feminist movement, still predominantly composed of nuns, has by now become so radical that its language and behaviour seem unbelievable and blasphemous to Catholics who do not share its revolutionary world view. Sister Theresa Kane, who publicly defied the Pope to his face about women's ordination during his 1979 visit to the United States, published in 1984 her own pastoral letter, with a new version of Mary's Magnificat: "Our souls magnify the holiness which dwells within us. . . . From this day forward all generations will call us blessed. Holy is our name!"[18] The 1983 Chicago convention of the National Assembly of Religious Women (NARW, formerly the National Association of Women Religious) had as its theme "Spirituality of Politics: A Woman's Concern." Participants sang, "I have a fury deep inside my very soul. I will not live forever on my knees. Waves of hate wash over me and wash me clean of fear," and celebrated a priestless "eucharist" featuring liturgical dance, stories of revolutionary struggle in Central America, and a "hip to hip" ritual during which the women "lowered and raised their bodies as they exhaled and inhaled." One NARW board member, arranger of the feminist liturgy, said: "In liturgy we bring spirituality and politics together."[19]

Also in Chicago, in November 1983, twelve hundred women gathered for "From Generation to Generation: WomanChurch Speaks," which included the Women's Ordination Conference, NARW, the Women's Alliance for Theology, Ethics and Ritual (WATER), and the pro-abortion group Catholics for Free Choice. At the "ritual meal" women danced and blessed bread and wine: "We now claim that bread to be holy by ourselves and we call on the name of God to offer thanksgiving." Theologian Marjorie Maguire, a member of Catholics for Free Choice, said: "I see the ritual as a Mass, a Eucharistic liturgy. . . . I encouraged the women who blessed the bread at our table to use the word *consecration*. I believe that the Real Presence of Christ was in that bread as much as Christ is ever present in Eucharistic bread."[20]

At the same time, a Conference for Catholic Lesbians held in conjunction with WomanChurch discussed what it means "to be a lesbian within the context of being a Catholic Sister."[21] The closing liturgy proclaimed mock-scripturally: "On day eleven in November in the year 1983, women of great knowledge and spirit did travel to the city called Chicago. . . . There in a large room 1200 women spoke of their lives, their calls to be holy, their pain and alienation . . . and of their wisdom gained by experience. . . . Claiming their gifts as those given by the Holy One, they celebrated for many days the birthday of a new church – WomanChurch."[22]

The August 1984 convention of NARW had as its theme "Breaking with the Old and Blessing the New." Sister Theresa Kane called for "new rituals of Eucharist" based on women's memories of pain and oppression. Sister Jeannine Gramick, SSND, board member of NARW and director of New Ways Ministry to homosexuals, said: "I'm beginning to believe that the greatest sin for lesbians and gay people is to want to be straight." Another participant charged that abortion was "a smokescreen of patriarchy" because it was so divisive.[23]

The August 1984 meeting in Kansas City of the Leadership Conference of Women Religious, the powerful organization of major superiors which is the official liaison to the Vatican for American nuns, discussed "a culture in crisis," prayed to "our mother God," watched a skit called "Bear Woman" in which a Benedictine nun mimed to loud-speaker words: "A long trek is ahead of us with no place to rest. We must find a place within us where the enemy cannot hurt us or take our young," and took part in a liturgy celebrated by a bishop in which "barefooted nuns in long white shifts danced with coloured streamers."[24]

Sister Judy Maier (who at thirty-four has "entered and subsequently left two religious orders") announced upon her founding of Canadian Catholics for Women's Ordination that "five years from now we intend to present ourselves to the bishops for ordination."[25] Upon the appearance of Cardinal Carter's pastoral letter on the priesthood which excluded the possibility of the ordination of women, fifty feminists demonstrated in front of the Toronto Chancery, including Sister Rosalie Bertell, an American anti-nuclear activist working for the Jesuit Centre for Social Justice and Faith in Toronto, and Laurie Bell, a writer for the leftist *Catholic New Times* and participant in the Chicago Conference for Catholic Lesbians (at which she led the singing of the lesbian theme song, "We are a gentle, angry people").[26]

Commenting on the transformation of religious orders in the United States, the American historian of the Catholic revolution, James Hitchcock, remarked that "a literal self-worship has now replaced the worship of God among nuns in the United States."[27] Before Vatican II, nuns were totally committed to the traditional eschatological world view. I remember with awe from my several years as a novice in a religious order the intensity of their sublimation of natural maternal yearnings and the energy and passion it lent to the work of the Church. The shock of the revolution was too much for many of them to bear. Their souls became like the empty house into which wandering devils enter and dwell. There is a real stink of brimstone at gatherings dominated by feminist nuns, especially at their liturgies, a creepy neo-paganism with strong suggestions of sexual perversion. This is no longer a secret; Mary Daly, an early radical who has left the Church but still teaches at the Jesuit Boston College, openly preaches lesbian witchcraft. Recently, a collection of confessions, called *Lesbian Nuns: Breaking Silence*, quickened the heartbeats of the pious readers of the pornographic magazine *Forum*, to which its feminist publishers peddled it.[28]

Nevertheless, there exists among orthodox Catholics a dismaying tendency to dismiss behaviour such as I have described as the isolated actions of bizarre extremists. I have sat fuming in too many conservative gatherings while intelligent people laugh as the latest feminist grotesqueries are retailed. They fail to realize that the attack by women on the Catholic cosmology strikes at the very heart of religion, the point at which the natural and the divine touch, at which incarnation natural and supernatural takes place. It was inevitable that rejection of the Catholic teaching on the transmission of human life must lead, especially for women, to rejection of the complex of mysteries that the idea of a sacrificial priesthood postulates. The argument against *Humanae Vitae* and the argument for the ordination of women, or, as it has developed, against any ordained priesthood, are one and the same argument.

Feminism, the most radical of the theologies of liberation, the one that strikes deepest at the roots of religion and society, was not even mentioned in the Vatican's recent condemnation of liberation theology, although no other branch of that theology has gone so far, or has the power to go so far, towards what the declaration calls "the politicization of existence." There is a Catholic joke that only Catholics know how to curse properly because only Catholics know enough names. Likewise, Catholic feminist theologians know exactly where to lay their hands on the roots of the sacred and the springs of existence. It is impossible, for instance, to imagine how anyone could be more "sacrilegious" about human sexuality than Germaine Greer, an ex-Catholic feminist. While male liberation theologians and the Vatican argue about the suitability of Marxist analysis in a critique of society, and the Vatican and the bishops try to buy off feminists with cosmetic changes, the feminists go right to the heart of the matter in a declared war against God the Father.

The developed state of the case appears in a 1983 work, *Sexism and God-Talk* by Rosemary Ruether, whom I quote again as a revolutionary always honest about the goals of the revolution and always logical about their consequences. In her view, the priesthood, the classical theology to which it belongs, and the codified traditions of the Catholic religion are based on male rather than on universal human experience. The image of a Father God is a product of "the Judeo-Christian formation of the normative image of transcendent ego in the male God image." The "underside" of this image is the male conquest of nature "imaged as the conquest and transcendence of the Mother."[29] Patriarchal control over the womb is the first of the sins of patriarchy against the earth and its peoples. Hierarchical stratification with the Divine as apex is nothing more than a patriarchal tool for the control of society. Therefore, "the critique of hierarchy must become explicitly the critique of patriarchy."[30] Feminist theology attempts "to transform the dominant consciousness."[31] "Feminism represents a fundamental shift in the valuation of good and evil."[32] We must get rid of the parent image of God and become autonomous. Ruether sounds the true note of revolution: "Patriarchal theology uses the parent image for God to prolong spiritual infantilism as virtue and to make autonomy and assertion of free will a sin."[33] Even the attractive human person of Christ will no longer serve as a model of "redemptive personhood" for women because "the Christological symbols have been used to enforce male dominance."[34] "Must we not say that the very limitations of Christ as a male person must lead to the conclusion that he cannot represent redemptive personhood for them? That they must emancipate themselves from Jesus as redeemer and seek a new redemptive disclosure of God and of human possibility in female form?"[35] Ruether proposes that we call the divine principle "God/ess."

Feminists insist that, as a means of liberation, the people must reclaim the sacraments into their own administration. "Eucharist is not an objective piece of bread or a cup of wine that is magically transformed into the body and blood of Christ. Rather it is the people, the ecclesia who are being transformed into the body of the new humanity."[36] At the 1983 WomanChurch conference, Ruether, to ecstatic applause, described the historic Church as an "idol of masculinity" and expounded the feminist revolutionary vision of liberation in messianic language:

> We are WomanChurch, not in exile, but in exodus. We flee the thundering armies of Pharaoh. We are not waiting for a call to return to the land of slavery and to serve as altar girls in the temples of patriarchy. Our brother Jesus did not come to this earth to manufacture this idol and he is not represented by this idol. We cry out – horror, blasphemy, deceit, foul deed. We call our brothers [here she named several liberal Bishops who were in her audience] to flee with us from this idol with flashing eyes and smoking nostrils who is about to consume the earth. . . . Together let us break up this great idol and grind it into powder, dismantle the great leviathan of violence and misery . . . and transform it back into the means of peace and plenty, so that all the children of the earth can sit together at the banquet of life.[37]

Golly. And these are the women whom the bishops expect to placate by the changing of a few pronouns. Amazing stuff, and I can hear my readers saying, "extremist" and "unrepresentative." Not so. This language has reached the elementary schools, where I heard local children sing a hymn to "God our mother," and to the teaching of teachers – I heard Ted Schmidt, a leftist educator, refer thus to the Holy Spirit at a conference of Catholic teachers: "Let us pray to Her because She too lives in the hearts of millions of beautiful Russian people."[38] It appeared in the Canadian bishops' intervention delivered by Archbishop Louis-Albert Vachon to the 1983 synod in Rome: "Let us recognize the ravages of sexism, and our own male appropriation of Church institutions and numerous aspects of Christian life";[39] and in the official position of the Canadian bishops, enunciated by Archbishop James Hayes: "Our church comes out of a male-dominated tradition. It has been male organized, male led, male taught and male celebrated."[40] Territory that only a short time ago looked like the wilder shores of revolutionary fanaticism has now begun to look, even to the Catholic hierarchy, like civilized terra firma.

Which brings us to the prospects for the future. Can they be bright when bishops who should be performing exorcisms on women possessed of devils instead take tuition from them? Jesuit John O'Malley, in the article already quoted, recalls how earlier attempts to bring about a "major paradigm shift" within the Church failed because they did not manage to institutionalize the new vision: "Only if the shift received firm institutional grounding has it had long range effects and resulted in a fundamental readjustment of religious consciousness and Church order."[41] Has the new consciousness of the post-Vatican II revolution in the Catholic Church managed to ground itself institutionally to the extent that it cannot be reversed or expelled? It is common to speak of the West as living in the "post-Christian era." Must we now begin to describe ourselves as living "after Catholicism"?

&~&

NINE

THE COUNTER-REVOLUTION
BEGINS

&~&

What of the future? Thomas Sheehan thinks things look good for the revolution:

> Perhaps the current regime in Rome will slap a few more wrists in a futile effort to stop the liberal movements launched by the Second Vatican Council. But it is more likely that, as the Church approaches the beginning of its third millennium, things will continue to follow the trajectory of the last two decades; an entrenchment of conservative forces in their shrinking pockets of power; the vigorous advancement of liberal exegesis and theology in scholarly circles; and the equally vigorous pursuit of the social gospel where issues of politics and morality are concerned.[1]

On the face of it, the revolution has good reason to feel confident. The "liberal consensus" is in unchallenged control on the local and national levels of every aspect of Catholic life. Many bishops now openly support the goals of the revolution, in return for which the revolutionaries keep them in power in all the important positions in the national conferences. The understanding that only by electing candidates acceptable to the revolution will bishops' conferences be allowed to lead a quiet life leads, for example, to the election of "leading progressive" Bishop James Malone as president and national spokesman of the NCCB on the first ballot over nine other nominees, though it meant breaking a precedent by choosing a prelate below the rank of archbishop.[2] Malone later produced the report, which in the opinion of many was a whitewash, on the condition of the post-Vatican II American Church prepared for the Extraordinary Synod held in Rome in 1985.

In the CCCB, Bishop Remi de Roo, from very early a disciple of revolutionary theologians, also wields power far out of proportion to his qualifications or episcopal rank. He fronted for the radical *periti* on the *Winnipeg Statement*, and again as head of the Social Affairs Commission which in December 1982 issued the leftist New Year's Statement on the economy. The grey eminence behind Bishop de Roo is Dr. Tony Clarke, a far-left lay bureaucrat who is the secretary of the Social Affairs Commission. Clarke has made his bureau the most powerful and radical department of the CCCB, but unlike his American counterpart in the USCC/NCCB, Father Bryan Hehir, he rarely emerges into the limelight. It is Bishop de Roo who gets his picture taken. At the 1984 assembly of the CCCB, Bishop de Roo championed an abusive feminist intervention based on one thousand "womanstories" as "a magnificent document," urging the bishops to accept it along with the model of "a community church with power shared by the membership" that it demanded.[3] He now occupies the very important position of head of the pastoral team, which sets the CCCB's priorities.

In contrast, the revolution has effectively sidelined Cardinal G. Emmett Carter, who, though once a powerful progressive in the early stages of the revolution in the Canadian Church, came to have second thoughts about it. When Cardinal Carter charged that most of the bishops had been bypassed over the economic statement, Bishop de Roo and Gregory Baum (an adviser for the statement) retorted that he was wrong, and, very significantly, Monsignor Dennis Murphy, general secretary of the CCCB, publicly supported Baum's and Bishop de Roo's version of events.[4] Moreover, Murphy's successor as secretary of the CCCB is William Ryan, a very liberal Jesuit and former national superior of English-speaking Jesuits in Canada, who had warmly praised the economic statement: "This prophetic statement, which has the advantage of being a clear, unexpected clarion call."[5] In his new job he will direct for the bishops a study of the pastoral impact of the Pope's visit to Canada.

Cardinal Carter suffered a similar humiliation over the issue of the report on the role of women in the Church at the 1984 annual conference. In spite of his scathing intervention, "one jarring voice" as the Toronto *Globe and Mail* editorially put it, Bishops de Roo and Vachon bullied the rest of the bishops into giving the feminists everything they wanted. Ex-priest Denys Horgan, the *Globe*'s religion editor, in his coverage, which was hostile to Carter, laudatory of deRoo, and warm towards the feminists, called it "a classic confrontation between the powerful and the oppressed" and provided a neat example of how revolutionary solidarity works.[6]

Even on the local diocesan front, where it might be hoped that non-revolutionized bishops might try to impede the doctrinal revolution, there is paralysis. One example that is exercising me very much at the moment is the "parish renewal" program called RENEW, based on the organizing tactics of the radical political activist Saul Alinsky as developed by the equally radical bureaucrats of the diocese of Newark under

Archbishop Peter Gerety. This activity is meant to develop in concentric circles, beginning with a centre that is inevitably composed of the most committed members of every parish, the few who do all the work, the perennial readers, ushers, and collectors, the daily Mass goers. Most of these Catholics have withstood the cultural shock of the post-Vatican II upheaval. Their cosmology is still more or less in place. It won't be for much longer. The revolution is pulling out all the stops to convert them by an intensive re-education effort. I cannot discuss RENEW in any detail here; it is too vast. One local example must do, the recent "large group event" run by RENEW which involved a member of Thomas Sheehan's "liberal consensus," David M. Stanley, S.J.

Stanley was in our town for a series of three lectures on the Gospel and Acts of St. Luke. The so-called "Infancy Narratives," those chapters of St. Luke's Gospel that describe Christ's birth and early childhood, are a favourite target of the theological revolution. If their incredible hold on the religious imagination can be broken, the revolution knows that the battle is over. The demythologizing position of the "liberal consensus," in Sheehan's summary, is this: "Most likely, Mary told Jesus what she herself knew of his origins: that he had a natural father and was born not in Bethlehem but in Nazareth, indeed without the administration of angels, shepherds, and late-arriving wise men bearing gifts. She could have told her son the traditional nativity story only if she had managed to read, long before they were written, the inspiring but unhistorical Christmas legends that first appeared in the Gospels of Matthew and Luke some fifty years after her son died."[7] The jeering note in this passage is typical of Catholic liberal consensus "scholars"; they tolerate no such levity towards their own constructions, having, as I earlier noted, provided for themselves a stable of bishops ready to defend their new orthodoxy against criticism.

So Father Stanley arrived in the sticks (Welland, Ontario) with the new good news: the Gospels are inspiring but unhistorical legends. For the believing and unsophisticated RENEW audience, present at an elaborately official catechetical event, Stanley was far more destructive than Hans Küng would have been. Küng would have provoked his audience, been outrageous, shocked his hearers, and been hissed by them. Stanley was so careful, so reasonable, so priestly. (Theologians intending to subvert an orthodox audience always wear their clericals; Jesuit William Ryan, appearing in unaccustomed clerical dress for a debate with me, said to me with disarming candour that he always wore it when facing "people like you.") Stanley undermined the historicity of the accounts of Christ's lineage and birth with the utmost delicacy, presenting the usual liberal ideological assumptions modestly, not as his own but as "the scholarly consensus": the Gospels are not biography but autobiography, recording each evangelist's "faith journey"; the sayings and deeds of Jesus as recorded in the Bible reflect each evangelist's understanding of what Jesus meant; none of the writers knew Jesus, since they lived several generations after His time (the average life-span in biblical times being, he said, only twenty-eight years!); the Gospels grew out of the felt needs of the early Christian community.

After he finished his masterful demolition exercise, there was a long uneasy silence. Finally, one woman, her voice quivering, asked: "You seem to be saying that the evangelists put words into Jesus's mouth. What does this do for my faith?" A sophisticated and honest question, piercing to the heart of the modern problem. Stanley's evasive answer seemed to be tailored to an audience of what he must have considered hicks: "Well, you know that the Gospels come to us in Greek. So of course the Bible puts words into Jesus's mouth. Jesus didn't speak Greek! Jesus spoke Aramaic!" And then he put his hand on his hip, assumed the stance and leer of the caricature Jew and grated: "Vell, I'm tellingk ya . . . !" I am happy to record that this piece of liberal scholarship drew only a nervous titter.

After the lecture, I talked to several holy, innocent, elderly Catholics, the backbone of RENEW in our parish. "I don't know," one said. "We used to read St. Luke in a Bible group with Sister —— a few years ago. But this is a whole different approach. I don't know what to make of it." I did. In my first rage I intended to make a public row about it as I've done on earlier occasions, obeying Newman's dictum that if we allow men to speak against the Church and its teaching without remonstrating with them, "We are deficient in jealous custody of the Revealed Truths which Christ has left us."

Then I thought, the hell with it. Let's all stop saying, as my friends did, "I wonder if the bishop knows." Yes, the bishop knows. He authorized RENEW, put up the large amount of money required, hired the radical young priest who directs it and who hired Stanley. The twenty-five or so priests who were at the lectures know. We all know. What are we going to do about it? God knows. My own useful contribution to the restoration of Catholic doctrine was to quarrel bitterly with two priest friends who also know and who do nothing. "But what *can* we do?" "You can get some priests together and go and tell the bishop." "But the bishop *knows!*"

This is the fact: whatever is left of the heart's core of the Catholic faithful is being subverted with the approval of its shepherds. That is hard to accept, but when one sits in a school auditorium in Welland, Ontario, listening under diocesan auspices to stuff like Stanley's or hears a fool of a nun chirrup after another recent local program for teachers: "I'm comfortable with thinking that the Resurrection wasn't a historical event. I can live with that," one has to admit that the revolution has succeeded in penetrating to the grass roots of Catholicism. They don't come any grassier than in Welland, Ontario. That this is the situation everywhere in the Church is the hard reality any counter-revolution has to face.

So, what are the chances of a Catholic counter-revolution, given the present unhopeful situation? Good, in the light of Catholic history. There is historical precedent for counter-revolution carried out with great success after other desperate schisms. It has been a pattern in Catholic history that general councils seem to be followed by periods of serious disorder. At the Council of Nicaea (325 A.D.), for example, all but two of the bishops signed the creedal formula that defined the divinity of Christ and repudiated Arianism, the Nicene Creed which we say today. Yet by 360 A.D., at the pseudo-Council of Constantinople, the bishops with "lamentable unanimity" had repudiated it; in St. Jerome's words, "The whole world groaned to find itself Arian."[8] In that crisis of faith, and in similar crises since then, the Roman primacy mounted and carried through a successful restoration of Catholic order. There are indications that a counter-revolution is already under way, centred upon the strong leadership of John Paul II.[9]

There can be no doubt that the election of the Polish Cardinal Wojtyla to the papacy was the critical turning point in the revolution, signalling the move of the magisterium from the defensive onto the offensive. The circumstances of his election, after the sudden death after only one month in office of John Paul I, the mild, unknown compromise candidate, generated an almost superstitious awe. It was for many as if the Holy Ghost, impatient with the cardinals' temporizing, had said firmly, "Now try that again!" John Paul II is in every way an extraordinary figure who has electrified the imagination of the world and who seems destined to loom as large in Catholic history as Pope Leo I, or Pope Gregory I (both deservedly called "the Great") whose times these much resemble. Both sides in the revolution see him as the most important factor in the future of the Church, and there is evidence that he believes himself destined by God to lead a counter-reformation. Shortly after his election on the feast of St. Charles Borromeo, one of the greatest figures of the Counter-Reformation, he wrote:

My beloved parents . . . could never have foreseen . . . that this name would open up for their child a path to the great events of today's Church. St. Charles! How often I have knelt before his relics in Milan Cathedral, how often I have thought about his life, contemplating in my mind the gigantic figure of this man of God and servant of the Church, Charles Borromeo, Cardinal, Bishop of Milan, and a man of the Council. He is one of the great protagonists of the deep reform of the sixteenth-century Church, carried out by the Council of Trent, which will always remain linked with his name. . . .

My patron saint! In his name my parents, my country, intended to prepare me right from the beginning for an extraordinary service of the Church, in the context of today's Council, with the many tasks united with its implementation, and also in all the experiences and sufferings of modern man.[10]

The revolution within the Catholic Church and its supporters without have from his election directed at John Paul II a stream of vituperation unparalleled in modern times. One constant theme is his Polish nationality, how it limits him, gives him tunnel vision, blinds him to the complexities of the Christian situation in the West. The ironic truth, however, is that the accident of his Polish experience has uniquely qualified him to deal with a hostile ideology, institutionally grounded in every area of government and culture, unchallengeable on its own terms. This man "born in the eye of the world's storm," as Paul Johnson puts it in his sympathetic study,[11] learned not only how to keep a private faith alive, but how to establish that faith as the victorious force of moral and spiritual liberation from materialist systems, whether on the left or the right. John Paul II knows how to reach the hearts of the faithful over the heads of jailors; he is used, too, to dealing with the traitorous clerks who form the government-sponsored national associations of "peace priests." He understands the tensions of the modern world.

Even an outsider who doesn't acknowledge the Holy Ghost's hand in the choice of John Paul II must at any rate see the election of this particular man at this particular time as evidence that the Catholic Church possesses extraordinary and perennial powers of survival of external and internal catastrophes, of resistance to secularization, and of unexpected rejuvenation that make it different from other human institutions. The election of John Paul II marks the point at which the idea of counter-revolution became tenable. I shall here touch briefly on the Pope's counter-revolutionary program under two heads, doctrine and discipline.

DOCTRINE

Catholics who suffer under the alien cultural norms imposed at present on Catholic life, especially in the liturgy, are impatient with the Pope for tolerating these, and even participating in them, as he does in the dreadful Masses arranged around him on his travels. But the Pope puts first things first. For him doctrine is the all-important thing. It is not that he does not understand or care about externals; he knows from his experience in Poland that symbols are of life and death importance. Where he can, as in Rome, he forbids Communion in the hand and enforces the wearing of religious dress. But he also knows that in Catholicism it is the doctrine that creates and sustains Catholic culture, Catholic societal behaviour, rather than the other way around, as modernists would have it. Clear and strongly maintained doctrine will quickly work to develop a culture that reflects it.

Immediately upon his accession, he began the precedent-shattering personal missionary travels which are the distinguishing public feature of his papacy. In January 1979, he presided over the Puebla (Mexico) Conference on justice and liberation. A similar conference at Medellin (Colombia) ten years earlier, unrestrained by Paul VI's frail presence, had marked the triumphal emergence of liberation theology as the new frame of reference for the Church's thinking about existence. The revolution had hailed Medellin as "the new Pentecost" and intended that at Puebla the new concepts would become doctrine. John Paul defused Puebla by his formidable presence. His speeches enunciated the working principles of his papacy: he affirmed the divinity of Christ, the hierarchical nature of the Church, its divine mission to teach objective truth, freedom from sin as the true meaning of liberation. He established the pattern of his social and political thought, denouncing liberation theology's secularization of the Christian message, but at the same time demanding that Catholics intensify their work for human justice.

In the years since Puebla, John Paul II has visited dozens of countries, carrying out in the process an incredible recatechizing of the world. He has done this single-handedly, the loneliness of his witness accentuated to an almost magical quality by the fact that his catechesis reaches the world, mainly through television, in a direct and singular contact. The cameras ignore the bishops and the crowds and centre on this one commanding priestly figure, symbol of timeless Catholic authority. It cannot be accident that this brilliant modern, who believes with all his mind and with all his heart, should also have an uncanny ability to project this faith utterly convincingly through the technology of modern communications. He is riveting on television; one television critic wrote during the Pope's September 1984 visit to Canada that the union of this man and the "iconographic medium" of television is "a match made in heaven."[12] Therefore, the secular media, though they hate him, cover him obsessively and with total effectiveness for his message. He is accused of manipulating the medium of television, and it is certainly true that he has triumphantly used this most potent political and cultural tool against the purposes of the secularizing revolution. And he does it, incredibly, simply by saying Mass. In Canada, in the United States, in Poland, he used Christianity's oldest mass medium to teach the world again about the Sacrifice of Christ and the Mystery of the Church.

When the Pope is off-screen, the media pull themselves together and present a line-up of hostile commentators, especially Catholics made virulent by feelings of guilt, to attack his world view. Television coverage in particular revealed as nothing else has so graphically done the face of the open but undeclared schism ravaging unchecked within the Church. During the U.S. visit, for instance, the institutional solidity of the revolution was alarmingly obvious. Here it was clearly the Pope, with his reiteration of the ancient faith, who was the dissenter, the disturbing radical; Mercy Sister Theresa Kane, who as president of the Leadership Conference of Women Religious, speaking for all the nuns in the United States, rebuked him humiliatingly to his face for upholding the Church's position on ordination, and Redemptorist Superior Francis X. Murphy, "Xavier Rynne," who knocked him on national television behind his back, were the pained upholders of the new orthodoxy. "But hasn't he set the Church back fifty years?" asked one CBS reporter in testament of John Paul's personal counter-revolutionary offensive.[13]

Yet what remains in the memory is not the sour heterodoxy of the parallel magisterium but the icon-screen image of the Pope, his arms outspread against the backdrop of the Capitol in Washington, proclaiming, "Human life is forever!" Or of him getting off the plane and saying to the Governor General of Canada: "I am the shepherd who follows in the footsteps of the first shepherd, the Apostle Peter. I am a father, which is what the word 'Pope' means. . . . My word . . . will offer you the light and the strength of faith in Jesus Christ as proclaimed by Peter himself in Galilee: 'You are the Christ, the Son of the living God.' "[14] "I don't believe I'm hearing this on the CBC," said one of the young people with whom I was watching this scene. Or of all of us on our knees before the television set, of all strange secular places, as the Pope, alone with the Body of Christ, turned against the windy sky in a slow circle to show Him to us and to other invisible millions. In the Canadian visit alone, there were twelve days of this iconography, twelve hours a day in the nationally owned Canadian Broadcasting Company's remarkable coverage. (My one regret was that Marshall McLuhan, the great convert Catholic, was not alive to enjoy this brilliant counter-revolutionary coup carried out in the service of the ancient faith to which he had converted in middle life, through the means of the modern communications technology McLuhan understood better than anyone else.) John Paul II, through his missionary travels and his understanding of modernity, has dispelled the post-Conciliar confusion. Everyone knows once more exactly what the Catholic Church believes and teaches in the name of Jesus Christ.

To my mind, the Pope's most interesting and important doctrinal contribution is his move to restore and strengthen the connection between supernatural and natural revelation, between grace and nature. I discussed earlier how the natural law provided Catholicism with a second seat of appeal complementary to and corroborative of the written scriptures. It is this continuity of faith and nature that makes up "the fullness of the Catholic universe," in Peter Berger's words, and which has served to arrest the process of secularization within Catholicism, whereas Protestantism's reliance on *sola Scriptura* has produced the outcome Berger describes: "With nothing remaining 'in between' a radically transcendent God and a radically immanent world except this one channel, the sinking of the latter into implausibility left an empirical reality in which, indeed, 'God is dead.' "[15] At its beginning, Catholicism carried out "a re-naturalization of ethics – a return to the divine-human continuity,"[16] thereby providing historic Catholicism with a "plausibility structure," to use Berger's phrase, both "massive and durable." It is fascinating to see the modern Catholic Church, in the creation theology of John Paul II, counter the current rationalist attack from within by re-emphasizing the link between nature and supernature.

Long before his election, Karol Wojtyla, by specialization a phenomenologist, by inclination a personalist, had begun to work out in *Love and Responsibility* (1960), the brilliant and original explanation of the relationship of men and women with each other and with God which he now calls "the theology of the body." Beginning soon after his election, in an extended commentary delivered piecemeal to the weekly general audiences the Pope holds when in Rome, he has been working out before a succession of bemused tourists a new synthesis of natural and sacred anthropology. Beginning at the beginning, in Genesis, before the Fall of Man, the Pope finds the psychological and spiritual roots of Catholic moral teaching on sexuality, procreation, marriage, contraception, abortion, and the dignity of the human person. In *Sign of Contradiction*, he described the Book of Genesis as "the key to understanding the world of today, both its roots and its extremely radical . . . affirmations and denials." In Genesis, "that fundamental ensemble of facts and situations," we "find the reason why man is man" and how by the "communion of persons" man becomes the image of God.[17]

From Genesis, the Pope moved through other books of the Bible. By 1984 he had reached the Church's reasons for the ban on artificial birth control. In a ten-week series of reflections, delivered this time to the summer crowd in St. Peter's Square, the Pope continued to develop his moral anthropology. It is impossible to summarize here the depth and richness of his theology of the body; it has begun to appear in collected form, the first volume being entitled *The Original Unity of Man and Woman: Catechesis on the Book of Genesis*,[18] and though received with the expected derision by the revolution, it has begun to make its influence felt, sometimes in unexpected quarters: the archdiocese of

153

Toronto, for instance, where Cardinal Carter's major pastoral letter (January 1984) *Upon The Sacrament of Priestly Orders*, based its Christology and its support of the traditional male priesthood upon the radical sexual differentiation built by God into creation, a clear borrowing from the Pope's theology of the body.

Doctrine in general is not defined until it has come under attack. Often, as in the cases of contraception or ordination, the traditional teaching has become so internalized through long assenting practice that when attack suddenly comes there are no compelling arguments, other than the fact of the tradition, ready for articulation. The arguments adduced by Paul VI's defence of the traditional doctrine on sex and procreation, other than the argument from authority, were found incomplete even by some of its defenders. John Paul II's theology fills the rational and emotional gap opened, or rather revealed, by the revolution's attempt to secularize human life, that is, to remove human conduct from the jurisdiction of the sacred. It provides arguments attractive to the religious imagination and acceptable to right reason, and, most important for the future of unity with Protestants, answers the question, "But where is it found in Scripture?" It is found everywhere in Scripture, as the Pope shows us. In this radical return to the beginnings, ethics will not be allowed to escape from nature on the one hand or grace on the other, but will continue to make manifest "the divine-human continuity."

This Pope's repeated, solemn, ubiquitous, public reaffirmation of the historic doctrine on contraception makes it highly unlikely that this teaching, together with the totality of the Catholic sexual ethics of which it is the keystone, can be rejected or retired in the future, in any way less than suicidal for the Church. It has become clear that John Paul II regards the doctrine on contraception as an infallible doctrine of the Church, requiring the assent of theological faith. This position is contrary to the opinion of Paul VI, as expressed in the statements at the time of *Humanae Vitae*, but what other interpretation can be made of John Paul II's statement to a natural family planning conference in Rome in September 1983 that "those who practice contraception or even believe it to be lawful are refusing objectively to acknowledge God"? Statements like this have led to widespread speculation that the Pope means to define the teaching on contraception as infallible in an *ex cathedra* pronouncement.

John Paul II seems to have effectively checked the institutional grounding of this particular part of the revolution's proposed "paradigm shift." Critics like Andrew Greeley lament that the Pope has effectively painted the Church into a corner from which it cannot withdraw with respect. Even the most convinced and obedient Catholics recognize the extent of the secular breach in the Catholic world view and the difficulty, if not impossibility, of repairing it. Both sides agree on gloomy short-term prospects for the Church, the difference for the believer being that the prognosis includes the conviction that the Church is divinely right about the nature and purpose of human sexuality, and that therefore the Pope's corner is shared by the Holy Ghost.

The public catechesis, missionary travels, and "theology of the body" are original features of the Pope's doctrinal counter-revolution. As well, there is a steady stream of papal teachings and legislation issued by the various congregations of the curia under his firm direction. I mention here only a few of what seem to me the most important:

In liturgy:
• The *Apostolic Letter on the Eucharist, Dominicae Cenae*, February 24, 1980, contained this amazing, unprecedented apology by Pope John Paul II: "I would like to ask forgiveness – in my own name and in the name of all of you, venerable and dear brothers in the Episcopate – for everything which, for whatever reason, through whatever human weakness, impatience, or negligence, and also through the at times partial, one-sided and erroneous applications of the directives of the Second Vatican Council, may have caused scandal and disturbance concerning the interpretation of the doctrine and veneration due to this great Sacrament. And I pray the Lord Jesus that in the future we may avoid in our manner of dealing with this sacred mystery anything which would weaken or disorient in any way the sense of reverence and love that exists in our faithful people."
• The October 15, 1984, permission by the Sacred Congregation of the Sacraments and Divine Worship for the qualified reintroduction of the banned Tridentine Rite Latin Mass stated: "The Pope, who is the father of the entire Church, . . . wishes to be responsive to such groups of priests and faithful" who, while accepting the validity of the new Mass, "remained attached" to the old. The revolution was outraged. The timing of the surprise late-evening press conference which announced the decision seemed calculated to irritate the heads of the world's liturgical commissions who were then gathering in Rome to celebrate the twentieth anniversary of the *Constitution on the Sacred Liturgy*. Father George Austin, chairman of the theology department and liturgical expert at Catholic University of America, said: "I see it as a terrible move. It will undermine the changes in the liturgy. . . . It belongs in another period of time." Father John Gurrieri, director of the liturgy secretariat of the American bishops, told the *Washington Post*: "I first heard about the latest Vatican directive when I opened the *Post* at breakfast. I nearly choked over my coffee. . . . By reforming the liturgy we reformed the Church." One of the liturgists gathered in Rome to discuss the theme "The Liturgical Reforms: Twenty Years After: Approval and Perspective" called the permission for the old Mass "the biggest act of betrayal in the Church since Judas."[19]

But the counter-revolution was jubilant. After twenty years we have the Mass back. Permission as yet is spotty, since implementation of the Indult was left up to the local bishop. My bishop, Thomas Fulton of St. Catharines, was generous. He restored the Mass without strings, and came and said the first one for us on July 14, 1985. We packed the chapel and sang the *Missa de angelis* and everybody wept. For the first time in many years I felt like kissing a bishop's hand as one used to, and I did so. We have the Tridentine Latin Mass every Sunday now. Oh, frabjous day.

• The September 8, 1983, Congregation for the Doctrine of the Faith *Letter to the Bishops of the Catholic Church on Certain Questions Concerning the Minister of the Eucharist* condemned "the erroneous conception that persons other than ordained priests can celebrate the mystery of the Eucharist and consecrate the Host." The letter was taken as an attack on the theories of Edward Schillebeeckx, in particular on his recent work, *Ministry, Leadership in the Community of Christ*. The letter also took aim at aberrations like the WomanChurch feminist liturgies and of the increasingly common "eucharistic communities" of women.

• In 1983, the Congregation of the Sacraments and Divine Worship announced that it had earlier rejected a 1980 decision by the U.S. bishops to "adopt eucharistic prayers revised to end the exclusively male tone of the original language."[20]

In catechetics:
• In April 1984, Cardinal Joseph Ratzinger, prefect of the Congregation for the Doctrine of the Faith, ordered the radical Archbishops Gerety (Newark) and Hunthausen (Seattle) to withdraw their *imprimatur* (episcopal assurance that the work in question contains no doctrinal or moral error) from, respectively, *Christ Among Us*, by former Paulist priest Anthony Wilhelm, and *Sexual Morality*, by Sulpician Father Philip Keane. Both bishops complied; Gerety, on Ratzinger's orders, told Paulist Press, publisher of both books, not to market or reprint Wilhelm's best-selling (1,600,000 copies) book, for seventeen years the staple of the catechetical revolution. *National Catholic Reporter*, reacting hysterically to the shock of the first official attack on the revolution's hitherto unchallenged domination of catechetics, initiated a continuing watch on "the chill factor being felt in certain circles of the U.S. Church."[21] A recent *NCR* roundup of new books was headed "Books To Read Before the Burning."[22]

In religious life:
• In April 1983, a papal commission was set up under Archbishop John Quinn (San Francisco) to study religious life in the United States, because of "the influence they have exerted on religious life through-

156

out the world." Perhaps not expecting much from this commission, given Quinn's constant assurances that there was nothing amiss in U.S. religious life, and the presence on the commission of radicals like Sister Bette Moslander and Father Michael Buckley, s.j., signers of petitions against the Pope, the Congregation for Religious issued in 1983 the statement *Essential Elements of Religious Life*. Among the essentials the Vatican listed were religious dress, cloistered areas in convents, community life, clearly defined united apostolates, and obedience to the Pope. The National Coalition of American Nuns (NCAN) rejected the statement as "sexist and classist."[23] Moreover, NCAN urged American religious to consider non-canonical status, outside the jurisdiction of Rome. "We do not need the support of the institutional Church."[24] The Conference of Major Superiors of Men rebuked Rome's "feudal, anti-modern authoritarianism."[25] However, 134 superiors of the Institute for Religious Life backed the papal commission's mandate in a letter to all American bishops.[26]

• Beginning in 1980, the Vatican began to enforce the prohibition against priests in politics contained in the Council documents and in the upcoming Code of Canon Law. Robert Drinan, s.j., prominent leftist Massachusetts Democrat (May 1980), and Father Bob Ogle, NDP member of the Canadian parliament (February 1984), were ordered not to run for re-election. Both obeyed.

• In 1983, after Vatican pressure, Detroit Archbishop Edmund Szoka ordered Mercy Sister Agnes Mansour to resign her post as head of the Michigan Department of Social Services because she would have to handle abortion funding (she supported such funding for the poor),[27] and Providence Bishop Louis Gelineau ordered Mercy Sister Arlene Violet to cease her bid for re-election as attorney-general of Rhode Island.[28] Both nuns chose instead to renounce their vows and leave their order. The radical auxiliary bishop of Detroit, Thomas Gumbleton, speaking at a RENEW session on social justice in Ohio, claimed that the Church had treated Mansour unjustly.[29]

• In December 1984, the Jesuit General, after much Vatican urging, expelled Father Fernando Cardenal from the order after his refusal to quit his post in the Sandinista government of Nicaragua.[30]

• In October 1983, the Vatican required Mercy Sister Theresa Kane to instruct her order's sixty-four hospitals to stop doing tubal ligations for contraceptive purposes.[31]

• In a decree of February 2, 1984, the Congregation for Religious ruled that Canon Law took precedent over the particular rules of individual communities where the two conflicted.[32]

Canon Law:
• The new Code of Canon Law came into effect November 27, 1983. If the revolutionary paradigm shift were to be institutionally grounded

anywhere, it had to be here, in the *lex fundamentalis* of the universal Church. It was not. John Paul II presided over its later drafts personally, in over twenty-four personal sessions with his own hand-picked group of experts. He reportedly sent the crucial provisions on marriage back fifteen times for revision, and personally scrutinized every one of the code's 1,752 provisions. The revolution reacted angrily to the new code. Speakers at the annual meeting of the prestigious Canon Law Society of America (CLSA) in 1982 attacked it as "historically dated," "anachronistic, inappropriate, ominous, regressive," to be interpreted only "within the larger context of the renewed ecclesiology of Vatican Council II," or better still, "to be ignored, which is what it deserves."[33]

The liturgical bureaucracy of the CCCB couldn't restrain its fury. Father Patrick Byrne, editor of the *National Bulletin on Liturgy*, lamented that "the prophets of doom were manoeuvring while the children of light were sleeping, in order to close the window that John XXIII opened." He charged the new code with a "lack of balance" in its treatment of the Mass: "It seems strange to find the Mass called a 'sacrifice' nine times" while "the term *banquet* is not used here at all. . . . Should one be tempted to suspect that some mandarins had axes to grind, or windows to close?"[34] Obviously, very good news indeed for the counter-revolution. For perhaps the first time since the *Constitution on the Sacred Liturgy* had been passed, traditionalist Catholics felt able to praise a Vatican initiative. "Dawn of Hope: the New Code," exulted Bryan Houghton, an English traditionalist priest. "I shall know that, long after my death, the Church shall once more be ruled by law."[35]

In politics:
• The Pope, having spent his life dealing with totalitarian systems, has no illusions about Marxism. The first political policy of his papacy was the ending of Paul VI's too conciliatory *Ostpolitik*, which had resulted, for example, in the forced resignation of the heroic Cardinal Mindszenty in favour of the Hungarian government's choice, Cardinal Lekai, as primate of Hungary. John Paul II has no time for "peace priests" and has made no more appointments from among them or their sympathizers. (He is said to have indicated his disapproval of Lekai by pointedly ignoring him at the conclave that resulted in his election.[36])

In 1973, Rosemary Ruether dismissed the possibility of "some sectarian split" in Catholicism on the grounds that "the relation of religious ideology to political power that caused every ideological change to be expressed in separate churches no longer exists in the same way. Therefore the reasons that were paramount in forcing ecclesiastical division do not obtain in Catholicism today."[37] I disagreed then, suggesting that the growing Marxist wing in the Catholic Church in Central and South America might very well ally itself with the new Communist dictatorships and under certain ambitious prelates form national "popular churches," in revolt from Rome.[38] In Nicaragua, whose Marxist junta boasts four Catholic priests in high office, the "popular church" disrupted the Pope's Mass with government-arranged demonstrations. The Nicaraguan situation is only the visible tip of an extremely serious problem that is beginning to occupy the Vatican's attention. The stakes involved are huge and the prospect of national schisms on the scale of those of the Protestant Reformation looking ever more likely.

Since the late 1960s, Latin American theologians have been developing a revolutionary "theology of liberation," so named after a book of that title by the leading proponent of the theory, Father Gustavo Gutierrez, a Peruvian theologian.[39] Liberation theology is a comprehensive system of thinking about existence which offers, in Cardinal Ratzinger's words, "a new global interpretation of Christianity" in which all reality is seen as political. Theology must, therefore, concern itself with political, practical ends, chief among these being the liberation of human beings from political and economic injustices. The ideological theory underlying liberation theology's view of social reality is that people are everywhere oppressed because of "unjust structures" kept in place by the beneficiaries of the class system. Therefore, the basic datum of liberation theology is the existence of the class struggle.

The original contribution of liberation theology to the familiar Marxist analysis of society is its use of the concepts and language of Christian faith to explain and justify political revolution and social violence. Liberation theology reads the Bible in an exclusively political way. The Kingdom of God is secularized; the "poor" of the Gospel are identified with the Marxist proletariat; salvation, which in Christian theology means liberation from personal sin, is now taken to mean liberation from temporal injustice. The lived experience of the suffering community is both source and test of Revelation. Power in society and ministry in the Church come from the people, who can no longer tolerate subordination to the dominant class. The "community from below" *is* the Church; from it flow sacraments and ministry.

There are now many thousands of "*communidades de base*" in Latin America, seventy thousand in Brazil alone. Latin American hierarchies are bitterly divided over the question of liberation theology and base communities. The powerful Brazilian cardinals Aloisio Lorscheider and Paulo Evaristo Arns accompanied Brazilian liberation theologian Leonardo Boff to a Roman inquiry into his theories in 1984 and defended him to Cardinal Joseph Ratzinger. On the other side, Brazilian cardinals Rossi and Sales, and Colombian Cardinal Alfonso Lopez Trujillo oppose liberation theology and pressed the Vatican to act against it. In March 1983, Cardinal Sales withdrew "canonical mission" from two leading liberation theologians, Clodovis Boff and Antonio Moser, professors at Rio de Janeiro's pontifical university.

The huge Catholic populations, the markedly uneven social conditions, the lack of modern structures of industry and capital, and the volatile political arrangements make very possible the emergence of national "popular churches" at the service of revolution from the left. The Pope is deeply concerned with the Latin American situation. "He has told us," one Latin American theologian is quoted as saying, "that he thinks liberation theology is going to cause a schism in Latin America and that he isn't going to let that happen."[40] I touched earlier on the cooling effect his presence had at Puebla. During his Third World visits (on which, with the exception of Nicaragua, he has been received rapturously) he warned the poor against accepting the fatal solutions of Marxism, but also passionately and angrily demanded that the rich and powerful be socially just. In one striking example, in the Philippines, he delivered his anti-Marxist message standing in the filth of the worst slum in Manila; with President Ferdinand Marcos sitting beside him, he denounced the government's extension of martial law and breaches of human rights.

In 1984, three leading liberation theologians, Gustavo Gutierrez, Jon Sobrino, and Leonardo Boff, were summoned to Rome to explain their ideas in person. (In 1985, Boff was "silenced," that is, forbidden to lecture or publish.)

In March 1984, Cardinal Joseph Ratzinger published a comprehensive attack on liberation theology in an Italian magazine, singling out for criticism Hugo Assman, Gustavo Gutierrez, Jon Sobrino, and Ignacia Ellacuria, linking their ideas, interestingly, not only with Marx, but with the rationalist theology of the great German modernist, Rudolf Bultmann.[41]

On August 6, 1984, symbolically on the Feast of the Transfiguration which commemorates Jesus's revealing Himself as God, the Congregation for the Doctrine of the Faith issued under Cardinal Ratzinger's name an *Instruction on Certain Aspects of the 'Theology of Liberation,'* a sustained attack on the theology's methods and world view. This is the most important document to issue from the Vatican since *Humanae Vitae* in 1968. For the first time the entire activating philosophy of the Catholic revolution is outlined and condemned as "a practical negation" of the faith of the Church (VI, 9). The *Instruction* recognizes "the global and all-embracing character of the theology of liberation" (X, 2) which "discredits *in advance*" (Ratzinger's italics) the arguments of the hierarchy and the Roman magisterium by means of a "new interpretation" of the Scriptures, "exclusively political," which "touches the whole of the Christian mystery" (X, 12, 13).

The importance of this statement cannot be exaggerated. It has enormous political importance for the future of western society, giving notice that the flirtation with Marxism of important elements in the

160

Church is officially over. For the first time since Pius XII, Marxism is explicitly condemned in a Vatican document. Communist regimes are called "this shame of our time. . . . While claiming to bring them freedom, these régimes keep whole nations in conditions of servitude unworthy of mankind" (VI, 10). This splendid honesty, or "gratuitous insult" as Peter Hebblethwaite angrily described it,[42] makes up for the silence of the Council and the fellow-travelling of the post-Conciliar years.

The revolutionary consciousness has come so to dominate modern Catholic theology that the Church's restatement of Christian principles sounds almost reactionary: "The New Testament does not require some change in the political or social condition as a prerequisite to this freedom [from the slavery of sin]" (IV, 13). "The acute need for radical reforms . . . should not let us lose sight of the fact that the source of injustice is in the hearts of men" and only by "interior conversion" will "that social change be brought about which will truly be in the service of man" (XI, 8). The *Instruction* criticized the ivory-tower romanticism of the theologians of revolution: "A major fact of our time ought to evoke the reflection of all those who would sincerely work for the true liberation of their brothers: millions of our own contemporaries legitimately yearn to recover those basic freedoms of which they were deprived by totalitarian and atheistic regimes which came to power by violent and revolutionary means, precisely in the name of the liberation of the people. . . . Those who, perhaps inadvertently, make themselves accomplices of similar enslavements betray the very poor they mean to help" (XI, 10). The last sentence of that passage was taken to mean the Church leadership of Nicaragua, whose co-operation with the Communist guerrilla movement against Anastasio Somoza brought the present Marxist government to power, and who now find themselves the target of persecution.

It was incredibly heartening to see the Church at last denounce the "fatal illusion" that Marxist revolution will "give birth to 'a new man' " and a world of justice (XI, 9). The ugliest feature of the Catholic revolution has been its totally selective indignation, its obscene sycophancy towards any revolution from the left, however brutal, however ill-disposed towards Christianity. How sickened many Catholics have been by the political behaviour of the official social-justice organizations in the post-Conciliar years – all the feverish energy displayed against the South and for the North during the Vietnam War; all the foolish nuns leading boycotts against coffee harvested in Portuguese Africa, against South African grapes, against Nestlés – yet when the curtain came down upon the miserable "liberated" countries, not another hard word was uttered about those particular pieces of geography. Angola, Mozambique, Vietnam, Cuba, Cambodia – where are they now? What, no nuns in front of the Russian embassy? A prize is hereby offered to anyone who can find a serious attack, *any* attack, on a Communist regime, anywhere in the enormous "educational" output of the huge official rich Canadian Catholic Organization for Development and Peace, especially in its newspaper *The Global Village Voice*, distributed free (and paid for by levies from parish funds) to all Catholic churches. (U.S. and British Catholics may substitute as required from their own social-justice publications.)

The Pope is a man neither of the right nor of the left; he is as critical of capitalist materialism as he is of socialist. The *Instruction* states that the warning against liberation theology "should in no way be interpreted as a disavowal of those who want to respond generously . . . to the 'preferential option for the poor' " nor to excuse "those who maintain an attitude of neutrality in the face of the tragic and pressing problems of human misery and injustice" (Introduction). No one could judge this Pope neutral, although in political arrangements he does what the Church always does, coexists with the city of this world, where possible choosing the system that is the lesser of evils, which allows the Church the greatest freedom to teach its redemptive message.

I think it very unlikely that this or any future pope will accept the argument of certain neo-conservative Christians that the system of capitalist democracy is inherently moral and altruistic, but he obviously does accept that it is morally superior to the alternative system, in that its "fallout," as someone recently put it, includes the very great social virtues of peace, freedom, and widely diffused plenty. Which is why John Paul II, an adamant critic of the arms race, summoned the bishops who were drafting the 1983 American "Peace Pastoral" to Rome to prevent them from declaring that nuclear deterrence was morally unacceptable and from demanding a unilateral freeze. At Puebla, John Paul II, in what Paul Johnson describes as his "majestic exposition of the Church's view on 'political commitment,' "[43] declared that human liberation depended upon "the truth about Jesus the Savior, the truth about the Church, and the truth about man and his dignity." These truths in their entirety are just as unacceptable to the post-Christian West as they are to the Communist East, a true sign that this Pope has brought the Church back to where it should be.

The statement on liberation theology is also of great importance for the doctrinal future of the Church. In considering liberation theology in the way Pius X approached modernism, as a synthesis of errors, each item depending on an underlying conception that is wrong and heretical, the Roman magisterium has begun the process of identification, isolation, and expulsion by which modernism was controlled at the end of the nineteenth century. The first ritual moves have been made on each side – Roman investigation has begun of certain key liberation theologians; and charges have been made by defenders of liberation theology that Rome "has made up a system which does not exist,"[44] exactly the same claim made by the modernists and their present defenders. In the present crisis, the revolutionary theology is getting more hierarchical support than did modernism. Not surprisingly, prominent Brazilian bishops publicly criticized Rome for bypassing collegiality and for Rome's own historical sins. In Cardinal Arns' province of São Paulo, twenty-eight bishops published a document affirming the existence of the class struggle and countering certain of the Vatican's criticisms of liberation theology.[45] Equally unsurprisingly, Colombia's bishops warmly agreed with the Vatican.[46] In June 1984, the editorial board of the radical theological journal *Concilium*, the revolution's *L'Osservatore Romano*, issued a strong statement expressing solidarity with Third World and feminist "movements of liberation and with their theology."[47] *Concilium*'s board is a roll call of the revolution's leadership – Hans Küng, Gregory Baum, Edward Schillebeeckx, Leonardo Boff, Marie-Dominique Chenu, Johannes Metz, David Tracy, Elizabeth Schussler-Fiorenza, John Coleman, Virgilio Elizondo, Gustavo Gutierrez, Jurgen Moltmann. . . . In October 1984, in two speeches, to a group of visiting Ecuadoran bishops, and to a plenary session of the Sacred Congregation for the Clergy, the Pope warned against the "serious danger" to Church unity posed by "basic Christian communities" and laid down rules to keep them from becoming an alternative to the institutional Church.[48]

These are only the opening shots of what is going to be a long and dirty war, one that will decide, once again, what the Church believes, how it should be governed, and by whom.

DISCIPLINE

The second heading under which the counter-revolution must be looked at is *discipline*. One cannot really separate discipline from doctrine. There is no point, as Paul VI found, in issuing the soundest of instructions to mutinous subordinates. Therefore, appointments are all-important. This Pope has a brilliant political sense. Having thoroughly familiarized himself with the running of the universal Church, he identified his men and moved them into key positions. Here are some high points in this process, from a counter-revolutionary perspective.

- The wholly unexpected and controversial appointment of the orthodox and eccentric Jean-Marie Lustiger as Archbishop of Paris in 1981. The result of this appointment is, in Peter Hebblethwaite's words, that "while no one was looking, the French church was totally transformed," in particular by Lustiger's de-emphasis of the episcopal conference and freeing of the individual bishop.[49]

- The extremely interesting general shake-up of the curia announced on April 9, 1984. The points of chief interest are the appointment of the African Cardinal Bernard Gantin, who is from the small hard-line Marxist state of Benin, to the very important Congregation for Bishops, to replace that quintessential old-style Vatican bag-man, Sebastiano Baggio. During his brief visit to Benin in 1982, John Paul II told the six bishops of the severely repressed Catholic Church: "You are in a political and social situation which I know well by experience."[50]
- The appointment of the tough Archbishop Jerome Hamer, O.P., to the Congregation for Religious, replacing the liberal Argentine Cardinal Eduardo Pironio. Hamer, a "hard man . . . out of sympathy with his fellow Dominicans," will certainly, as the *National Catholic Reporter* gloomily noted, provide a less "sympathetic ear" for dissident U.S. religious.[51]
- The disappearance from any office (back to a parish) of Archbishop Jean Jadot, the very liberal apostolic delegate to the United States, who during his tenure from 1973 to 1980 changed the face of the American Church by his appointment of over eighty young, "progressive" bishops. An earlier warning of papal displeasure was his failure to be made cardinal, the first such omission since the U.S. office was established in the late nineteenth century.
- The appointment of Monsignor George Kelly, long-time critic of the U.S. theological establishment and of the bishops who supported it,[52] as consultant to the Sacred Congregation for the Clergy, which is also in charge of catechetics.

Apart from this curial shake-up, there was "the unprecedented event," in the Pope's own description, of the private Dutch synod held in Rome in January 1980. Holland since Vatican II has been the craziest area of the Church; the private synod with the Pope was an attempt to get the Dutch episcopate to restore order themselves. The synod produced forty-six propositions asserting traditional Catholic belief and order. This project having failed to curb Dutch excesses, the Pope set out to replace the radical majority among Holland's seven bishops, who, since the days of the Dutch Pastoral Council, "Red October," had backed every revolutionary trend in the Dutch Church. In 1983, his appointment of the conservative Bishop of Rotterdam, Adrianus Simonis, to Utrecht, to replace the very liberal Primate Cardinal Jan Willebrands (safely kicked upstairs to a curial sinecure) caused public demonstrations of dissent; appointments at the same time to Rotterdam and Haarlem were equally unpopular. The radical bishop of Haarlem, Theodore Zwartkruis, was widely reported to have dropped dead in fury when he learned who was picked to succeed him (missionary Henry Bomers). By 1984, when Jan Bluyssen, the most liberal of the Dutch bishops, "received permission" from the Vatican to retire at the age of fifty-seven "for reasons of health," the Pope had brought about a complete ideological change-over. He managed this by routinely bypassing the lists of candidates submitted by local episcopal conferences and other official groups, on the sensible presumption that their suggestions would simply mean more of the same. This now routine papal behaviour has produced unexpected choices, all good news for the counter-revolution. Recent pleasant surprises include the appointments of Archbishop John O'Connor to New York and Archbishop Bernard Law to Boston; these bishops managed to make abortion the single most pressing issue in the 1984 presidential campaign, discrediting the mealy-mouthed "personally opposed, but . . ." stance of leading Catholic contenders; they have united millions of orthodox American Catholics left leaderless in the ethical and political storms of the contemporary cultural and religious revolutions. The surprise appointment of Bishop Adam Exner to the Archdiocese of Winnipeg is also reported to have been by the Pope's personal intervention.

In another most unusual move, acting upon a deluge of lay complaint, the Vatican in late 1983 launched an investigation into the administration of the dioceses of two of the most radical U.S. bishops, Raymond Hunthausen (Seattle) and Walter Sullivan (Richmond). Hunthausen complained that the Vatican had listened to "reactionary elements which seem bent on undoing the renewal begun . . . by the Second Vatican Council."[53]

TEN

THE FUTURE OF THE COUNTER-REVOLUTION

In the previous chapter I suggested that an active counter-revolution has begun in the universal Church. But it has a sad long way to go before Catholic faith and order can be widely restored, if indeed they ever can be to any sizeable part of Catholicism. From my own vantage point on the scruffy edges of the revolution, it too often seems as if Rosemary Ruether is right, and that the revolutionary consciousness is too deeply absorbed into Catholicism to be isolated and expelled. But there is another vantage point, from which the long view is more comforting, the eminence of Catholic history. I console myself, as Catholics must have done in the Roman persecutions, in the chaos after Nicaea, during the scandal of the Western Schism, in England after the Reformation, in Japan after the expulsion of Christians in the seventeenth century, in Russia after 1917, in China after 1950, in Vietnam after 1976, that there were worse times for the Faith, yet it lived, "in spite of dungeon, fire and sword." Which does not in any way weaken the truth of the perception that things are very bad now.

Human societies become corrupt from the top down; the Catholic Church is no exception. Moreover, the clear and coherent hierarchical structure of the Catholic Church is extremely responsive to direction, or lack of it, from above. Nevertheless, in the present crisis, amid the widespread collapse of the upper level of hierarchy and defection at the second level, a large part of the laity has remained faithful, brave, and combative.

Lay people have until very recently, for instance, been the whole strength of the anti-abortion movement, faithful to the Mystery of the Incarnation and the divine-human continuity, unflagging in the face of hostility and even open opposition from the Catholic theological and social-justice offices. Except for self-serving politicians, Brian Mulroney, John Turner, and Ed Broadbent in Canada, Geraldine Ferraro, Mario Cuomo, and Edward Kennedy in the United States, the lay Catholic, no matter how liberal in every other way, tends to remain adamant on this issue. What is more, the anti-abortion crusade has laid a solid base of genuine ecumenical co-operation among orthodox Christians and kept one bridge open on which bishops and others can escape back to the Catholic cosmology. In 1984, Daniel Maguire, an ex-priest and a leading theologian of the revolution, was able to obtain fewer than one hundred signatures for his full-page ad in the *Times*, "A Diversity of Opinion Concerning Abortion Exists Among Committed Catholics,"[1] designed to minimize the damage being done to Ferraro's candidacy by Archbishop O'Connor's uncompromising stand. Ed Broadbent, himself involved in an election campaign, quoted Maguire gratefully on television in support of his own position. But even Elizabeth McAlister, radical activist, ex-nun, wife of ex-priest Philip Berrigan, writing from prison attacked the pro-choice-on-abortion signatories,[2] and Notre Dame's James Burtchaell, C.S.C., whose bitter attack on *Humanae Vitae* I quoted earlier, has emerged in *Rachel Weeping* and in his *National Catholic Reporter* debate with Maguire as one of the most eloquent voices in defence of the sacredness of human life.[3] It is very hard to kill the incarnational aspect of Catholicism.

The laity has done its best; even those Catholics who left the church over the issue of contraception display an intellectual honesty lacking in their mentors. But though the laity can hold fast to the faith forever, as in England, Japan, and China, it cannot reform the Church. In the present flurry about the Vatican's "book-burning," an American lay organization, Catholics United for the Faith (CUF), was often attacked in the *National Catholic Reporter* as the devil behind the scenes. Certainly CUF and other orthodox Catholics had taken to complaining directly to Rome about heretical catechetical texts after years of trying to interest their local bishops, but, as the *National Catholic Reporter* editorially wondered, what made Rome suddenly act over *Christ Among Us* after seventeen years?[4] Lay Pilgrimages of Grace are of themselves politically ineffective. If they lack hierarchical leadership, they historically end in martyrdom – though some of us think this not the worst way to end.

It is a decisive moment in a revolution when the government stops trying to conciliate its enemies and starts accepting the help of its friends. There is, as I have tried to indicate, good evidence that this point has been at last reached. (Even a lowly guerrilla like me has experienced a distinct warming of episcopal manners lately.) But the Catholic faith cannot begin to be restored unless all the bishops speak with one voice and act in practical directions to disengage themselves from the revolutionary parallel magisterium they themselves created. The cold truth is that if Catholic faith and order are to be restored, the whole of the revolutionized post-Vatican II bureaucracy has to be repudiated and replaced, or better still, dismantled. But by now the revolution is so strong, so established at every level of Catholic life, so ruthless in self-preservation and savage in attack that bishops not unnaturally quail at the prospect of attempting to dismantle it. Yet if they do not, all is lost anyway. A society that is not prepared to defend itself by the use of force does not deserve to survive. At the moment, it is only too obvious that even good and orthodox bishops don't have the nerve to act against the revolution since it is grounded in their local administration. Yet, as revolutionaries themselves charge, nothing could be more destructive than the present episcopal solution of teaching the traditional faith while tolerating and even protecting its revolutionary contradiction.

Let us briefly consider the behaviour of the bishops in one crucial area of Catholic morality. No aspect of the moral and doctrinal revolution has been more distressing to those of us who grew up in and still adhere to the reformed morality of the pre-Vatican II Church than the corruption of Catholic sexual morality. This corruption reaches into everything, even, most dismayingly, into the seminaries. This is a matter Catholics have been very reluctant to discuss publicly; the trouble is, if it doesn't become public knowledge, the hierarchy won't act. To take one local instance: for several years, it was common knowledge in academic and clerical circles in Toronto that at St. Augustine's, the major English-speaking seminary in Canada, the theory and practice of homosexuality were openly tolerated. In the spring of 1984, several students at the University of Toronto, where seminarians attend classes at the ecumenical Toronto School of Theology, complained that they had been sexually propositioned by seminarians. Amid warnings of expulsion if they talked, non-homosexual seminarians tried to interest influential Catholics to make representations to the archbishop about correcting the situation. Meanwhile, an extraordinary document written by the rector, Father Brian Clough, called "A Dialogue in Trust," which urged sensitivity and tolerance upon the non-homosexual seminarians, was leaked to the public.[5] Cardinal Carter launched an investigation which, after an initial attempt to cover things up, resulted in the dismissal of the rector and two professors (one of whom was suspended from the exercise of his priestly faculties). The public was informed that though there were in fact a number of "homosexually oriented" seminarians, there had been no homosexual behaviour.

All this was shocking enough, but the really worrying thing was the behaviour of the hierarchy. One of the dismissed priests, Father Thomas Dailey, moral theologian and dean of students at the seminary, in return for submitting his resignation without making a legal row, was given written recommendations by the three rectors under whom he had taught, and the promise of two years' pay if he couldn't find a job in that time. "You're much too compassionate," Cardinal Carter quotes himself as telling Dailey, and adds, "He's a good man and we would not hesitate to give him a recommendation to teach moral theology. . . . We won't stand in his way. . . . He's certainly not slavish to what has been the traditional teaching of the church in many areas, that's for sure."[6]

One sympathizes with the desire to minimize the damage, but the kicker in this story is that the same Father Thomas Dailey had been dismissed from Bishop McNulty's seminary in 1968 for public dissent from *Humanae Vitae*, a qualification which for some strange reason inspired the then Rector of St. Augustine's (now bishop of Thunder Bay) John O'Mara to hire him at once to teach moral theology to future priests. When Dailey was fired this time, O'Mara added to Cardinal Carter's kindnesses by asking Dailey to stay with him and giving him a job teaching adult education, where his unslavish attitude to Church teaching ought to advance the revolution another useful little bit. The one comforting thought is that, as long as John Paul II reigns, O'Mara is unlikely to get the archbishopric of Toronto, open in a few years, a post for which he has been widely touted.

Stories like this about seminaries don't usually hit the news as this one did but they are numerous. Episcopal action is usually confined to disciplining non-homosexual students who complain. The American and Canadian bishops are firmly on record as teaching that homosexual acts are gravely sinful. Yet groups such as Dignity, the Catholic homosexual network, and New Ways Ministry, both of which take issue with Catholic teaching,[7] operate under episcopal patronage. Dignity's Seattle convention in 1983 featured videotaped greetings from Archbishop Hunthausen, who was out of the country. Gregory Baum, long-time officer of Dignity, teaches at St. Michael's College in the University of Toronto and at the Toronto School of Theology. The chaplaincy at St. Mike's, which my children attend, co-sponsored in 1984 as its contribution to Gay Awareness Week three sympathetic sessions on homosexuality, "a breakthrough at the college," in the chaplain's words, at which Father Norbert Brockman, a sex therapist, concluded fashionably that the prejudice against homosexuals is more immoral than the homosexual act itself.[8]

In 1977, a study commissioned by the powerful Catholic Theological Society of America rejected the old concept of universal moral norms and concluded that sexual behaviour is "wholesome and moral" if it is self-liberating, other-enriching, honest, faithful, socially responsible, and joyous. (As long as it enhances your horse's self-image and doesn't hurt his chances for the Queen's Plate, it's okay?) No wonder that some heated young student (let us hope it wasn't a heated old professor) in the St. Mike's library copy I consulted underlined in red this statement: "Christians must therefore be encouraged to embrace their sexuality joyfully and in full consciousness,"[9] and wrote beside it the poignant and heartfelt words, "I agree! I agree!" But of course it isn't funny. This book is used to train teachers of the compulsory sex-education programs in Catholic schools; our local ex-nun sex-ed co-ordinator was brandishing it when last I caught her act.

I mention the book here because it contains a perfect jewel of a sentence that encapsulates the argument on both sides of the Catholic revolution: "A homosexual engaging in homosexual acts in good conscience has the same rights of conscience and the same rights to the sacraments as a married couple practising birth control in good conscience."[10] Exactly, if such a right exists. If sex divorced from procreation is good sometimes, why not all the time? If singular "good conscience" is the only norm, what is the purpose and function of Catholic authority? This fine exercise in revolutionary logic strikes fatally at the Achilles' heel of the post-Conciliar episcopal position. Until the bishops go back to the beginning, until they anchor their cosmology once again on the point where man and woman and God combine in creation, they will continue to get everything wrong. They must go back to the beginning because it *is* the beginning; one cannot take one's stand halfway along the line of the Catholic argument, at homosexuality, or at abortion.

At present, the behaviour of many bishops suggests that they no longer operate from any coherent Catholic world view. This position leaves them utterly at sea when they try to understand and deal with feminism, for instance. What can possibly be the view of the world and the Church of the Canadian bishops who (a) lately hired a group of radical feminists, all vocal agitators for women's ordination and the new model of the Church, to staff their Ad Hoc Committee on the Role of Women in the Church, which wrote a report for the cccb's annual meeting, and who (b) at that meeting, in November 1984, rightly condemned the report for its revolutionary liberation theology and wild, abusive language, and who then (c) adopted the report unanimously! How is one to describe the idea of the family, "the domestic Church" as the Pope calls it, held by bishops who – unanimously – promised bursaries in every diocese to pay for tuition and baby-sitting for mothers who want to train for Church "ministries"? "Bravo!" said Cardinal Carter. "What we have done at this assembly will have far-reaching effects on the Canadian Church," said Bishop James MacDonald, chairman, unnervingly, of the Episcopal Commission for Theology. "We got less than we wanted but perhaps more than we hoped for," said one of the bishops' salaried feminists.[11] What they got was no less than the Canadian Catholic Church's commitment to the whole radical feminist agenda for the Church and for society. Was it just male panic or episcopal cowardice that led the whole Canadian hierarchy to adopt the feminist program? Can they have understood the revolutionary cosmology embodied in the twelve resolutions (which appear in the Appendix of this book) and in the revolutionary "lesson-plans" based on "womanstories" designed for consciousness-raising in the parishes?

The Canadian bishops submitted all the papal speeches prepared in Canada for John Paul II's September 1984 visit to the feminists' Ad Hoc Committee on the Role of Women in the Church to be vetted for "sexist" language. Mary Malone, a former nun, reported thus to Canadian Catholics for Women's Ordination (CCWO): "Another big area of work was overseeing the language used in the documents used during the Pope's visit. We spent a lot of the time working on all of the documents, all of the press releases, all of the Pope's talks . . . to make sure that it was inclusive language. The Pope, as you remember, was not accustomed to speaking inclusively, and . . . while he was in Quebec, he . . . said: 'My brother and sister (bishops).' He had been warned every time he said brother to say sister. He caught himself just in time."[12] The Canadian bishops ensured that even the Pope had to say, "How high?" when the feminists said, "Jump!"

Malone's report to CCWO details how the six women on the Ad Hoc Committee, working closely with Bishop Sherlock (London), president of the CCCB, and Bishops de Roo and Vachon (Quebec), pushed the twelve resolutions on the role of women in the Church past the very reluctant majority of bishops, whose instincts were against granting feminist demands, but whose nerves and political sophistication were no match for the women and their allies. When it looked as though the majority might prevail, especially after a strong letter of objection from Cardinal Carter, Bishops de Roo and Vachon got together with some Ottawa feminists not invited to the bishops' assembly, and worked out an intervention for Archbishop Vachon to present. It contained an expression of gratitude, for "the intelligence and unselfishness of their [the Ad Hoc Committee's] participation in the building of an ecclesial community which is truly attentive to the signs of the times," and an apology for "certain questions or objections raised during our exchange [which] have been perceived and received as a judgment of premeditated intention on the part of the Ad Hoc Committee members."

Archbishop Vachon read his ladies' words to the Plenary Assembly of the Canadian Bishops: "I propose, therefore . . . that the executive committee address a letter to each member of the Ad Hoc Committee . . . to express our profound gratitude and that in this same letter we express our strong wish to continue the dialogue started several years ago with a view to new understandings between women and men in the Church and that despite the delays in dealing with the recommendations of the committee members, we assure them of our desire to allow ourselves to be questioned together by the Spirit of God."

"The result of that intervention by Archbishop Vachon," said Malone triumphantly, "is again that for the first time in history, we made another kind of history, the bishops changed their agenda. Apparently, they had never done that before. They changed their Thursday agenda, took up the recommendations again and passed them all unanimously."

The bishops know, because their salaried feminists have told them, that the women they habitually choose as advisers want the end of the traditional authority structure of the Catholic Church because they think it is a "patriarchal" structure "based on structures of dominance and subordination. . . . This is where the bishops are coming from, without exception. That's the whole biased thing – the official traditional teaching of the Roman Catholic Church."[13] Therefore, one cannot blame the feminists for the outcome of the bishops' meeting. Malone recounted, to laughter and applause from the ccwo, that the Ad Hoc Committee women had charged their gins and tonics to "whichever bishop gave the most trouble." Impotent counter-revolutionaries can only admire their success. "My workshop, everything was approved eventually. Bishop Sherlock and myself, between us. He had the things approved because he wanted them pushed through and I tried to get them approved . . . on principle," says Mary Malone. The gals deserved their drinks.

Have the Canadian bishops named by Malone embraced the goals of the revolution? Or have they a death wish?

And who can trace the logic of their U.S. counterparts who, preparing their upcoming pastoral letter on women, appointed as consultants four extreme feminists: Sister Ann Carr, who signed Maguire's *New York Times* ad, is pro-abortion; Sister Sara Butler and Sister Toinette Eugene are for women's ordination; and Pheme Perkins embraces the whole radical feminist argument about patriarchy – that is, that the Church is "built upon the backs of women, slaves and the lower classes."[14] Present-day bishops seem to be entirely without an objective point of reference.

The original episcopal loss of nerve over *Humanae Vitae* paralyses the Church in those areas where the "truth about Jesus Christ, about the Church and about man and his dignity" is hardest to affirm and to practise in the circumstances of modern secular culture in the West. The hard, hard truth of the indissolubility of Christian marriage, for instance, has become too onerous to maintain, and "divorce Catholic-style" is reaching scandalous proportions. In 1968, the year *Humanae Vitae* was issued, 338 annulments were granted in the United States; in 1983 there were approximately 52,000.[15] In Canada in 1982, there were 3,000 annulments.[16] In the past, three or four notorious annulments provided staple fodder for generations of Catholic-bashing; now every Catholic has experience of some openly cynical annulment decision. Catholics file for annulment in easy dioceses – Los Angeles is tough, Brooklyn easy. (A current joke has it that when you go into a parish office in Brooklyn diocese to arrange your marriage, they give you your annulment forms on the way out.) Before the Council, Catholic marriage was amazingly resistant to modern secular pressures; today it is completely demoralized, and the blame for that demoralization has to be laid at the door not of the dissenting theologians but of the bishops, by Christ's appointment the principal pastors and teachers of the Church.

Catholics keep saying about the revolution, "You can't turn the clock back." Of course you can, and must, if it's telling the wrong time. There are certain moves vital to the counter-revolution. First, all bishops must publicly, solemnly, wholeheartedly, affirm the supernatural and natural truth of the whole of the Church's teaching on the transmission of human life, and require that no one should undertake to teach in their name who cannot give internal assent to that teaching. They can point for support to Canon 812 of the new Code of Canon Law, which rules that anyone who wants to teach theology in a Catholic school must seek a mandate from the bishop. The Canadian bishops must publicly take back the disastrous *Winnipeg Statement*, which has crippled their apostolic work for society in the related matters of divorce, abortion, and family life. And while we're on the subject of recanting past error, let us demand that the theologians who persuaded the bishops that contraception was *necessary* to preserve the Christian values of marriage admit, at least in this one case, that they were absolutely, tragically wrong, in the light of the overwhelming empirical evidence to the contrary. And would it be too extravagant to insist that, when the bishops wish to consult experts on how best to explain and teach the faith, they consult the *faithful*, those of us who in our lives have tested and proved the soundness of the doctrines of the faith? If the bishops wish to understand the beautiful truths reaffirmed by *Humanae Vitae*, they should ask genuine *periti*, who learned it by living it, sore hard as it was at times, as sharp and full of splinters as the Cross of Christ. The *sensus fidelium*, the feeling and judgement of those who *practise* the faith, has always throughout Catholic history served as a touchstone of faith; today it is the *sensus infidelium* that so serves. (Newman, if he were writing today, would have to call his famous essay "On Consulting the *Unfaithful* in Matters of Doctrine.") The *faithful* could explain to the bishops that the Church's teaching is even more crucially relevant to the modern situation than it was in the Age of Faith. The *faithful* might lead them to see that it is, after all, not so odd that the fate of Christ's Church should hang on what it says to the modern world about the transmission of human life since the fate of humanity hangs upon the Incarnation of God as man, of which sweet Mystery human incarnation is a humble analogy.

Therefore, once the bishops have made the initial counter-revolutionary move in the place where the revolution emerged, they must start choosing *periti* from among the *faithful*. Otherwise, it will be business as usual. Feminist appointees can do no other than produce lies about the nature of men and women for the bishops to sign; theological modernists cannot produce sound liturgy; Marxist theologians must incline to totalitarianism. There are any number of wise and scholarly faithful, lay and clerical, anxious to serve; a bishop with guts could restaff his bureaucracy quite quickly. Some years ago, before an American presidential election, the three hundred or so staffers of the USCC threatened to submit their resignations if the NCCB went ahead with a strong statement urging Catholics to vote for anti-abortion candidates. The bishops cravenly backed down. What a God-sent opportunity lost: "Dear Mr./Fr./Ms/Sr. — : It is with deep regret that I accept your resignation operative as of this moment. . . ."

Every counter-revolutionary has his own list of bureaucrats who never would be missed. We know where the good guys are too; just ask us, Your Excellency. References supplied.

It has often been said that all revolutions fail since the ideals of the early reformers are inevitably betrayed by the dynamics of the very process intended to secure them. James Hitchcock, in his early study of the post-Conciliar revolution, *The Decline and Fall of Radical Catholicism*, noted this. The radicals had wanted a Church "more open, more honest, less authoritarian and more humane than at present." But they soon discovered that "it is also impossible to have effective revolution . . . without having authoritarianism, strong discipline, enforced orthodoxy, the sacrifice of individuals to the cause – all the abuses which revolutionaries object to in the establishment . . . have already begun to appear within radical American Catholicism."[17] To survive in power over a large number of unwilling subjects who still adhere to the older idea, a revolution is forced to maintain a more rigid and punitive orthodoxy than the one it is trying to supplant. Twenty years after Vatican II, the revolution, though it has failed to behead the king, has for all intents and purposes become the establishment. Yet the horrid truth has begun to dawn that the teaching authority of the Church, centred upon the Roman magisterium, is not after all going to abdicate, scrap its cosmology, become a constitutional monarchy or a parliamentary democracy or a revolutionary commune. Therefore, instead of being able to settle down to consolidate its gains, the revolution has had to step up its attack. Though the post-Conciliar hierarchy, up to and including Pope John Paul II and Cardinal Ratzinger, have been consistently patient and gentle – the traditionalist Archbishop Marcel Lefebvre is suspended, Hans Küng is not – the charges of brutality directed against it by the revolution become ever more outrageous. Typical of the approach is a sneering article in the *National Catholic Reporter* by Peter Hebblethwaite, entitled "Roman 'Heat' on the Church Worldwide" under a cartoon of a Roman prelate walking the national churches on a leash, with the caption, "The only good dog is an orthodox dog."[18] The U.S. bishops' own official service, *National Catholic News*, which supplies news to the many Catholic papers, is also consistently slanted in favour of the revolution. The 1984 convention of the Catholic Press Association criticized the Vatican's pressure on the bishops to withdraw imprimaturs and suggested that "It might be time for a primal scream."[19] The recent study by James Hitchcock for the National Committee of Catholic Laymen shows the dispiriting extent of institutionalized "frenetic anti-papalism" among American dissenters.[20] The revolution is not going to go quietly.

It is now time for conciliation of the revolution by the magisterium to stop. It had to be tried, but it hasn't worked; it never does. If the counter-revolution is to have any bite, it needs some dramatic symbolic move from Rome against the heart of the revolution. Some egregious dissenter needs to be made an example of, and it shouldn't be only theologians. The Vatican, as I've noted, has been quietly removing bad bishops. It would be salutary at this time to remove one and say why. Everybody has a favourite contender, though few of us go as far as Archbishop Hunthausen's critics, who expressed their displeasure by fire-bombing his rectory.[21] My own candidate is the Canadian Archbishop Jean-Marie Fortier (Sherbrooke, Quebec), who, during a United Church ordination held in his own cathedral, "in a moving ecumenical gesture . . . strode from his seat in the chancel into the main body of the huge cathedral to receive bread and wine from a newly ordained woman minister."[22] One of the ordinands was a former Catholic priest, a fact known to Archbishop Fortier. It would have been comforting to see something done about that.

The place where a symbolic move against the revolutionary consciousness would have most impact is the Mass, the Church's oldest and best means of communication on the subliminal level. I said earlier that all revolutions fail, but it is also true that all revolutions succeed, since some of their "gains" have to be more or less left in place because the cost of removal is too high. Nowhere has the revolution's ideology been so universally or so institutionally grounded as in the official liturgy. Though it cuts me to the heart to say it, I do not have much hope that the old liturgy can now be universally restored, no matter how strong the case for such restoration. I expect the recent Indult for the limited use of the Tridentine Rite to have some small mitigating effect, but it will be scattered and unofficial unless the Vatican, as seems possible, revises the Indult to allow its unrestricted use for those priests and laity who want it.

I realize with unutterable sadness that, barring a miracle (and I do not bar one), I will for the rest of my life feel a stranger at the official worship of the Church, and that the Catholic world to which I belong is dead. Our bishop and some others, I gather from my traditionalist friends, have kindly received requests for occasional access to the old Mass; I will attend when I can. But it is bitterly hard for someone with an unreconstructed Catholic heart to bear that the glorious universal prayer of all the Catholic ages in which, whatever his race and station, he unselfconsciously used to join, has been remaindered into a barely tolerated cultural survival. The Catholic who cannot worship without the Church yet finds the present form of worship almost intolerable is in a pitiable situation. I will search out old Missals and take my children to the Mass of the Catholic ages, and they will be devout and impressed and strangers. Yet they are no better off, having fallen between two stools; they do not know the old and they do not love the new.

Nevertheless, something counter-revolutionary can be done at once to begin to move the Mass back towards being the complete expression of the Catholic world view it used to be. If an angel allowed me one suggestion as to what more than anything else would most quickly restore the sense of the sacred to the Mass it would be this – to do away with Mass facing the people. I am convinced that the position of the priest at the altar is the single most important liturgical "external" symbol, the one that carries the most doctrinal baggage. To put the priest back on our side of the altar, facing with us towards God, would at one stroke restore the Mass from an exercise in interpersonal relationships to the universal prayer of the Church to God our Father. This reversion to the correct symbol wouldn't even need new or corrective legislation. It may surprise even Catholics that the turning around of the altar (or rather, of the priest) was not legislated in any Vatican II document or in any document since. The only remarks pertaining to the *versus populum* (facing the people) mode of the altar and Mass are to be found in the *Instruction on the Liturgy* (October 16, 1964) issued hot off the mark by the radical Cardinal Lercaro, president of the new Commission for the Implementation of the Constitution on the Sacred Liturgy, after the *Constitution* had been passed but before the end of the Council: "It is proper that the main altar be constructed separately from the wall, so that one *may* go around it with ease and so that celebration *may* take place facing the people" (V, 91: my italics). That's all. Ideology, not law, transplanted the priest. As in the Protestant revolution, the radical intent was to replace the idea of an altar of sacrifice with that of a table for a community meal.[23] In Rome, Mass is still commonly said *contra populum*, facing away from the congregation; the famous Brompton Oratory in London never departed from the tradition. Orthodox priests changed because it was made to seem hopelessly old-fashioned not to, and they thought, mistakenly, that it was a change without theological cost. With the priest facing God once more as leader of the people, the importance of the microphone will diminish, and the priest can stop making faces at us. He and we can go back to thinking only about what is happening in the Mystery.

But we must leave the shape of the counter-revolution to the Holy Ghost. No one, angel or otherwise, is likely to consult the laity about what to do, and there is no disagreement with that from this quarter. Most of us will never be in a position to influence Church policy and few of us want to. The layman's role remains what it always was, to hold fast to that which seems good, to provide a touchstone of the faith.

In an earlier book on the post-Conciliar unpleasantness, I used a quotation that became the wry watchword of traditionalist circles – "Don't let the bastards drive you out of the Church!" The beloved friend whose irreverent motto this was has died since then, bravely in the faith of his fathers, after a dreadful illness. No Catholic of my acquaintance understood better what had happened to Catholicism, and no one was ever more broken-hearted about it. Or more bad-tempered. Going to Mass was a real penance to him, but he went. The bastards didn't drive him out, and I expect that now he has forgiven them and been forgiven for the furious maledictions he fervently bestowed on them. He was buried with a Latin Mass, the Novus Ordo, but in beautiful solemn celebration by his Oratorian friend. ("Pity a feller has to die to get a Latin Mass!" said one of his Irish mourners.) And this past July, after we had got the old Mass back, we had it offered for him. In your charity, pray for the soul of James Daly, traditionalist, Catholic, Irishman, scholar, wit, counter-revolutionary. *Ipsi, Domine, et omnibus in Christo quiescentibus, locum refrigerii, lucis et pacis, ut indulgeas, deprecamur.*

Well, we haven't been driven out, though the bastards are as plentiful as ever. Here we are still, not notably in a better temper. Where else is there to go? But it is more than ever important for defenders of the Church and conscripts to the counter-revolution to remember, as patience wears thin and charity with it, what every deathbed must remind us – that the purpose of the Christian life is first and foremost the imitation of Christ, that Our Lord will judge not the number of our successes but the purity of our witness. Everything temporal, no matter how useful, should be seen in the light of eternity.

ELEVEN

ROMAN REMAINS

In the English county of Sussex, a few miles inland from the port of Hastings, there is a valley exquisitely lovely and serene, a place that more than any other now speaks to my heart. Almost the whole of it is in farm as it has been for over a thousand years, though the land-use has changed with the centuries. It was mostly apple orchards when I first entered it twenty-five years ago, and there was an encampment of gypsies, hired to pick the apples. The hop-gardens are still there, though the oast houses no longer pungently smoke, having gone the way of windmills and become conversation-piece dwellings. Much of the land was in grain when I saw it last, wheat (corn, as the English confusingly call it), red-gold on both slopes, and barley white on the drained bottoms near the river. Sheep graze in steep meadows. In every light and in every weather it is beautiful.

It was not its beauty alone that won me. I was born and grew up in a wonderfully beautiful place, at the confluence of a fine river and a long fjord on the west coast of Newfoundland, far more striking and noble than this gentle English countryside. What attracted me at once, years before I learned anything of its history, was the almost tangible sense of a benevolent past still harmoniously bound into a present that has forgotten it. There is no rustic charm to be romantic about, no wise old peasants; the farms are run by the latest technology and a few men good at tending complicated machinery. But the countryside remembers. The past lies upon it, not like a weight but like a fragrance. Many people who grew up in the wild empty places as I did will know the feeling that one is the first human being to intrude into a certain place, the consciousness of a hostile non-human regard directed at one's back. In this valley, I felt instead for the first time that indefinable communication from a place that has been inhabited peacefully for time out of mind and because of this breathes a sense of fullness and experience, of blessedness. Even at its busiest, when the farm machinery works all night to catch the fine weather, there lies upon it "an influence luminous and serene, a shining peace," while at its most restful, on a Sun-

day evening in summer when the famous peal of bells in Salehurst Church rings the changes, the air shimmers with religious joy. I sit on a bench facing the sunset and hope that in the many mansions of heaven I will find this valley and its bells.

My husband was not a Catholic when he first took me to visit his home, so I went with him to Evensong in the beautiful village church of Saint Mary the Virgin, a mixture of Norman remains and several styles of Gothic, and felt the usual Catholic pang that churches like these, so lovely, so holy, are no longer ours. English and Irish Catholic churches are uniformly cringing and ugly, the result of persecution and poverty and of having to be built after the Age of Faith. The parish church of Salehurst is all that is left standing of the old Catholic possession of the area. Only some low ruins remain of the large Cistercian Abbey dedicated to Our Lady, as all Cistercian foundations were, that stood beside the Rother. The monks were driven out in 1538, but traces of their civilizing presence are everywhere, their clearings and boundaries, their dikes and ditches. Wherever you dig on the Abbey Farm you are likely to turn up a piece of carving, a stone flower, a broken angel. Wherever you walk, you see the big dressed golden sandstone blocks taken from the abbey after its destruction, forming part of farm kitchens, cowbyres, pigsties, farm buildings, stone walls; sunk as stepping-stones in the miry path that leads to the church, used as mounting-blocks. I always feel sad when I come upon these mute reminders of a European Catholicism at the height of its spiritual and cultural confidence. Catholicism disappeared as a public presence from this place which it had so saturated with its spirit, and it has never managed to return. The traces of its long habitation are visible only to antiquarians.

Today I see the same obliteration once again threatening Catholicism. As before, the monasteries have been destroyed, their buildings sold to Hare Krishna or for golf courses, their books bought up by the pound by second-hand-book dealers. Salehurst Church lost its stained glass and its statues to the Reformation. Every modern Catholic church has, in the wake of Vatican II, been savaged by a liturgical reform more destructive of Catholic religious symbolism even than that of the sixteenth century. Most terrible of all, the Mass disappeared from Salehurst's altars. In modern Catholicism, the centre of the Mass, at least, endures, though much denuded; but for how much longer? Traditional eucharistic doctrine is under subtle attack in every parish, as the continuing thrust of the reform tends inexorably towards the disappearance of the sacrificial aspect in favour of the communitarian. I kneel in Salehurst Church; I do not genuflect.

The Real Presence remains, though often under sufferance, in the tabernacles of most Catholic churches; it might as well not be reserved for all the attention paid to it. A whole generation of Catholics has been subtly instructed that Christ is present in the sacramental Species only symbolically, at the moment when the gathered community communicates, a Protestant reductionism clear in every new catechism and in bulletins from official liturgy committees. The practice of making visits to the Blessed Sacrament has virtually ended; even if one wanted to visit them, most Catholic churches are now locked up except during Mass. Devotion to the reserved Sacrament has been officially excluded from modern catechetics. Complaining about its total absence from the official, ruthlessly enforced *Canadian Catechism*, one of its critics, now a bishop, asked: "Why should we neglect this firmly established way of preparing for, and continuing our awareness of, the death and resurrection of Jesus made present for us in the Eucharist?"[1] Why indeed, if we still believe it? The revolutionaries in unchallenged charge of catechetics, seminary training, and liturgy since Vatican II do not believe it.

RENEW, the latest attempt to push the revolution down to the grass roots in the parishes, has for its hopeful symbol an old dead-looking tree stump breaking out into new leaves, an image of what its developers want to believe about the condition of modern Catholicism. "Expect a miracle!" RENEW's bumper stickers and ubiquitous banners advise. (RENEW must be one hell of a shot in the arm for the banner industry: there must be a thousand square feet of banner in one of the local churches.)

A miracle is certainly called for if the Catholic Church is not to disappear from places where it survived or regrouped after the Reformation, or triumphantly established itself anew in missionary territory. It has already disappeared from tens of millions of hearts which only lately were committed to it in countries where, on the surface, it still exhibits an imposing official presence. The ecclesiastical establishment is actually much swollen since the bureaucratic explosion after Vatican II, during the national churches' grab for power, but its bustling show, much as it fills the eye and the media, is a mushroom growth; under its shadow the troops have quietly deserted. The impressive bureaucracy creates an atmosphere of excited renewal ("ferment" is the preferred word) but it is rapidly destroying its base. Every new "outreach" of the modernist revolution liberates a few more Catholics from their principles; these quite quickly stop practising.

It was supposed to work the other way. If the Catholic dogmas were made more relevant, easier to accept, we were assured, if the sexual ethic were revised in the light of modern social conditions, the Church would retain its present members and be enormously more attractive to those outside it. The opposite has happened. It must be obvious to everyone now that theological modernism is not going to work towards the reinvigoration of Catholicism in the late twentieth century any more than it has for Protestant bodies which earlier embraced it.

180

Salehurst and the thousands of exquisite Anglican parish churches of England and Ireland have long been empty. Preservation societies keep them in a poignant state of preparedness for worshippers who do not come. Whenever I visit one, I contribute a pound to the box set for tourists at the door and pray to the souls of the Catholics who built them. (The last time I was in the glorious fragment that remains of Winchelsea Church, I found an altar to Our Lady, a water-filled font and a burning sanctuary lamp; some Anglo-Catholic priest, keeping a light burning to an ancient love.)

But modernists seem only to be spurred on by mass defections. The latest battle over the ordination of women split the Episcopalian and Anglican Churches of the United States and Canada, driving into schism the most Catholic elements in both. The extremely liberal leadership of the United Church of Canada recently proposed that practising homosexuals be accepted into the ministry. The standard purpose of "coming to terms with the twentieth century," in this case by the approval of homosexual behaviour, was applauded by Bruce Hunter of Dignity, the Catholic homosexual organization: "I think it's terrific. It's just great, a very positive development."[2] A schism has been promised by evangelicals horrified by the move.

It is a curious testimony to the uniqueness of the religious impulse that corruption in priests does not seriously weaken it. Catholics have always endured bad priests as long as these priests maintain the truth of the mysteries to which they grant access. Nor does persecution, of itself, extinguish faith. The blood of martyrs is the seed of Christians. Catholicism thrives in Poland because its leadership there has remained firm, teaching the faith with one voice; it perished in England because at the beginning of the Reformation, the bishops wavered, temporized, compromised, conciliated. The laity resisted desperately, as it always does, and was betrayed by its shepherds, as it always is. Popular risings against the looting of the monasteries, the Act of Supremacy, and the teaching of the new German heresies coalesced into that unique insurrection, the ill-fated Pilgrimage of Grace. Non-violent, devout, doomed to betrayal, it has had no counterpart until the recent remarkable peaceful religious resistance movement in Poland. The lay leadership, lords and commons, were put to death, some of them hanged at their own doors; sixteen priests, six abbots, and thirty-eight monks, Cistercians prominent among them, were executed. The bishops, as they too often do, led their army from behind; they found it less exciting. Only one, St. John Fisher, resisted to the death. By the end of Elizabeth's reign there was only a handful of Catholics left in England.

I visit the English valley only in the summer, which no doubt colours my perception of its character, but does not, I think, falsify it. For that time, whose ruins remain so poignantly, was the high summer country of the Catholic Church. Newman, in his magnificent sermon upon the

restoration of the Catholic episcopate to England in 1850, joyfully pre-
dicted "A Second Spring": "A second temple rises on the ruins of the
old. Canterbury has gone its way, and York is gone, and Durham is
gone, and Winchester is gone. It was sore to part with them. The Church
in England has died, and the Church lives again. Westminster and Not-
tingham, Beverley and Hexham, Northampton and Shrewsbury, if the
world lasts, shall be names as musical to the ear, as stirring to the heart,
as the glories we have lost; and Saints shall rise out of them . . . and
Doctors once again shall give the law to Israel, and Preachers call to
penance and to justice, as at the beginning."[3] But Newman was too
hopeful. An incredibly loyal and stoical band of recusants had kept the
faith alive after the Reformation, but the Catholicism that crept back
to England in the nineteenth century was largely the import of the
despised Irish diaspora; pure and total as it was, it never recaptured
the imagination of the secularized England to which it was reintro-
duced nor was it able to exert influence over social policy. The last of
the punitive measures under which it had suffered since the Reforma-
tion were removed in the late nineteenth century, but only at the insis-
tence of liberal Anglicans.

And now the universal Church is in ruins. In a spectacular act of
public suicide it has destroyed its cult and the culture it had informed.
The world view that created Europe and kept the Word incarnate is
shattered. There is little argument from either side of the revolution
about the presence and extent of the ruins, only about their significance.
To orthodox hold-outs, the only question is whether what is left of the
Church will collapse quite quickly or whether it will settle down instead
to a long dismal dilapidation; the most optimistic among us envisage
at best a counter-revolution, resulting in a much shrunken Catholic
Church. On the other hand, the men who made the revolution have a
vested interest in believing that the ruins mean the rebirth of a better
Catholicism. Yes, said the bishops of Quebec recently, the Church does
resemble "a house in ruins," but this is no cause for despair; it is rather
"an old house under renovation." French Canada had been the one part
of North America where the Church did not exist on sufferance, where
its pre-Vatican II presence was as total and confident as in pre-
Reformation England. "In 1960, we had more than 80 per cent of the
Catholic population coming to Mass every Sunday. Now, it's 25 per
cent; on Christmas and Easter, it does not go over 60 per cent."[4] Only
18 per cent of Quebec high-school students go to Mass regularly. But
this is not, the bishops note, because of "an absence of a spiritual quest."
In the void left by the Church's abdication, new sects and cults are
mopping up the very religious populace. Nor is it because the Church's
traditional morality and doctrine are unacceptable to modern
Quebeckers. People have turned to the cults, it seems, precisely because

the Church has abandoned its certainty. Charismatic and evangelical sects, say the Quebec bishops, "propose a coherent and simplistic dogma that we cannot offer without betraying the integrity of our message." Perish the thought that the Church might return to offering its old coherent dogmatic imaginative faith, to which it has been true since the Resurrection, that faith so deeply satisfying to the religious heart, so sanctifying, so accessible and truly egalitarian, so transforming of human society, so beautiful. It is precisely because the integrity of its message has been betrayed by those in whose care Christ left it that the Catholic Church is in ruins.

The more a religion demands in the way of commitment, the greater the response of faith. Yet even now there are converts, of exceptionally high quality, and my own perception is that their number is increasing with the tenure of the present Pope. They are refugees fleeing the increasing moral laxity of the mainline Protestant bodies, their defection a tragic loss to their former churches, as they were usually the most committed and active members. Catholics watched with a mixture of pity and amusement as the whole staff of the excellent Anglo-Catholic *New Oxford Review* argued and agonized itself into the Catholic Church over the issues of the ordination of women and homosexuals. I now know a substantial number of recent converts like this (in counter-revolutionary groups they usually outnumber "cradle Catholics") and am much edified by their purity and ardour. Seven of them are my godchildren, and I must confess that some of us, to our shame, earnestly tried to delay them, on the grounds of the growing disorder in the Catholic Church. They forced their way past us anyway, thank God; though the priest I brought them to for instruction and I could not resist saying, when they had their first shocking confrontation with revolutionary priests and nuns over their children's education: "Well, you can't say we didn't warn you!" The point is, these converts remind one of what one asks of the Church of God, as the old baptism question went; the answer being, "Faith!" They come, like St. Peter, because they have found that for them there is nowhere else to go to hear "the words of eternal life." They come because at the highest level of Catholic teaching, the doctrine of the faith, though much embattled, remains uncompromised and is as fearlessly proclaimed by John Paul II as by Peter, Paul, Ignatius, or Augustine.

These new Catholics and the extraordinary Pope to whom they belong as personally as the converts of Pentecost belonged to St. Peter are a very present comfort when one is tempted to despair. "Don't always be so negative," people say to critics of the post-Conciliar Church. "Aren't there *any* good things?" Yes there are, though they don't ever emanate from the parallel hierarchy and the revolution it is trying to institutionalize. Nothing comes from that quarter but endless destructive talk.

Some of the good things have caught the public imagination – the missions of Mother Teresa to the lepers and the poorest of the poor, of Jean Vanier to the retarded, of Father Bruce Ritter to the street waifs in big cities. Mother Teresa, in particular, has served as a sign of the faith and charity of the Catholic Church during the past two decades of confusion. But there are many others, not as well known, who keep the Catholic world view alive. I mention the two following because they have been so important to my family and me, not because they are singular. As I walk about in the valley of my life, these are the boundary walls and byres and stepping stones and bells that incarnate Catholicism for me.

The first is a small group of priests and brothers of the Canadian house of the Oratory of St. Philip Neri. The oratory, founded in Rome in the sixteenth century, is not a religious order but a family of secular priests and brothers who nevertheless lead a regulated community life. Newman after his conversion brought the oratory to England where it flourishes in his own Birmingham house and in the more famous Brompton Oratory in London. Now, as then, many of the recruits to its English-speaking houses are converts. They bring to the priesthood that heightened appreciation of the central Mystery that converts have and so freshly convey to cradle Catholics who too often take it for granted; converts always remember what they came for. I hasten to add, before I irritate them, that there is about their beautiful decorous liturgy none of the exaggerated and too often precious application of "Catholic" aesthetics to "high" Anglicanism. The Protestant doctrinal content of Cranmer's Communion Service cannot bear the weight of the Catholic centuries' accumulation of ornament and reflection and when it tries it looks ridiculous, because the heart has long ago been cut out of it. Hence the contradiction that the "highest," most ritual-conscious Anglicans, for example, Episcopalian Bishop Paul Moore of New York, are also the most theologically modernist. Oratorian liturgy is beautiful and correct, and it is one of the reasons we go there when we can, but not the principal reason.

It was a happy accident of history that the most frequent and simplest Mass was adorned by the glories of Latin language and Gregorian plain-song. But Catholics, celebrant or layman, generally gave little thought to aesthetics. When Catholics of all tempers complain about the ugliness, chaos, and banality of the new Mass, they think they are lamenting the disappearance of some constant universal beauty of celebration that existed prior to the changes. Memory misleads them; Catholic worship in general, before the Council, was just as scruffy and unaesthetic as it is now, the priests just as ignorant and even more slipshod; actually, priests today try much harder to make Mass "meaningful." The irreplaceable quality of the pre-Conciliar Mass was its unselfconscious certainty about the truth of the Eucharistic Mystery. What critics of the new rite are reacting to is not the disappearance of the Mystery but the disappearance of *certainty* about it. The sudden, ruthless destruction of the externals that long reflection upon the Sacrifice and the Real Presence had produced, and the doubts sown in the seminaries by modernist professors which reappear in the diffidence or panic of the new priests, are responsible for the air of desperation, the frantic addition and manipulation of externals that characterize modern liturgical practice. (Every time I go into a certain local church, for example, the organ, the choir, the "presidential chair," and "the president of the assembly" have been shifted to a new spot.)

Religious truth and the beautiful expression of it do not always go together, but when they do, the combination is irresistible. Having experienced it, one feels that one can never do without it again. The Oratory of St. Philip Neri is the only place now within our reach where the combination occurs. We live a long way from it, but we go when we can to have our Catholic batteries recharged. It has been interesting to see the changing reaction of our children, who grew up in the throes of the revolution, to the oratory's now exotic-looking brand of Catholicism. At first they couldn't tolerate its difference from the local Sunday offerings. One by one they have succumbed; the oldest throughout his university years has gone with many other students to attend the Sunday Latin High Mass. He said to me lately: "I'm so glad the oratory is there. It's made me understand what the Church could be like." And it's made him understand me, and why I have been so unreconciled to many of the new departures, why Catholics like me are so brokenhearted about the collapse of Catholic certainty and practice, why we have carried on so bitterly and sometimes extravagantly about it, and why finally we cannot go away.

But if it were only a nice place for the nostalgic to go to Mass it wouldn't be worth the trip. The oratory church is in one of the roughest parts of Toronto. Its congregation yields that wonderful cross-section of society for which the Catholic Church was uniquely famous. There is a remnant of the original Irish community, but the core is now the recent bustling flamboyantly religious Filipino influx. There is also a component of university professors and students, and well-heeled refugees from modernist parishes; there are Haitians, West Indians, and Vietnamese. And then there are the bums and drunks, the mental hospital out-patients, the religious fanatics and bag ladies, the welfare state's pensioned-off rejects, for whom this area has become a dumping-ground. One of these is usually gibbering and twitching at one's elbow. Towards the area's wounded the oratory exercises a large tolerance and compassion, distributing unostentatiously and unsentimentally many thousands of dollars of emergency aid and following up its cases.

Whenever I visit, there is a sandwich being made for a bum, or a food voucher written for a girl with a black eye and a baby, or some cash advanced to a desperate young father whose paycheque has bounced. They are philosophical and amusing about the rip-off artists. And the young madman whom they call "our resident demoniac," who keeps turning up and rending his garments, gets taken out on his birthday by one of the brothers; this year, much to our amusement, the brother took him to the Canadian National Exhibition.

The oratory's work wouldn't have seemed very remarkable before the revolution. They do what religious orders were expected to do as a matter of course – pray constantly, live in community, sing beautiful Masses, write scholarly works on Hegel and Thomas Aquinas, run an orthodox seminary to train their priests, draw the young of the parish into the life of the Church, dispense unjudgemental charity, hear confessions a lot. But religious orders on the whole don't do that anymore; members are generally to be found in the academy and the media tearing down Catholic truth, or at conferences, telling each other how this might be better and faster done. Modern religious tend to see themselves as prophets, not as servants of the servants of God. So the oratory looks out of step. The establishment simply dismisses it as old-fashioned and therefore irrelevant. Even some of its friends, anxious for it to be influential for good, urge it to co-operate more with the revolution. "You've missed the boat!" one of them said angrily. "This is not where the action is!"

It is true that the oratory's concerns are not what much of the present Church is active about but that is because the present Church is all too often active about the wrong thing, and not because the oratory has lost track of Catholicism or failed to adjust to Vatican II. The Canadian oratory is a post-Conciliar foundation; only its superior was ordained before Vatican II. Moreover, it is scrupulously obedient to all the official reforms even when it doesn't like them. This obedience, ironically, earns them enmity from both sides. The revolution considers their exact obedience a reproach, while certain conservatives, followers of Archbishop Lefebvre, charge them with having done more than anyone else to reconcile orthodox Catholics to the new Mass, especially to the new Mass in the vernacular, and I must agree that at least in my case this is true. Their one Latin Sunday Mass and their regular English Mass and Vespers prove that the new liturgy, when the letter of the Council's *Constitution on the Sacred Liturgy* is followed, can be acceptable. Of course, the revolution neither intended nor has rendered obedience to Vatican II, invoking its name only to legitimate modernist practice. It is a sobering sign of how fast the revolution has moved that it is the oratory, entirely obedient to both the Conciliar reform and the new Code of Canon Law, that looks outrageous and dissident, while genuine brazen disobedience has succeeded in becoming accepted as orthodoxy.

Nevertheless, despite all this, the fact that the oratory *is* here on the ground, a post-Vatican II venture that is orthodox, obedient, cheerful, confident, brave, rapidly expanding, scholarly, non-élitist, pastoral, prayerful, in short, truly Catholic, is a most hopeful sign of the tenacity of the Catholic idea. I owe it very much: the rescue of the vocation of my young cousin after he left the diocesan seminary, disillusioned, at the nadir of the post-Vatican II delirium; the guiding of many friends and of my husband's parents into the faith; some indication to my children of what the Church used to look like and could again; a Catholic port in this storm; a place to retreat to, if it becomes impossible in the future to go to Mass without intolerable distraction in our own locality.

The second bright habitation among the ruins that I want to mention is the Molesey Venture, a home for retarded boys and young men, founded by Father Paul Bidone of the Sons of Divine Providence. (Malcolm Muggeridge, who introduced me to them, calls them the Sons of Divine Improvidence, because of their unnerving habit of not letting the little matter of being totally broke stand in the way.) The home literally rises from ruins, occupying several dilapidated and abandoned houses on waste ground used until lately as a garbage dump, at the edge of the small village of East Molesey near the Thames and well into the urban sprawl of London. I first met Father Bidone in circumstances very stirring to a Catholic with my cultural background. As a student in England, he had been a protégé of Hilaire Belloc, often visiting him in Shipley, Sussex, in the private chapel of which the Blessed Sacrament was reserved by permission of Pius X. Father Bidone said Mass for us there, the Novus Ordo in Latin; one of my sons served. Permission had been obtained from the apostolic delegate for Mr. Muggeridge, who was not then a Catholic, to receive Holy Communion in recognition of his services to the Church. I have reservations about such permissions, but this was properly acquired and it seemed cavalier to object, since my family had prayed so long for such an event. It was, needless to say, deeply moving.

Mr. Muggeridge is a patron of the Molesey Venture; so, most fittingly, is the woman who lives in the Abbey Farm, built upon the ruins of the Cistercian Abbey. When the venture celebrated its birthday, my family and I were invited. I hadn't yet gathered whether the foundation was Catholic or ecumenically run. I found out upon arrival in their garden, when a stumbling boy immediately handed me a glass of wine (sorely needed after several hours in Greater London traffic in their van which runs by faith alone). There used to be a catechism question: What are the marks of the true Church? Answer: One, holy, catholic, apostolic.

A certain amount of dry ecumenical togetherness over the past decade leads me to add another: You can get a drink on the premises. Good wine, too, as at Cana of Galilee. This place had the comfortableness with the flesh apparent of all ascetical Catholic places, a comfortableness very apparent in this home of distressed humanity. These young men, whom no one else will have, made us a meal, got us a drink, showed us around; this really is their own home. The girls from another home the order runs were invited to dinner. The boys who tend the livestock bore off my little daughter, who returned clutching a large warm duck's egg. Father Bidone and the boys who take care of the chapel took us to pray there. The coloured glass behind the altar had been smashed by local hooligans sometime since morning Mass. The boys' faces looked as pained as if the stones had struck them. But most of the local hostility has been disarmed, they told us. One of the house-parents, a young Irishman who lived at the venture with his wife and two babies, told us that he had started to take the older youths to the pub in the evening for a "shandy." They were at first made extremely unwelcome. The publican slapped down their change and tried to hurry them off. But no one is going to hurry an Irishman over his beer; they stuck it out and came back again, and now, when they don't come, there's a disappointed "Where's the boys this evening?" from the locals. The young Irishman was just back from a strenuous camping trip with a vanload of boys to Ireland. "Lord, when did we take Thee on the rides at the CNE, or when did we camp with Thee for two weeks in Ireland in the soft cold rain . . . ?"

The Molesey Venture and the eight similar homes this order runs for the retarded and old are post-Conciliar foundations, though the order itself is older. Here, too, there is nothing singular, in a Catholic sense. Yet they also capture the religious imagination of modern Catholics, especially the young, who come to this humble, hard work with sacrificial dedication. The basic conviction of modernism has always been that if Christianity is to survive, it must ask less in the way of belief and morality. That large part of the Church, especially among the religious orders, which is testing this conviction in universal experiment is rapidly disintegrating, having alienated even its own citizens. Those few Catholic endeavours that are succeeding in the post-Conciliar world, such as the two I have described, are living proof that exactly the opposite is true.

Since the beginning, Christianity has been communicated by absolutists, by people who believed utterly and practised to the utterance. Modernity has changed nothing in this respect. No one is going to give up his whole life to an ethical or psychological understanding of Christianity. No one was ever converted by a seminar. Whatever form the witness of the Catholic takes – martyrdom, care of the helpless, instruction in the faith, the priesthood, the religious life, the increasingly difficult fidelity to the Church's sexual morality in marriage, or in the single life in the world – can proceed and continue only from confident belief in the actual intervention of God in history. Only witness from faith can inspire faith in others. It was the overpowering historical event of the Resurrection that created the faith of the Apostles, and their faith, passionately communicated, that begot the faith of the Church. No psychologically understood "resurrection experience" can have the power to transform the lives of modern men and to reconcile them to the world of suffering and death. Christianity radically transformed the pagan and savage societies it found, and the residue at least of Christian values continues to make bearable the modern society we call the West. Only a total missionary faith in the truth of the Redemption can become incarnate in charity redemptive of society. The belief that we are all fallen inspires true egalitarianism and brotherly compassion. We are equally stricken, our intellect darkened, our will weakened and inclined to evil, our bodies subject to disease and death. The belief that Christ atoned for us to God gives us a second chance, destroys despair. And the crown of belief, Christianity's great promise made in Christ's name that we shall live forever, makes sweet the sorrows of life led in the light of eternity.

I earlier recorded the standard argument that if Catholic modernism had been given its head in its first appearance, it would soon have settled down into a faithful and renewing force within the Church. Now we have tested that thesis. Theological relativism has had a free run for more than twenty years, virtually unresisted at any level of the Church, even by the papacy until recently. No heresy since Arianism has had a more authoritative airing. Its missionary zeal has ensured that every Catholic has been exposed to its ideology. Even the impermeably orthodox have had to come to terms with important elements of the revolution now institutionalized, in liturgy and discipline. Now we can answer the question: Has modernism worked? Has it renewed the Church, made the Gospel more reasonable to alienated modern man? Has it been redemptive of secular society? What are its fruits? It has undermined the faith of millions. It has emptied the churches of North America and western Europe and has begun to move Africa and Asia on the road back to paganism. By its relativizing of morality, it has legitimized within the Church that relapse into pagan sexual behaviour that is occurring in secular society. That this was not the intent of good modernists, I readily admit. I recognize, too, that the final collapse of what remained of Christendom and its moral restraints must exert pressure upon the relative sanctuary of Catholicism. The modernist charge a hundred years ago and again at the Second Vatican Council was that the Church was not speaking to modern man. To whom is it now speaking? Is it speaking to anyone?

We have in my family what amounts to a test group in the post-Vatican II modernist experiment. Our oldest child was in the first classes to be exposed to that early neo-modernist masterpiece, the *Canadian Catechism, Come to the Father*. We objected to that catechism at the first indoctrination meetings and we are still objecting to it. Most of the religious who developed and enforced it have since left their orders and the Church. It is now by several revisions even less Catholic, if that is possible. Last year, we were forced to remove our fifth child from First Holy Communion class, since the parish and school refused to prepare her, in obedience to Church law, first for Confession. During practices, therefore, she had to sit in the last pew with the class's only Protestant student. We ourselves prepared her for the sacrament of Penance and she made her First Confession and Communion privately, with our new convert godchild, at the hands of our former parish priest.

Over the years, tension between the faith professed at home and that officially presented through the Catholic system has produced some exceedingly nasty arguments with our children. Rearing them as Catholics has increasingly involved angry descents on the schools, removal from particular classes, constant contradiction of what they have been taught by people they rightly want to believe, expostulatory letters to various levels of hierarchy, *sotto voce* arguments with priests after Mass and louder ones in less sacred forums. When orthodox parents lose this civil war for hearts and minds, their children first accept the whole relativist proposal, second, abandon Catholic faith. Unbelief begets unbelief. And if the parental world view prevails, the result is a precocious cynicism, destructive to Catholic community but often what one must settle for.

There seems to be no way out of this trap. The purpose of the Catholic life is not argument. One cannot pray with one eye open for sacrilege, nor learn about the imitation of Christ with one ear tuned for heresy. Yet neither can one let sacrilege or heresy go unchallenged when the matter at stake is one's children's immortal souls. So teaching them Catholic truth necessarily involves correcting falsehoods taught them by people teaching with the Church's mandate. The most charity that one can then manage is the assumption that those people are sincere but mistaken. Parents make those comforting noises we've all learned: "He/she is really a very good priest/nun. . . . He/she picked that up in the seminary/Toronto School of Theology/Divine Word. . . . They're really good pious Catholics, but they've been told that by religious education class/RENEW/inquiry class. . . . It's the bishop's fault. He knows what's going on and doesn't correct it. . . ." Our children are left with the happy choice between thinking their teachers knaves or thinking them fools.

And belief begets belief. Four times now we've stood with our children and heard the oratory's highly educated young moderns make the ancient vows of Catholic ordination. Lives lived in the strong hope of the Resurrection, not as a metaphor but as a solid promise to be fulfilled quite soon, are irreplaceable carriers of Christianity. Every time we go back to Sussex, yet another of Father Bidone's lay recruits descends upon us with another vanload of big wild boys for tea. Last year, Father Bidone's order in England ordained another priest and professed four novices.

The Catholics who stay in the Church and the converts who come do so through the inspiration that incarnations like these provide. I speak from grateful experience. I saw that kind of Catholic faith prove in the end irresistible. As I've mentioned, my husband was not a Catholic nor a Christian at the time of our marriage. I was a foolish young liberal then (than which there is no one more self-righteously enlightened), and I was opposed to the common Catholic urgency to "turn" the non-Catholic partner before marriage. (Nor was I softened by having an ass of a priest badger my mother about it on her death-bed.) When the sensible reasons for the Church's discouragement of mixed marriages quickly revealed themselves to me, it took several years of penitent petition to Our Lady before my husband suddenly believed.

His parents were not Christians, though they respected Christianity. In his first letter to me, my father-in-law, Malcolm Muggeridge, wrote that, though he could not believe it, he thought the Christian explanation of the human condition to be the most satisfying that the world had produced and that he envied people who held it. My first conversation with him and my mother-in-law was about the Catholic Church and why I adhered to it. They were deeply religious people, disillusioned by the failure of all the modern gods, without a spiritual home. Their long odyssey is perhaps known to readers of this book. Over the years they came to profess an unaffiliated Christianity. As the moral and cultural revolution in the West quickened, Mr. Muggeridge increasingly found himself defending unpopular Catholic positions. Ironically, as in the case of *Humanae Vitae*, he was opposed by Catholic spokesmen. "I do not doubt," he wrote to the *London Times*, at the beginning of the uproar about the encyclical on human life, "that in the history books when our squalid moral decline is recounted, with the final breakdown in law and order that must follow (for without a moral order there can be no social, political, or any other order), the Pope's courageous and just, though I fear . . . largely ineffectual stand will be accorded the respect and admiration it deserves."[5]

Early in the Council years, in an article called "Backward, Christian

Soldiers!," he predicted what would happen from the Council and I said, confidently, that he was wrong. I saw when we were at Mass together that Mrs. Muggeridge came quite soon to believe in the Real Presence and I longed for her to be able to come with us to Holy Communion, but it could not happen separately for them. As the confusion in the Church grew, I gradually lost hope (though we never stopped praying) that they would come to Church. He said, and I was hard put not to agree with him, that what we were experiencing was the collapse of western civilization into a new dark ages, and the Church, being the western institution par excellence, was perishing with the world it created. I reaffirmed, as orthodox Catholics always do, the Petrine Promise, Christ's assurance to Peter that He would be with the Church unto the consummation of the world; which perhaps, we agreed, is upon us.

In the summer of 1982, Father Paul Bidone, who knew their hearts, suddenly wrote urgently to Mr. Muggeridge. Come now, he said. There is no reason to hesitate any longer. This is where you must both be. And in November of that year they were both received into the Church, with a delegation of Father Bidone's kids chirruping away around them. Three years ago Malcolm Muggeridge was writing articles about "Why I Am Not a Catholic." Now he writes to us about "our Church," brought to it in the end not by arguments, nor beauty, nor order, but through the witness of Catholics whose lives are faith incarnate.

When we were last in Sussex, we went to Mass with them on the Feast of the Assumption, August 15, still a Holy Day of Obligation in England. It had been a perfect English summer day; we had walked to Salehurst by the monks' path to the Church and had found to our joy that a statue of the Mother and Child again occupies the niche over the main door, empty since the Reformation; the Virgin Mary has come back to her valley. The nearest Catholic Church is several miles away at Hurst Green, a modest but beautiful little chapel dedicated to Our Lady built on the land and with the assistance of the Earl and Countess of Longford, convert Catholics, old friends and godparents of the Muggeridges. We went up through the beautiful golden fields in the golden evening light. There was the usual Catholic handful and an old priest who preached an Assumption sermon full of an old priest's chivalrous love of the Mother of God. He, too, dwelt on the Catholic history of the place, recalling the time of persecution after the Reformation, when recusant Catholics were fined the large sum of a shilling every Sunday that they attended Catholic Mass instead of the Reformed Protestant service. In that time, the recusant Catholic nobleman into whose family William the Conqueror's Battle Abbey had fallen after Henry VIII's dissolution of the monasteries pulled down and sold part of the abbey to pay the fines of his tenants. How hopeless things must have seemed then to that remnant, how bleak the future.

It struck me during the sermon that I was wrong in thinking that Catholicism had never returned to that place. All the people I had come to Mass with that evening were converts to Catholicism, come back to the old faith; Frank and Elizabeth Longford, my husband, Malcolm and Kitty Muggeridge. I felt utter thankfulness to be with them there in our beloved country the Catholic Church, on a great feast day of St. Mary the Virgin, in that holy Catholic place, in the high golden summer. We sang the national anthem of the Catholic English:

> *Faith of our fathers, Mary's pray'r*
> *Shall keep our country close to thee;*
> *And through the truth that comes from God*
> *Mankind shall prosper and be free.*
> *Faith of our fathers, holy Faith,*
> *We will be true to thee till death!*

How, at the end of this examination of the revolution within Catholicism, do I sum up the present state of the Church and the prospects for the future? Not a great deal more cheerfully, at least for the short run, than the way I began this book. Comforting and hopeful as was that Catholic moment I described above, I cannot pretend that it is typical. Our company at that Mass was as out of tune with the prevailing spirit of the secular or Catholic culture we live in as the Catholics of the Reformation were in that same place four hundred years ago. We are just as much a remnant; in worse case, indeed, since we were debarred from the Mass that comforted our ancestors.

One can state, cautiously but with growing confidence, that the revolution has been checked and the counter-revolution formally begun. I offer as a symbolic mark of that development the announcement in December 1984 by Charles Curran, instigator of the revolution in America, that he "is in correspondence with the Vatican" about his teachings.[6] But the devastation of the faith has been incalculably great. No matter how energetic the Catholic counter-revolution, it cannot reasonably be expected that many of those tens of millions who have abandoned the Catholic world view can be reconverted to it. And though the spread of the revolution may have been slowed, it has not been halted. Liberation theology will continue to subvert Central and South America, perhaps with serious political consequences; syncretism resulting from "inculturation" will continue to debauch Catholicism in Asia and Africa. Those "who hold and teach the Catholic faith that comes to us from the Apostles" are already a remnant.

The only kind thing about the future is that not one moment of it is foreseeable. Perhaps the army of occupation can be forced to abandon the country of Catholicism more quickly than we think it can; perhaps it will not leave behind it too scorched a countryside. Whatever happens, our times are in His hands, Who has promised to be with us to the consummation of the world. Hans Küng, gloomily noting that a counter-revolution had begun, advised his colleagues, "to stay, to fight and to work and prepare for the future." Yes, indeed we will, as we have done for the past twenty years; Küng, I think, will not. The front ranks of the revolution are much thinned since we began this struggle.

Remnant we may be, but it must be great cause for hope not only for the Catholic Church but for the civilization it created that this remnant includes the greatest man of our times, Pope John Paul II. In 1925, the Soviet Foreign Minister Chicherin said to Father Michel d'Herbigny, the Jesuit whom Pius XI made a bishop and sent to Russia to consecrate other bishops and appoint underground liaison with Rome, that communism felt quite confident of being able to destroy capitalism, but that Rome would be much harder to deal with. Without Rome, he said, religion would die. This is certainly true for what we call the West; without Rome, religion will cease to animate our civilization and mitigate the savageries of the human condition. All other branches of Christianity depend upon Rome as children upon their mother. Without Rome's cosmic view, we will be left to depend upon the values of the Politburo, of the boardroom, and of the laboratory.

Quomodo sedet sola civitas plena populo: facta est quasi vidua domina Gentium . . . non est qui consoletur eam ex omnibus caris eius; omnes amici eius spreverunt eam, et facti sunt ei inimici . . . omnes portae eius destructae: sacerdotes eius gementes: virgines eius squalidae . . . Et egressus est a filia Sion omnis decor eius. . . . Jerusalem, Jerusalem, convertere ad Dominum Deum tuum.

&~&

TWELVE RESOLUTIONS OF THE AD HOC COMMITTEE ON THE ROLE OF WOMEN

&~&

Here are the 12 recommendations on the role of women as adopted by the Canadian bishops during their plenary assembly in Ottawa:

1. That the bishops of Canada continue to take all steps necessary to ensure that principles of social justice are enunciated, upheld and applied with respect to women employed by or otherwise involved in the Church;

The bishops of Canada continue to speak out clearly and courageously against the injustices which are still being perpetrated against women throughout society.

2. At the national level, that the Commission for Liturgy continue to negotiate more firmly for corrections in liturgical texts and that all commissions of the CCCB be more attentive to use of inclusive language;

The bishops of Canada develop policies to foster a growing awareness of the importance of inclusive language in a Church of communion and take steps to implement them (liturgies, homilies, hymns, etc. with pastoral prudence).

3. That those women, as well as men, who exercise functions and services recognized by the bishop receive an official, pastoral mandate.

4. That bishops of Canada, by whatever measures available, ensure that all the instruments they use to educate on the vocation of marriage (catechetics, family education programs, marriage preparation courses, engaged and marriage encounters, retreats, etc.) be revised in the light of recent cultural developments as well as the teaching of Vatican II on the equality of women so that married women be recognized and promoted as equal partners the same as married men both in private and in public sectors, in accord with their personal vocation.

5. Each diocese set aside a bursary and scholarship fund for the use of lay women. These funds would be used to assist in payment of tuition, registration, babysitting, accommodations, etc., as applicable. The applicant would assure that the training obtained would be such as to further her ability to serve the Church community.

6. That adequate representation of women and men who are competent and/ or experienced be assured at all levels of the diocesan church;

When organizing consultations or forming committees at national, diocesan or parish levels, equal numbers of competent women and men be considered.

7. Priests and future priests be conscientized to the fundamental equality of women in the new humanity instituted by Christ, "equality of origin and destiny, equality of mission and commitments" (Canadian Bishops at 1983 Synod);

Priests recognize in their attitudes and pastoral activities the fundamental equality of women and men in the Church;

In the professional formation of future priests, the question of the role of women in the Church be considered as a question of prime importance;

Women be actively involved in the formation of future priests.

8. That the CCCB encourage the establishment of fully representative diocesan ad hoc committees to study ministries of women. These committees would collaborate with national and/or regional episcopal commissions.

9. That a revised kit prepared by the Pastoral Team by made available to dioceses for use in parishes and to Church organizations, with the understanding that it may be adapted to their particular needs;

The appointment of a committee or of a woman who will foster the promotion and the pastoral co-ordination of the revised working kit at the diocesan level.

10. A study be undertaken on the situation of women involved in the diocesan Church (who and where they are, what they are doing, etc.).

11. Women be accorded a larger participation within the Pastoral Team of the CCCB;

A permanent member of the Pastoral Team have as her primary responsibility the issue of women in the Church.

12. That the CCCB encourage the regions and dioceses to hold gatherings where women can meet together and establish dialogue;

That the CCCB pursue its theological and pastoral reflection on the lived experience and mission of women in the Church;

That the CCCB set itself a schedule of ongoing review of the situation of women in the Church and that this ongoing review be carried out with women and men.

NOTES

❧

Chapter 1: Revolution: The Background

1. James Hitchcock, *The Decline and Fall of Radical Catholicism* (New York: Herder and Herder, 1971), p. 43.
2. For instance, Michael Novak, the famous sixties radical Catholic, who, having undergone a conversion, is now attempting to stake out a "neo-liberal" position in the Church, insists that he now disagrees with "the teaching authority of the Church" only "in its condemnation of artificial contraception." *Confession of a Catholic* (San Francisco: Harper and Row, 1983), p. 118.
3. Sources for this outline include: Peter Shaw, *American Patriots and the Rituals of Revolution* (Cambridge: Harvard University Press, 1981); Aristotle, *The Politics*, trans. Ernest Barker (London: Oxford University Press, 1950); Walter Laqueur, "Revolution," *International Encyclopedia of the Social Sciences*, 1968; Alfred Muesel, "Revolution and Counter-Revolution," *Encyclopedia of the Social Sciences*, 1967; Gunter Lewy, *Religion and Revolution* (New York: Oxford University Press, 1974); Michael Walzer, *Regicide and Revolution* (London: Cambridge University Press, 1974).
4. For a recent example, see Peter Shaw's extremely interesting study of the psychology of the men who made the American Revolution, *American Patriots*.
5. Ibid., p. 231.
6. For the classic study of religious antinomianism, see Ronald Knox, *Enthusiasm* (Oxford: Clarendon Press, 1950).
7. Peter Berger, *The Sacred Canopy* (New York: Doubleday, 1967), p. 112.
8. Ibid., p. 113.
9. For a different view of the consequences of the Reformation and the American Revolution, see John Courtney Murray, *We Hold These Truths* (New York: Sheed and Ward, 1960) and Russell Kirk, *The Roots of American Order* (La Salle, Ill.: Open Court, 1974). These Catholic scholars, one liberal, one conservative, do not admit of any necessary dichotomy between "the American proposition" and "the Catholic proposition."
10. John Henry Newman, *Apologia Pro Vita Sua* (New York: W. W. Norton, 1968), p. 38. Newman's "note A" on the meaning of *liberalism*, ibid., p. 216, remains the best exposition of the Protestant principle.
11. See for instance A. R. Vidler, *The Church in an Age of Revolution* (Harmondsworth, Middlesex: Penguin Books, 1961) or Gabriel Daly, O.S.A., *Transcendence and Immanence: A Study in Catholic Modernism and Integralism* (Oxford: Clarendon Press, 1980). For a different view, unsympathetic to modernism, see John A. Hardon, *Christianity in the Twentieth Century* (Garden City, New York: Doubleday, Image Books, 1972).
12. Quoted by Pierre Elliott Trudeau in *Federalism and the French Canadians* (Toronto: Macmillan of Canada, 1968), p. 110. The passage occurred in the program "Prières du matin." In the chapter in which he quotes this passage, "Some Obstacles to Democracy in Quebec," Trudeau blames the Catholic Church for "the complete lack of a democratic frame of reference for French-Canadian political thinking." Ibid.

Chapter 2: The First Modernist Crisis

1. Vidler, *Church*, pp. 188-9. In 1982, in his foreword to Ellen Leonard, *George Tyrrell and the Catholic Tradition* (New York: Paulist Press, 1982), Dr. Vidler notes that "the modernist movement which was condemned by Pope Pius x . . . has to a large extent come into its own since Vatican II."
2. Ibid., p. 188.
3. Alfred Loisy, *My Duel with the Vatican* (New York: Greenwood Press, 1968), pp. 102-3, 111.
4. Rudolf Bultmann, "New Testament and Mythology," in *Kerygma and Myth*, ed. Hans Werner Bartsch (London: S.P.C.K., 1964), vol. I, p. 39.
5. George Tyrrell, *Christianity at the Crossroads* (London: George Allen and Unwin, 1963), pp. 105, 109.
6. See, for example, Rosemary Ruether, *Sexism and God-Talk: Towards a Feminist Theology* (Boston: Beacon Press, 1983), pp. 122-3.
7. Ibid., p. 125.
8. James Breech, *The Silence of Jesus* (Toronto: Doubleday, n.d.), p. 218.
9. John Malcolm Muggeridge.
10. Stephen Neill, *The Interpretation of the New Testament 1861-1962* (New York: Oxford University Press, 1962), p. 209.
11. Adolf von Harnack, *What Is Christianity?* (New York and Evanston: Harper Torchbooks, 1957), p. 56.
12. Bultmann, *Kerygma*, p. 309.
13. Breech, *Silence*, pp. 22, 47, 71, 80.
14. Adolf von Harnack, *The Sayings of Jesus: The Second Source of St. Matthew and St. Luke* (New York: Putnam's, 1908). As a cheering antidote, see Rev. Dr. A. M. Farrar, "On Dispensing With Q," in *Studies in the Gospel* (Oxford: Blackwell, 1955).
15. For a recent critique of the historical-critical method, see Stephen Neill, *Jesus Through Many Eyes: Introduction to the Theology of the New Testament* (Philadelphia: Fortress Press, 1976); George Kelly, *The New Biblical Theorists: Raymond Brown and Beyond* (Ann Arbor: Servant Press, 1983); Stephen B. Clark, "Modern Approaches to Scriptural Authority," in *Christianity Confronts Modernity* (Ann Arbor: Servant Press, 1981).
16. Bultmann, *Kerygma*, p. 5.
17. Ibid., p. 10.
18. All quotations from Vatican II documents taken from Rev. J. L. Gonzalez, s.s.p. and the Daughters of St. Paul, comps., NCWC translation, *The Sixteen Documents of Vatican II and the Instruction on the Liturgy with Commentaries by the Council Fathers* (Boston: Daughters of St. Paul, n.d.).
19. Karl Jaspers and Rudolf Bultmann, *Myth and Christianity* (New York: The Noonday Press, 1958), p. 69.
20. Newman, *Apologia*, p. 87.
21. Ibid., p. 51.
22. Thomas Molnar, *Theists and Atheists* (The Hague: Mouton Publishers, 1980), p. 190.
23. Raymond E. Brown, *The Virginal Conception and Bodily Resurrection of Jesus* (New York: Paulist Press, 1973), p. 117.
24. Tyrrell, *Crossroads*, p. 146.
25. Brown, *Conception*, p. 68.

Chapter 3: Interim: The Revolution Underground

1. Ludwig Ott, *The Fundamentals of Catholic Dogma* (St. Louis, Miss.: B. Herder Book Co., 1954), p. 16.

2. Newman, *Apologia*, p. 200.
3. Daly, *Transcendence*, p. 215.
4. Ibid.
5. Philip Hughes, *A Popular History of the Reformation* (Garden City, New York: Hanover House, 1957), p. 267.
6. Quoted in Robert Speaight, *Teilhard de Chardin* (London: Collins, 1967), p. 162.
7. Ibid., p. 112.
8. Ibid., p. 233.
9. Review of *The Divine Milieu*, quoted in *Flannery O'Connor: Her Life, Library and Book Reviews*, ed. Lorine M. Getz (Toronto: The Edwin Mullen Press, 1980), p. 161.
10. Ibid., review of *Letters from a Traveller*, p. 196.
11. Quoted by Thomas Corbishley, S.J., in "Teilhard and Original Sin," *Teilhard Review*, vol. 9, 2, pp. 36-7.
12. Speaight, *Teilhard*, p. 290. Flannery O'Connor entitled one of her short stories, and a later collection, "Everything That Rises Must Converge."
13. Ibid., p. 280.
14. *Teilhard Review*, vol. 1, p. 17.
15. Letter from Teilhard, September 1950, to a priest who had left the Church to join the Old Catholics, the group who went into schism as a result of Vatican I. Quoted from *Approaches*, March 1966. My translation.
16. Ibid.
17. Quoted in Jean-Pierre Demoulin, *Let Me Explain* (London: Collins, 1970).
18. Speaight, *Teilhard*, p. 139.
19. Teilhard, *Approaches* letter. The reference is to the recently promulgated *Humani Generis*.
20. Speaight, *Teilhard*, p. 299.
21. Rosemary Ruether, "Continuing Reform After Vatican II," *The Month* (March 1973), p. 97.
22. Speech to OECTA, Ontario English Catholic Teachers' Association convention, Toronto, 12 November 1983.
23. *National Catholic Reporter*, 20 July 1984: "When Chill Sets In, 'Stay and Fight' – Küng."
24. Speaight, *Teilhard*, p. 300.
25. *Conception*.
26. *National Catholic Reporter*, 2 December 1977.
27. Kelly, *Biblical Theorists*, p. 137 ff.
28. Ibid., p. 7.
29. Gregory Baum, *Man Becoming: God in Secular Experience* (New York: Herder and Herder, 1971), p. 188.
30. Ibid., pp. 189-90.
31. Ibid., pp. 283, 284.
32. Quoted in James Hitchcock, "The Gospel According to Cuomo," *National Catholic Register*, 16 September 1984.

Chapter 4: The Revolution Surfaces
1. Michael Novak, "Marriage: The Lay Voice," *Commonweal*, 14 February 1964, pp. 587-90.
2. See Julien Benda, *The Betrayal of the Intellectuals* (Boston: Beacon Press, 1955) and Paul Hollander, *Political Pilgrims* (New York: Oxford University Press, 1981), especially chapter 2: "Intellectuals, Politics, and Morality," and chapter 9: "Conclusions Concerning the Nature of Intellectuals, Estrangement and Its Consequences."

3. See Richard McCormick, S.J., "The Relation of Theological Reflection and Analysis to the Magisterium," *National Catholic Reporter*, 7 August 1968; and idem, *Notes on Moral Theology 1965 Through 1980* (Lanham, Maryland: University Press of America, 1981), for his discussion of the relationship of theologians to the teaching office of the Church.

4. This summary is taken from Alphonse de Valk, C.S.B., *The Canadian Catholic Review*, May 1983, pp. 5, 143, correspondence.

5. Stefan Cardinal Wyszynski, *A Freedom Within* (New York: Harcourt Brace Jovanovich, 1983), p. 10.

6. American figures taken from the *Official Catholic Directory* (New York: P. J. Kenedy) for the relevant years.

7. *Annuaire/Directory of Canadian Catholic Conference* (Ottawa: Concacan, Inc.) from 1968 to 1984.

8. Edward Schillebeeckx, O.P., *The Real Achievement of Vatican II* (New York: Herder and Herder, 1967), pp. 84-5.

9. Space does not allow me to go further into this matter here. For a thorough critique of the double voice in the Vatican II statements, see Michael Davies, *Pope John's Council* (Chawleigh, Devon: Augustine Publishing Company, 1977), especially chapter 6, "Time Bombs."

10. Quoted in Ralph M. Wiltgen, S.V.D., *The Rhine Flows into the Tiber* (Chawleigh, Devon: Augustine Publishing Company, 1978), p. 59.

11. Peter Nichols, *The Pope's Divisions* (Toronto: Clarke Irwin, 1981), p. 44.

12. Henri Fesquet, English title, *The Drama of Vatican II*, trans. Bernard Murchland, American introduction Michael Novak (New York: Random House, 1967). Indicative of the importance Fesquet had for the most "progressive" Council fathers, the book sports congratulatory prefatory letters from Helder Camara, the "red archbishop" of Olinda-Recife; Archbishop Athenagoras, patriarch of Constantinople; the president of the Académie française; Roger Schultz, prior of the ecumenical monastery Taizé.

13. Robert Kaiser, *Inside the Council* (London: Burns and Oates, 1963).

14. Ibid., pp. 105, 107.

15. Ibid., p. 21.

16. Ibid., p. 225.

17. Ibid.

18. Ibid., pp. 34, 35, 33-42.

19. Ibid., p. 241.

20. Speech, Burtchaell, 2 October 1981, quoted in *Catholic Mind* (April 1982).

21. Wiltgen, *Rhine*, p. 5.

22. Ibid., p. 23.

23. Ibid.

24. Ibid.

25. Ibid., p. 17.

26. Peter Hebblethwaite, "Catholics," CBC Radio, 6 May 1984.

27. Wiltgen, *Rhine*, p. 114.

28. Ibid., p. 228.

29. Ibid., p. 242.

30. Ibid., p. 232.

31. Remi de Roo, "Catholics," CBC Radio, 6 May 1984.

32. Ibid.

33. Quoted in Wiltgen, *Rhine*, p. 210.

34. Quoted in Wiltgen, *Rhine*, p. 59.

35. Wiltgen, p. 80.

36. Cardinal Joseph Siri, *Gethsemane: Reflections on the Contemporary Theological Movement* (Chicago: Franciscan Herald Press, 1981), p. 274. Siri accuses not only Rahner but also Jacques Maritain, Henri de Lubac, and a large number of other influential theologians of an historicist perspective on Catholic faith.
37. Joseph Jungmann, *The Mass of the Roman Rite* (Maryland: Christian Classics, 1978), p. 124.
38. Wiltgen, *Rhine*, p. 42.
39. For the best account of the liturgical revolution see Michael Davies, *Pope Paul's New Mass* (Dickinson, Texas: The Angelus Press, 1980).
40. Quoted in Wiltgen, *Rhine*, p. 91.
41. See letter, Rev. Joseph W. Oppitz, c.s.s.r., in *America*, 15 April 1972.
42. Nichols, *Divisions*, p. 98.

Chapter 5: The Triggering Incident
1. John T. Noonan, Jr., *Contraception: A History of Its Treatment by the Catholic Theologians and Canonists* (Cambridge: Harvard University Press, 1965), p. 6.
2. Maurice J. Moore, *Death of a Dogma: The American Catholic Clergy's View of Contraception* (University of Chicago: Community and Family Study Center, 1973), p. 48.
3. Ibid., p. 4.
4. *America*, 4 November 1961.
5. Ibid., 9 December 1961, 22 December 1961, 17 February 1962.
6. Ibid., 27 April 1963, 25 May 1963, 1 June 1963.
7. John C. Ford, s.j., and Gerald Kelly, s.j., *Contemporary Moral Theology* (Westminster: Newman Press, 1971), vol. 2, *Marriage Questions*, p. 277.
8. Andrew Greeley, "Family Planning Among American Catholics," *Chicago Studies* (Spring 1963).
9. Donald Thorman's memoir was reprinted in *National Catholic Reporter*, 30 November 1984.
10. Robert Blair Kaiser, *The Politics of Sex and Religion* (Kansas City: Leaven Press, 1985). See also idem., "The Long Road to Birth Control Control," *National Catholic Reporter*, 3 May 1985, from which this quotation is taken.
11. Gregory Baum, "Report from Rome: 'Birth Control and the Council,' " *Commonweal*, 20 November 1964, p. 284.
12. Quoted in Wiltgen, *Rhine*, pp. 269-70.
13. For a good summary of the collaboration between secular and religious moral revolutionaries in the years 1963-68 see James Hitchcock, "The American Press and Birth Control: Preparing the Ground for Dissent," *Homiletic and Pastoral Review* (July 1980).
14. Moore, *Death*, pp. 3-4.
15. Ibid., p. 19.

Chapter 6: The Consequences of Humanae Vitae
1. For a recent defence of this position see John C. Ford, s.j., and Germain Grisez, "Contraception and the Infallibility of the Ordinary Magisterium," *Theological Studies*, vol. 39 (June 1978).
2. Quoted in *National Catholic Reporter*, 7 August 1968.
3. Text of Curran's statement and of the Vatican statements quoted here taken from *National Catholic Reporter*, 7 August 1968. See this issue of NCR for a

very good account of the reaction to *Humanae Vitae* from both sides of the controversy.

4. Charles Curran, "Growth (Hopefully) in Wisdom, Age and Grace," in *Journeys*, ed. Gregory Baum (New York: Paulist Press, 1975), pp. 87-116. All quotations from this essay unless otherwise specified.
5. See Hitchcock, "Preparing," p. 21.
6. *National Catholic Reporter*, 7 August 1968.
7. Ibid.
8. Ibid.
9. Quoted in William Shannon, *The Lively Debate* (New York: Sheed and Ward, 1970), p. 215.
10. Canadian *Catholic Register*, 5 October 1968.
11. Curran, "Growth," p. 105.
12. Quoted in *National Catholic Reporter*, 7 August 1968.
13. *National Catholic Reporter*, 9 October 1968.
14. Ibid., 23 October 1968.
15. Ibid., advertisement and editorial, 6 November 1968.
16. Ibid., 20 November 1968.
17. Ibid., 23 October 1968.
18. For text of U.S. bishops' statement, see *National Catholic Reporter*, 20 November 1968.
19. Quoted in Andrew Greeley, "Church Authority: Beyond the Problem," *National Catholic Reporter*, 26 September 1980.
20. Anne Roche, *The Gates of Hell* (Toronto: McClelland and Stewart, 1975), chapters 6 and 7.
21. Canadian *Catholic Register*, 3 August 1968.
22. Ibid., 17 August 1968.
23. *Western Catholic Reporter*, 1 August 1968.
24. Canadian *Catholic Register*, 10 August 1968.
25. *Globe and Mail*, 7 August 1968.
26. Quoted in Edward Sheridan, s.j., "Canadian Bishops on 'Human Life,' " *America*, 19 October 1968, p. 349.
27. Canadian *Catholic Register*, 5 October 1968.
28. Rahner's rebuttal, based on a sophisticated theory of dissent, had appeared in the German Jesuit magazine *Stimmen der Zeit*. The translation circulated at Winnipeg was made by another Regis College Jesuit, Richard Roach. In 1982 Roach publicly retracted his dissident statement on *Humanae Vitae*, charging that he had "left the [Jesuit] seminary expertly trained in deviant moral theology." See "Jesuit Educator Retracts Moral Theology Views," *National Catholic Register*, 7 March 1982.
29. *Western Catholic Reporter*, 3 October 1968.
30. Moore, *Death*, p. 114.
31. Sheridan, "Canadian Bishops," p. 349.
32. Canadian *Catholic Register*, 5 October 1968.
33. Elizabeth Anscombe, "You Can Have Sex Without Children," in *The Collected Philosophical Papers of G.E.M. Anscombe* (Minneapolis: University of Minnesota Press, 1981), vol. 3, pp. 82-96.
34. Canadian *Catholic Register*, 23 November 1968.
35. Charles Curran, "Ten Years Later," *Commonweal*, 7 July 1978, p. 429.
36. Ibid., p. 426.
37. Ibid., p. 427.
38. *Concilium I* (New Jersey: Paulist Press, 1964).
39. Curran, "Ten Years," p. 428.

40. Quoted in *National Catholic Reporter*, 7 August 1968.
41. Ibid., 23 October 1968.
42. Richard McCormick, S.J., "Raises Questions on the Nature of Magisterium," *National Catholic Reporter*, 7 August 1968, p. 9.
43. Richard McCormick, S.J., "Notes on Moral Theology," *Theological Studies*, vol. 29 (December 1968), p. 738.
44. Charles Curran and Richard McCormick, S.J., ed., *The Magisterium and Morality* (New York: Paulist Press, 1982), p. 472.
45. Ibid., p. 486.
46. Ibid.
47. Max Weber, *The Theory of Social and Economic Organization*, trans. Talcott Parsons (New York: Oxford University Press, 1947), p. 324.
48. Greeley, "Church Authority."
49. Moore, *Death*, p. 115.
50. Curran, "Ten Years," p. 430.
51. *National Catholic Reporter*, 20 November 1968.

Chapter 7: The Phases of the Revolution
1. Dan Donovan, "Issues in Theology," *Catholic New Times*, 25 March 1984.
2. Louis Bouyer, *The Liturgy Revived: A Commentary on the Constitution* (Notre Dame, Indiana: University of Notre Dame Press, 1964); Hans Küng, *The Changing Church: Reflections on the Progress of the Second Vatican Council* (London: Sheed and Ward, 1965).
3. Louis Bouyer, *The Decomposition of Catholicism* (Chicago: Franciscan Herald Press, 1969).
4. For opposite views of the USCC, see Arthur Jones and Joseph Feuerherd, "USCC, NCCB and We the People," *National Catholic Reporter*, 9 November 1984; and Joop Koopman, "USCC Finds Itself Focus of Scrutiny," *National Catholic Register*, 29 May 1983.
5. *Globe and Mail*, 21 April 1984, Letters.
6. *National Catholic Reporter*, 20 November 1968. NCR's excited account includes a picture of the priests sitting at Miss Harris's feet.
7. Ibid., 30 October 1968.
8. Ibid., 23 October 1968, Letters.
9. Ibid., 27 November 1968.
10. See Rosemary Ruether, "Beginnings: An Intellectual Autobiography," in *Journeys*, ed. Baum, p. 45: ". . . my devotion to Mary was somewhat less than my devotion to some far more powerful divine females that I knew: Isis, Athena, and Artemis."
11. Ruether, "Continuing Reform," pp. 96, 93.
12. Thomas Sheehan, "Revolution in the Church," *New York Review of Books*, 14 June 1984, p. 35.
13. Ibid.
14. My article appeared in the *Globe and Mail*, 19 December 1980; Archbishop MacNeil's letter, *Globe and Mail*, 24 December 1980; my answer, Letters, *Globe and Mail*, 10 January 1981; Monsignor Murphy's answer, Letters, *Globe and Mail*, 17 January 1981. Monsignor Murphy is now (October 1985) General Secretary of the CCCB.
15. Sheehan, "Revolution," p. 38.

Chapter 8: The Battlefronts
1. Bouyer, *Revived*, p. 6.
2. Bouyer, *Decomposition*, p. 105.

3. Richard Toporoski, "The Language of Worship," *Communio* (Fall 1977), p. 256. The best treatment of the revisionism carried out by ICEL in its translation of the official Latin text into English.

4. Claude Poirier, O.P., *Fragments*, vol. 28 (February 1984).

5. Transcript of appeal by Roseanne Skoke-Graham, Christopher MacFarlane, Veronica MacFarlane, Rosalie Hifey, Kathryn Skoke, Margaret Martin, against their conviction for wilfully disturbing the order or solemnity of religious worship; 4-18 August 1982, p. 93.

6. "Faith without Doubt Called 'No Faith at all,' " *National Catholic Reporter*, 6 July 1984.

7. See *Crusade for a Christian Civilization* (April 1977). Photographs and text of the "mass" in my possession.

8. E. Michael Jones, "Fidelity Attends the Feast of Fools," *Fidelity* (October 1984).

9. Patrick Byrne, ed., *National Bulletin on Liturgy*, vol. 92 (January-February 1984). A sustained and vituperative attack from the Canadian bishops' liturgy office on the new code's traditionalist approach to the liturgy.

10. John O'Malley, S.J., "The Jesuits' Congregation," *America*, 19 November 1983, p. 308.

11. Sheehan, "Revolution," p. 39.

12. John Godey, *The Taking of Pelham One Two Three* (New York: Putnam, 1973), p. 214.

13. Brian Moore, *Catholics* (Toronto: McClelland and Stewart, 1972), pp. 70-71.

14. Parish bulletin, 18 November 1984, St. Vincent de Paul Church, Niagara-on-the-Lake, Ontario. Copy in my possession.

15. *Instruction on Certain Aspects of the 'Theology of Liberation,'* Sacred Congregation for the Doctrine of the Faith. Vatican translation, St. Paul edition. Issued in Rome on 6 August 1984, significantly, on the Feast of the Transfiguration of Christ.

16. Ruether, "Continuing Reform," p. 93.

17. *Catholic Book of Worship II* (Ottawa: Canadian Conference of Catholic Bishops and Gordon V. Thompson, Ltd., 1980). See for example p. 465: "Good Christian men, rejoice" has become "Good Christians all, rejoice"; "and man is blest for evermore" becomes "and we are blest . . ." On p. 462: "Hark the Herald Angels Sing!" has had "man" and "sons" changed to "we" and "us." Etcetera. This high-handed piece of vandalism was carried out by the National Committee for the Revision of the Catholic Book of Worship, composed of seven priests, including Patrick Byrne, who produces the *National Liturgy Bulletin*, four nuns, and four laymen. No textual footnotes accompanied these changes, although the editors were more respectful of the integrity of the lachrymose "sacred song" "How Great Thou Art," to which the two slight changes were carefully footnoted. The changes in the carols were made after many nuns refused to sing the original "sexist" words.

18. *National Catholic Register*, 4 March 1984.

19. Ibid., 27 November 1983.

20. Ibid.

21. Ibid.

22. *Catholic New Times*, 11 December 1983, report by Laurie Bell.

23. *National Catholic Register*, 26 August 1984.

24. Ibid., 18 September 1984.

25. *Maclean's*, 22 June 1981.

26. *National Catholic Register*, 27 November 1983.

27. Ibid., 4 March 1984.

28. Rosemary Curb and Nancy Manahan, *Lesbian Nuns: Breaking Silence* (Tallahassee, Florida: Naiad Press, 1985). Naiad also published *Old Dyke Tales*, *Black Lesbian in White America*, and *Labiaflowers*.
29. Ruether, *God-Talk*, p. 47.
30. Ibid., p. 32.
31. Ibid., p. 38.
32. Ibid., p. 160.
33. Ibid., p. 69.
34. Ibid., p. 114.
35. Ibid., p. 135.
36. Ibid., p. 209.
37. *National Catholic Register*, 27 November 1983.
38. Ted Schmidt, "Russians: Myths and Realities," lecture delivered at Ontario English Catholic Teachers Association convention, 12 November 1983.
39. *Catholic New Times*, 3 June 1984.
40. Ibid., 17 June 1984.
41. O'Malley, "Congregation," p. 308.

Chapter 9: The Counter-revolution Begins
1. Sheehan, "Revolution," p. 38.
2. *Hamilton Spectator*, 19 November 1983.
3. *Globe and Mail*, 27 October 1984.
4. "Bishops Attack on Ottawa Not Church View, Carter Says," *Globe and Mail*, 1 January 1983; "Bishops' Disagreement Exaggerated," *Toronto Star*, 15 January 1983; "Book Says Carter Wrong on Bishops' Support," *Globe and Mail*, 12 April 1984; "Catholic Collegiality Was Lost," Cardinal Carter, *Globe and Mail*, 21 April 1984, Letters.
5. "Jesuit Joins Debate on Economy," *Globe and Mail*, 10 March 1983.
6. "RC Debate on Women's Issues: Power Remains Solely for Men," *Globe and Mail*, 27 October 1984; "Provide Women Larger Role, Canadian RC Bishops Urged," *Globe and Mail*, 23 October 1984; "In Reasonable Tones," *Globe and Mail*, 29 October 1984, Editorial; Cardinal Carter, *Globe and Mail*, 12 November 1984, Letters.
7. Sheehan, "Revolution," p. 36.
8. Philip Hughes, *A History of the Church* (London: Sheed and Ward, 1979), vol. 1, p. 213. Still the best history of the Catholic Church.
9. See Paul Johnson, *Pope John Paul II and the Catholic Restoration* (London: Wiedenfeld and Nicolson, 1982).
10. Tony Castle, ed., *Through the Year with John Paul II* (New York: Crossroads Press, 1981), p. 215.
11. Johnson, *Restoration*, p. 4.
12. Rick Groen, "Close Encounters of a Heavenly Kind," *Globe and Mail*, 11 September 1984.
13. James Hitchcock, *Pope John Paul II and American Catholicism* (New York: National Committee of Catholic Laymen, Inc., 1980), p. 7.
14. Pope's speech of 9 September 1984 reprinted in the Canadian *Catholic Review*, 19 October 1984, pp. 5, 321.
15. Berger, *Canopy*, p. 112.
16. Ibid., p. 122.
17. Castle, *Through the Year*, pp. 37, 38-9.
18. Pope John Paul II, *The Original Unity of Man and Woman* (Boston: St. Paul Editions, 1981).

19. The above quotations on the Indult from *Christian Order* (March 1985), pp. 150-152.
20. *National Catholic Reporter*, 16 November 1984.
21. Ibid., 20 July 1984. See also for "the chill factor," ibid., 27 April, 4 May, and passim.
22. Ibid., 16 November 1984.
23. *National Catholic Register*, 17 June 1984.
24. Ibid., 6 November 1983.
25. Ibid., 20 October 1983.
26. Ibid., 6 November 1983.
27. Ibid., 10 April 1983.
28. Ibid., 17 June 1983.
29. Ibid., 27 January 1984.
30. *Catholic New Times*, 23 December 1984.
31. *National Catholic Register*, 11 December 1983.
32. Ibid., 19 February 1984.
33. *The Wanderer*, 4 November 1982.
34. Byrne, *National Bulletin on Liturgy*, pp. 15, 30.
35. *Christian Order* (May 1984).
36. Nichols, *Divisions*, p. 274.
37. Ruether, "Continuing Reform," p. 113.
38. Roche, *Gates*, p. 29.
39. Gustavo Gutierrez, *A Theology of Liberation: History, Politics and Salvation* (Maryknoll: Orbis Books, 1973).
40. *National Catholic Reporter*, 20 April 1984.
41. *30 Giorni* (March 1984). Reprinted in translation by *Catholicism in Crisis* (September 1984). In a later interview in *30 Giorni*, Cardinal Ratzinger amplified his criticisms. Interview reprinted in translation by *National Catholic Register*, 12 August 1984.
42. *National Catholic Reporter*, 2 November 1984.
43. Johnson, *Restoration*, p. 96.
44. Nicholas Lash, Cambridge historian and member of the editorial board of *Concilium*, quoted in *National Catholic Reporter*, 14 September 1984.
45. *National Catholic Register*, 4 November 1984.
46. Ibid., 7 October 1984.
47. *Catholic New Times*, 8 July 1984.
48. *National Catholic Register*, 4 November, 10 November 1984.
49. *National Catholic Reporter*, 22 June 1984.
50. *National Catholic Register*, 28 February 1982.
51. *National Catholic Reporter*, 10 April 1984.
52. As in: George Kelly, *The Battle for the American Church* (Garden City, New York: Regnery Gateway, 1979); idem, *The Crisis of Authority* (Chicago: Regnery Gateway, 1982); idem, *Biblical Theorists*.
53. *National Catholic Reporter*, 6 November 1983.

Chapter 10: Future of the Counter-revolution
1. *New York Times*, 7 October 1984, advertisement. See also Maguire's unspeakable "Visit to an Abortion Clinic," *National Catholic Reporter*, 5 October 1984.
2. Elizabeth McAlister, "Dear Friends of Pro-choice," *National Catholic Reporter*, 16 November 1984.
3. James Burtchaell, c.s.c., *Rachel Weeping and Other Essays on Abortion* (Kansas City: Andrews and McMeel, 1982). See also Burtchaell, "To Abort

is to Destroy One's Son or Daughter," *National Catholic Reporter*, 5 October 1984.

4. *National Catholic Reporter*, 4 March 1984.
5. "Document by Priest Praised by Gays," *Globe and Mail*, 10 September 1984.
6. *Globe and Mail*, 7 September 1984.
7. See for example: "Dignity Defies Church Teaching," *National Catholic Register*, 25 September 1983; James Hitchcock, "No Dignity in This Agenda," *National Catholic Register*, 3 June 1984; "Hickey on New Ways," *National Catholic Register*, 1 April 1984. See also the long, heavily documented study by Enrique Rueda, *The Homosexual Network* (Old Greenwich, Conn.: Devon Adair, 1982), especially chapter 7, "Relationship Between Religious Organizations and the Homosexual Movement: The Roman Catholic Church."
8. *The Mike*, 9 March 1984.
9. Anthony Kosnik, William Carroll, Agnes Cunningham, Ronald Modras, James Schulte, *Human Sexuality: New Directions in American Catholic Thought* (New York: Paulist Press, 1977), p. 99.
10. Ibid., p. 216.
11. Canadian *Catholic Register*, 10 November 1984.
12. Mary Malone, member of Ad Hoc Committee on the Role of Women in the Church, to Canadian Catholics for Women's Ordination (of which she is also a member), 24 November 1984 at the Faculty of Theology, St. Michael's College, University of Toronto. Transcript in my possession.
13. Ibid.
14. *National Catholic Register*, 4 November 1984.
15. *National Catholic Reporter*, 16 November 1984.
16. *Globe and Mail*, 10 November 1983.
17. James Hitchcock, *Decline and Fall*, p. 43.
18. *National Catholic Reporter*, 22 June 1984.
19. Ibid., 8 June 1984.
20. Hitchcock, *Pope John Paul II and American Catholicism*.
21. *National Catholic Register*, 5 February 1984.
22. *Ottawa Citizen*, 6 June 1981.
23. The best discussion of the import of this and other changes in liturgical symbols, and the parallels with the Protestant revolution, is in Michael Davies, *Cranmer's Godly Order*; and idem, *Pope Paul's New Mass* (Chawleigh, Devon: Augustine Publishing Company, 1976; 1980).

Chapter 11: Roman Remains
1. Aloysius M. Ambrozic, *Remarks on the Canadian Catechism* (Toronto: Mission Press, n.d.), p. 9.
2. *Globe and Mail*, 30 March 1984.
3. John Henry Newman, "The Second Spring," reprinted in *A Newman Treasury* (New Rochelle: Arlington House, 1975), p. 219.
4. Most Rev. Charles Valois (St. Jerome), *Globe and Mail*, 28 November 1983, interview.
5. *London Times*, 2 August 1968, Letters.
6. "Theologians Getting Nervous about Canon 812," *National Catholic Register*, 6 January 1985.

INDEX

Acknowledgements

❧

A lot of people provided me with information for this book and I am grateful. I wish to thank in particular: Mrs. Janet Daly, for access to the papers of her late husband, James Daly; James Scheer, president of Una Voce, Canada; Father John Marvyn; Father Jonathan Robinson, Father David Roche, and the Fathers and Brothers of the Oratory of St. Philip Neri, Toronto; Father Paul Bidone of the Sons of Divine Providence in England; Monsignor Vincent Foy; Father Alphonse de Valk, CSB; Father J.F. McIsaac; William and Elise Mathie; Betty Hamon of Burlington Right to Life; James Likoudis, president of Catholics United for the Faith; Professor Richard Toporoski of the classics department of St. Michael's College, University of Toronto; Mrs. Margaret McGrath, head of the reference department at the Kelly Library, St. Michael's College, who knows where everything is, and the rest of the helpful staff at the Kelly; Brent Wallace of the curriculum design unit of Niagara College of Applied Arts and Technology, Welland, Ontario, who helped in the preparation of the index. I wish also to thank Jennifer Glossop, my long-time editor at McClelland and Stewart, and John McConnell, an extremely knowledgeable reader for this manuscript. Most of all, I thank my husband, John Muggeridge, with whom I discussed every idea in this book before I wrote it down. He always added something or spotted some flaw in my argument. Moreover, he read the manuscript several times and was murder on dangling participles. He gave me, unstintingly, time taken away from his own work, and I am very grateful. And I want to thank my beloved children, John, Charles, Peter, Matthew, Rosalind, for being always patient with their frequently absent-minded mother. But, far better than that, they stand up gallantly and without embarrassment for the Catholic truths we have tried with God's help to teach them.